Her Turn on Stage

Her Turn on Stage

The Role of Women in Musical Theatre

GRACE BARNES

McFarland & Company, Inc., Publishers
Jefferson, North Carolina

Library of Congress Cataloguing-in-Publication Data

Barnes, Grace, 1965–
 Her turn on stage : the role of women in musical theatre /
Grace Barnes.
  p. cm.
 Includes bibliographical references and index.

 ISBN 978-0-7864-9861-1 (softcover : acid free paper) ∞
 ISBN 978-1-4766-2045-9 (ebook)

 1. Women in musical theater. 2. Women musical theater
producers and directors. 3. Musical theater producers and directors.
4. Musicals—History and criticism. I. Title.

 ML82.B33 2015
 792.6082—dc23   2015020268

British Library cataloguing data are available

Front cover image of dancer © 2015 isitsharp/iStock

Printed in the United States of America

McFarland & Company, Inc., Publishers
 Box 611, Jefferson, North Carolina 28640
  www.mcfarlandpub.com

Table of Contents

Acknowledgments   vii

Preface   1

The Interviewees   3

Introduction: How to Handle a Woman   7

1. Superboy and the Invisible Girl: The Lack of Women in
   Creative Positions   15

2. Loving You Is Not a Choice: Women as Martyrs to
   Heterosexual Love   41

3. He's No Good, but I'm No Good Without Him: Great Roles
   for Women?   63

4. If a Girl Isn't Pretty: Male Gaze and the Musical   85

5. It's Not Just for Gays Anymore! The Influence of Gay
   Culture on Musical Theatre   109

6. Why Can't a Woman Be More Like a Man? Difference and
   the Musical   130

7. A Secretary Is Not a Toy: Revivals and the Contemporary
   Audience   150

8. New Ways to Dream   179

Bibliography   203

Index   205

Acknowledgments

A number of people were extremely helpful and supportive to me during the writing of this book. Sherry Cohen, Eric Schaeffer, Lewis Rae, and Terry Eldridge arranged for me to speak with women I would not otherwise have been able to interview. Tom Gilling at the University of Technology in Sydney gave valuable feedback on early chapters. Peter Eyres in Sydney made many helpful suggestions and listened (and argued) for hours as I endlessly spouted my theories. So too did Martin McCallum and Anthony Blair.

My grateful thanks to all of the wonderful, talented, and tenacious women who gave me their time and shared their thoughts:

Rebecca Caine, Wendy Cavett, Kellie Dickerson, Anneke Harrison , Christine Toy Johnson, Melanie La Barrie, Toni Lamond, Nina Lannan, Rebecca Luker, Gillian Lynne, Jodi Moccia, Elaine Paige, Joanna Riding, Vanessa Scammell, Susan H. Schulman, Lucy Simon, Susan Stroman, Geraldine Turner, and Beth Williams.

My profound thanks to Cameron Mackintosh and Des McAnuff for so clearly demonstrating to me just how deeply prejudice against women in musical theatre can run and for inspiring me to write this book.

And finally, thank you to my lovely, late dad, Robin, for introducing me to musical theatre. He would have been horrified by my views on *My Fair Lady*!

"There's too many bloody women in that building."
   —Sir Cameron Mackintosh in 2001, referring to the Theatre
   Royal, Drury Lane, where *The Witches of Eastwick* was playing.

Preface

I don't remember a time when musical theatre was not a part of my life. I grew up in a household full of music—both my parents played the piano well, and my sisters and I played an assortment of musical instruments. Singing around the piano was something we did regularly and loved. My Dad had been taken to the theatre by his parents from a very young age and had, over the years, amassed a record and sheet music collection from musical theatre. As a result, I was more familiar with Rodgers and Hammerstein, Lerner and Loewe and Noël Coward than I was with the current musical trends of my generation. I was entranced by Dad's record collection of musicals and operettas. I would read the synopsis on the back of the cast album, and as I listened to the music, I realized that the story was being told through song and dance. People sang instead of speaking. They danced their emotions. Like Liesl and Rolf, I fell in love.

I was determined to have a career in musical theatre. I knew I wasn't a performer, but I did have a vague notion of what a director did, and I fixed my eyes on that goal—only to realize that women didn't seem to be musical theatre directors. I moved to London in the early eighties and immersed myself in theatre, becoming more and more aware of the lack of women. At that time there were many areas of society where women were conspicuous by their absence, but there was a feeling that this was all changing. Margaret Thatcher came to power, women were more visible in the workforce, and a vigorous debate was underway about women's place in society. Surely it was only a matter of time before women infiltrated musical theatre? Yet 30 years later, it still has not happened.

I did make a career in musicals, mainly as an assistant or associate/resident director, in both Australia and the U.K. But the longer I spent in the business, the more I noticed the gender inequality. Often, apart from the female performers, I was the only woman in the room.

Frequently, I began to bristle at a depiction of women onstage that was at odds with my reality. Why were all the women onstage bimbos or victims? Even more frequently, I became conscious of being ignored or dismissed because I was a woman in a group of men. When I discussed this with women who worked in different positions within the industry, I discovered they felt the same way and had experienced the same dismissive treatment. But there was an understanding among us that in order to retain any kind of career, we were obliged to follow in a code of silence.

This book is an attempt to break that silence by igniting a debate around gender and musical theatre—to have an honest and frank discussion about the gender inequality rife throughout the industry, onstage and off. No accusations, no threats; just a truthful exploration of the current state of affairs. I have worked in the U.S., the U.K., and Australia and currently reside in Sydney, which is why I include perspectives from three continents.

This book began life as a dissertation for a master's degree in nonfiction writing I undertook at the University of Technology in Sydney. I decided up front only to interview women for the project, as it is the female voice that is consistently lacking in musical theatre. There are many books on musical theatre in which men have their say. I wanted to hear how women in the industry felt about gender issues and musical theatre. I interviewed women in New York, London and Sydney, but as the early interviews were conducted for academic research, they are not all included in the book. All of the women I spoke with were extremely generous with their time, and I thank them wholeheartedly for their honesty and their willingness to voice personal opinions on potentially contentious issues.

Not everyone will agree with everything that is written or claimed in the following pages. We are all individuals and will invariably see the same situation from different angles. What I set out to do was to add a female viewpoint and a woman's voice to the current literature on musical theatre—to hear from the women themselves what it is like to be part of an industry dominated by men. Some have issues with it; some don't. Some readers will acknowledge that sexism is alive and well in musical theatre; some will deny it. Some will be angered by what is said, and just as many will be dismissive. But at least we are having the debate.

The Interviewees

Rebecca Caine was Cosette in London's original cast of *Les Misérables*. Prior to that she had been seen as Laurey in *Oklahoma!* and Eliza in *My Fair Lady*. Following *Les Misérables* she joined the original cast of *Phantom of the Opera* to play Christine opposite Michael Crawford. Her work with the Canadian Opera Company includes turns as Lulu, Vixen, Pamina, Despina, and Micaëla. Elsewhere, roles include Pamina in *The Magic Flute* (English National Opera); Ophelia in *Hamlet*; Aminta in *Il re pastore* (Opera North); Clomiri in *Imeneo* (Handel Opera Society); Leila in *The Pearlfishers* (Atlanta Opera); Marguerite in *Faust* (Opera Festival of New Jersey); and Adina in *Adina* (New Zealand Opera). World premieres include roles as *Jezebel* at the Toronto Symphony, Fotis in *The Golden Ass* for the Canadian Opera Company and Mme. Forestier in the Edinburgh Festival production of *Mathilde*.

Wendy Cavett is a musical director based in New York City. Her Broadway credits include *A Tale of Two Cities* (additional arrangements), *The Scarlet Pimpernel, The Most Happy Fella* and *Mamma Mia!* (as the musical director). She has toured with the National companies of *Mamma Mia!* (Las Vegas), *The Who's Tommy*, and *A Chorus Line*, and was also musical director of *A Year with Frog and Toad* (Off Broadway). Other music directing credits include premieres at Boston's A.R.T., North Shore Music Theatre, CTC in Minneapolis, Prince Music Theater in Philadelphia, and St. Louis Repertory Theatre.

Anneke Harrison trained as a stage manager in London and now lives in Sydney. She has worked in all genres of theatre for more than 30 years and has been the production stage manager on musical productions in Hong Kong, Singapore, the Philippines, Japan, Korea, Russia, the Netherlands, South America, Mexico, New Zealand, and Australia. She specializes in foreign language productions. Production credits include *The Phantom of the Opera, Joseph and the Amazing Technicolor Dream Coat, Les Misérables, Miss Saigon, War Horse, Billy Elliott, The Music of Andrew Lloyd-Webber, Mamma Mia!, The Boy from Oz—Hugh Jackman Arena Tour, We Will Rock You*, and *Strictly Ballroom: The Musical*. She is a guest tutor at the National Institute of Dramatic Art in Sydney and regularly gives talks at theatre training institutions wherever she travels.

Christine Toy Johnson is an award-winning playwright, actor, and filmmaker living in NYC. Her plays have been developed at the Roundabout Theatre Company,

Crossroads Theatre Company, Diverse City Theatre Company, Queens Theatre in the Park, and Leviathan Lab, and her documentary feature *"Transcending—The WatMisaka Story"* was released in 2010. As a performer she has worked extensively on Broadway, off Broadway, in regional theatres across the U.S., in film and television, and in concerts worldwide for over 25 years. In 2010 Christine was honored by the JACL, the nation's oldest and largest Asian American civil rights organization, as an "Outstanding Woman Champion."

Melanie La Barrie played Mrs. Phelps the Librarian at the Cambridge Theatre, London, in Dennis Kelly's and Tim Minchin's production of *Matilda: The Musical* for the Royal Shakespeare Company, directed by Matthew Warchus. She also appeared in *The Wiz* as Aunt Em/Addaperle at the Birmingham Rep and West Yorkshire Playhouse, directed by Josette Bushell-Mingo. Other credits include *Christmas Carol* and *Once on This Island* (Birmingham Rep), *Les Misérables, Mary Poppins, Daddy Cool, Ragtime*, and *The Sunshine Boys* (West End Playhouse), *Ma Rainey's Black Bottom* (Liverpool Playhouse).

Nina Lannan is a graduate of the University of California at Berkeley. Her professional career began in 1977 and spans more than 75 major shows on Broadway and multiple Broadway touring productions as general manager and/or executive producer. She was the first female to serve as chair of the Broadway League in the organization's 80-year history. In 2009, *Crain's Business* named her one of the 50 most powerful women in New York, and in 2010 The League awarded her its Distinguished Lifetime Service Award. She is an active supporter of the New York Civil Liberties Union and a member of the Broadway Cares/Equity Fights Aids board.

Rebecca Luker has performed leading roles on Broadway, including Winifred in the original Broadway production of *Mary Poppins,* Claudia Nardi in *Nine,* Maria in *The Sound of Music,* Magnolia in *Showboat,* Lily in *The Secret Garden* and Christine in *The Phantom of the Opera.* She appeared in *X* (*The Life and Times of Malcolm X*) and *Brigadoon* with the New York City Opera. Off Broadway she starred in *Death Takes a Holiday,* the world premiere of *Indian Blood* (Primary Stages), *Can't Let Go* (Keen Company) and *The Vagina Monologues.* She has also performed leading roles at regional theatres throughout the country including Clara in *Passion* at the Kennedy Center, Julia in *Time and Time Again* at the Old Globe, Mary in *Harmony* at the La Jolla Playhouse, and Amalia in *She Loves Me* with the "Reprise!" series in Los Angeles.

Susan H. Schulman was nominated for a Tony award for her production of *Sweeney Todd* and a Drama Desk Award for *The Secret Garden.* She received another Drama Desk Award nomination for her direction of *Violet* at Playwrights Horizons. On Broadway she has directed productions of *The Sound of Music* and the premiere of *Little Women.* She also directed a highly successful touring production of *Sunset Boulevard.* Her work for the Stratford Festival includes *Fiddler on the Roof, Man of La Mancha, The King and I, The Music Man, Hello, Dolly!* and *To Kill a Mockingbird.* She currently heads the graduate directing program at Penn State University.

Lucy Simon began her professional career at age 16 with her sister Carly as part of the Simon Sisters. She made her Broadway debut in 1991 as the composer of *The*

Secret Garden for which she received a Tony and Drama Desk nomination. She wrote and produced the songs and soundtrack for the award-winning HBO movie *The Positively True Adventures of the Alleged Texas Cheerleading Murdering Mom*. She received two Grammy awards for her *In Harmony* albums, which she co-wrote and produced. She also composed the score for *Dr. Zhivago*, which began development at La Jolla Playhouse in 2005 and had its Australian premiere in 2011.

Susan Stroman was the first woman to win two Tony awards simultaneously for both direction and choreography for *The Producers* in 2001. She also won Tony awards for choreography of *Crazy for You*, *Show Boat*, and *Contact*. On Broadway, she also choreographed *Big: The Musical* and *Steel Pier*, and for the Royal National Theatre *Oklahoma!* For Lincoln Centre Theatre, she directed and choreographed *Thou Shalt Not* and *The Frogs*. Other Broadway credits as director and choreographer include *Young Frankenstein* and *The Scottsboro Boys* and a 2000 revival of *The Music Man*. In 2004, she was the first woman to choreograph a full-length ballet for New York City Ballet—*Double Feature*—with music by Irving Berlin and Walter Donaldson. The production is now in the New York City Ballet repertory.

Geraldine Turner has appeared in numerous musicals, including *Wicked*, *A Little Night Music*, *Into the Woods*, *Company*, *Chicago*, *Anything Goes*, *Cabaret*, *Kismet*, *Oliver*, *Guys and Dolls*, *Call Me Madam*, *Noel and Gertie*, *Mack and Mabel*, *Ned Kelly*, *Grease*, *The Witches of Eastwick*, *Jacques Brel Is Alive and Well and Living in Paris*, and operettas *La Belle Helene*, *HMS Pinafore*, and *The Mikado*. She was the first person to record an all–Sondheim album, *The Stephen Sondheim Songbook*, which was followed by a second volume due to its popularity worldwide. She's also been a recipient of the Order of Australia for services to the arts.

Beth Williams is the CEO of the Theatre Division for Key Brand Entertainment, parent company of Broadway Across America and Broadway.com. Her productions include *How to Succeed in Business Without Really Trying*, *Million Dollar Quartet*, *Memphis*, *Godspell*, *Jesus Christ Superstar*, *Priscilla Queen of the Desert*, and *Tuck Everlasting*. Prior to joining Key Brand, she produced *Grey Gardens* with East of Doheny, was the president of production for Clear Channel Theatrical, where she was a producer of *The Producers*, *Hairspray*, *Sweet Smell of Success*, *Fosse* (Broadway and Tour), *All Shook Up*, and *Cabaret* (Tour). In her 25-plus year career in the theatre, she has also worked as a conductor (*Les Misérables*, *Dreamgirls*), pianist (*Miss Saigon*, *Phantom*) and company manager (*Dreamgirls*, *Dangerous Games*).

Introduction

How to Handle a Woman

I accepted a job to go on the road as one of the pianists on *Les Mis*[*érables*]. This was in the late eighties and I was about 28. I went on the road knowing that there was a conductor and an assistant already. I had spoken with [the musical director] when I was first hired and [he] had said that when I was ready I could learn the conducting book. They would need other covers and I could work towards being one of them. I was there for maybe a month and I went to talk to—I don't actually remember who said this to me, but it was one of my bosses—and I said, "OK, I'm in. I'm ready to take on the challenge of learning the conducting score." And they said, "Oh, but you're a woman." And I said, "What?" And they said, "Claude-Michel has made it very clear that no woman will ever conduct *Les Mis*." I was stunned and I asked what that meant. He said that Claude-Michel felt that *Les Mis* was three hours and twenty minutes of music and it would be too difficult for a female to conduct it. He has made it very clear that no woman will ever conduct *Les Mis*.

—Beth Williams

After retreating to her hotel room and "crying her eyes out" for two hours, Beth Williams "got mad." And nine months later she became the first woman—with great support and approval from composer Claude-Michel Schönberg—to conduct a performance of *Les Misérables*. Ms. Williams went on to conduct the Broadway production for five months and was associate musical director on the same production for six years. Apart from serving as a lesson in tenacity, this story illustrates the underlying attitude—some might say antipathy—towards women in the musical theatre profession. Yet this is an industry aimed at, marketed to, and consumed by women—attend a performance of *Mamma Mia!* or *Wicked* and you will be left in no doubt of this. But scratch the surface of this product and examine what, or who, is beneath it, and the reality behind the façade tells a different story. A picture quickly emerges of an industry controlled by men, subtly—or not so subtly—reinforcing a patriarchal view of society. Tales from female performers of being ignored or humiliated in the rehearsal room by a male director are commonplace, as are instances of women in the middle creative tier—the associates, the residents—being unable to progress to the next level. Examples of deserving creative women not being considered for positions because of their gender are too numerous to relate. Two years ago I was present backstage at a preview of a new musical when the male director shouted at three female members of management that they were "pussy bitches." Admittedly, this was Australia—not a country known for its progressive views on gender—but in any other industry, this would have resulted in a lawsuit. In musical theatre, apparently, it is perfectly acceptable. When I discuss any of this with other women working in musicals I am met with eye-rolling and shoulder-shrugging, but not much outrage. The overriding response is recognition and a resigned, "What do you expect?" Women in the industry put up with the abuse, the chauvinism, and the inequality without complaint because to question it would, in all probability, cost them their careers. Yet this is an industry that relies on women and their financial input for support. Remove them from the audience, and the few gay men who are left will not be enough to guarantee the genre a future.

In an interview with journalist Roya Nikkhah, published in *The Telegraph* in 2011, U.K. lyricist Tim Rice gave his view of why musical theatre in the U.K. was approaching a crisis. "The crisis is not with performers, it's with new writers. All the British guys who have written successful, good new musicals in the last 20 years have been getting on a bit. There's Elton [John] and Andrew and I, but where are all the young guys?" It never occurred to Sir Tim to ask, "Where are the women writers?"

Yet the history of the Broadway and West End musical is not exclusively male. Unquestionably, there are more men than women, but that is a reflection of the times and the same could be said of the judiciary, politics, academia, science, medicine, etc. But while women in the latter fields have increased their presence and influence over the last two decades, women in musical theatre—both on and off the stage—have become an increasingly rare sight. Gone are the days when composer/lyricists such as Rodgers and Hammerstein, Jerry Herman, John Kander, and Fred Ebb created a new musical around the talents of a particular female star, and investors only had to hear the names of Ethel Merman, Julie Andrews, Mary Martin, Barbra Streisand, or Chita Rivera to have the confidence to back the show. The "great" performances discussed reverentially by musical theatre devotees on both sides of the Atlantic were almost unanimously given by women—Julie Andrews in *My Fair Lady,* Ethel Merman in *Gypsy,* Patti Lupone in *Evita,* Betty Buckley in *Cats,* Carol Channing in *Hello, Dolly!,* Angela Lansbury in *Mame* or *Sweeney Todd,* Gwen Verdon in *Sweet Charity,* Liza Minnelli in *Flora the Red Menace,* Barbra Streisand in *Funny Girl,* Chita Rivera in *West Side Story* or *Kiss of the Spiderwoman,* Bernadette Peters in *Into the Woods* or *Sunday in the Park with George,* Idina Menzel in *Wicked*; the list goes on. Yet the great female roles that defined musicals such as *Mame, Hello, Dolly!, Call Me Madam, Gypsy, Kiss of the Spiderwoman, Funny Girl, Evita, Anything Goes, Calamity Jane, A Little Night Music, Sweet Charity,* and *Sunset Boulevard* have all but disappeared, overtaken by the Valjeans, Mormons, the boys of the Four Seasons, newsboys, boxers, ballet dancers, bodyguards, and an assortment of drag queens, or by the show itself, now marketed as the primary attraction.

Are male writers and producers deliberately removing women from center stage and demoting them to ensemble roles, or is this simply a reflection of the changing style of the genre? Whatever the answer, women in musical theatre today are no longer celebrated onstage in the way they once were. And while women on Broadway are finally being allowed to make their creative presence felt, the same cannot be said of women in the West End of London (or Australia), where musical theatre remains resolutely in the hands of men. What intrigues me most about this is the fact that no one questions it. Society regularly debates the under representation of women in politics, the judiciary, or on corporate boards, and yet the absence of women from key creative roles on current musical theatre productions passes without comment. This is odd, given the fact that musical theatre is now a multimillion dollar industry.

Perhaps the predominance of men in positions of power accounts for the fact that musicals, more often than not, portray women in a way that men might prefer them to be—secondary characters, existing purely to support the dominant male—rather than how they actually are. Male control over the creation of the product often results in female roles more influenced by "camp" or theories of chivalry than the authentic experience of contemporary women. Female characters are still defined by their relationships to male characters, and women who express any individuality are frequently left alone or dead by the closing scenes, punished for their non-conformity to gender rules favoring female compliance and sacrifice.

If, as is generally accepted, musical theatre reflects the prevailing societal attitudes (or offers unadulterated escapism in periods of recession), what does the modern musical tell us about attitudes towards women in America, the U.K. and Australia today? Have we regressed to the 1960s, when fears of the rising women's movement resulted in shows that vilified the single girl as immoral and exhorted her to find a man? Could this be another strand of the backlash against the liberation of women, explored by Susan Faludi in *Backlash: The Undeclared War Against Women* (1999), creeping its insidious way into the arts?

In the last twenty years, the musical has insinuated itself back into popular culture to a point where hugely successful television reality shows ask viewers to vote for the next star of a Broadway/West End show. The final episode of the U.K.'s *How Do You Solve a Problem Like Maria?* (2006)—Andrew Lloyd Webber's search to find an unknown actress to play Maria Von Trapp in his new production of *The Sound of Music*—saw over two million votes being cast by the public. Lloyd Webber repeatedly declared his desire to create a new young star of musical theatre, but the television show was clearly a marketing ploy to generate public and media interest in the musical before it had even gone into rehearsal. *How Do You Solve a Problem Like Maria?* had nothing at all to do with the artistic integrity of the new production of *The Sound of Music*; it was conceived purely to sell the show to a potential audience by bestowing upon them a sense of ownership. If viewers voted for the girl who won, they were more likely to buy a ticket to the show.

Musical theatre today has been rediscovered by a whole new generation, and producers are staging shows that are actively designed to appeal to this audience. Following on from the massive success of *Mamma Mia!,* savvy producers have invented a new genre of "jukebox musicals" (*We Will Rock You, Jersey Boys, Rock of Ages*) that rely on familiarity with the music to entice an audience. Or they have turned to mainstream films as source material for new musicals (*Billy Elliot, Dirty Dancing, Legally Blonde, Catch Me If You Can*) in an attempt to lure new patrons into the theatre. And let's not forget the "kiddie dollar" onslaught—*Beauty and the Beast, Mary Poppins, High School Musical, The Little Mermaid, Chitty Chitty Bang Bang*, and *Shrek*. The result of this is that musical theatre has become big business, a money train that people who previously exhibited little interest in the genre are eager to board.

The rediscovery of the movie musical, with recent film versions of *Chicago, Mamma Mia!, Nine, Hairspray, Dreamgirls*, and *Les Misérables* making it to the big screen, has brought the genre to the attention of non-theatre goers, and the popularity of TV shows such as *Glee, American Idol, The X Factor,* and *Smash* has introduced a younger generation to the concept of musical theatre. Even cruise lines have jumped on the bandwagon, offering

Baltic and Mediterranean musical-themed cruises hosted by luminaries such as Patti LuPone, Sutton Foster, Christine Ebersole, and Norm Lewis. Statistics prove that the genre is today more prominent in the public consciousness and appeals to a wider range of consumers than ever before, but what messages are women—particularly young women—absorbing about gender role definitions from musical theatre? Can the "escapism" excuse justify the fact that a genre that has moved to the forefront of the performing arts and is now described as populist, continues to promote a patriarchal view of society? Is the audience being diverted from the often dubious content onstage with reassurances that what they are seeing is harmless fun, not to be taken seriously? Yet soap operas, video games, computer games, and "chick flicks" are considered worthy of deconstruction within a cultural debate.

Broadway is generally regarded as the home of musical theatre, and in the U.S. the genre is regarded as an art form. Musicals are viewed within a historical context as an important factor in the development of a national cultural identity. A more disparaging attitude towards the genre exists in the U.K., where the commercial success of shows by composer Andrew Lloyd Webber and producer Cameron Mackintosh have resulted in musicals being viewed as mass entertainment or a purely commercial product. Detractors on both sides of the Atlantic accuse the musical of being "lowbrow," appealing to coach parties of women from the suburbs and offering manufactured emotions to elicit an audience response. But the recent upsurge of interest in musical theatre suggests that an evening of easy emotions is exactly what the audience is seeking. Attending a musical is less intimidating for the inexperienced theatre-goer than going to Shakespeare or a contemporary drama. It may well be insubstantial fluff, but for many people, the musical is the only experience of live theatre that they will have. So to dismiss it as irrelevant within a cultural debate is to ignore the growing number of people attending and their reasons for doing so. Susan H. Schulman observes,

> We've had difficult times in the last ten years and musical theatre has always been really popular in the most difficult of times. Especially economically.... It's really kind of quixotic that way. It thrives in times when people are more uncertain. They want to go to the theatre and be made to feel better. They don't want to go to the theatre and come out feeling worse than they did going in. I mean, even if you look at Hollywood movies during the depressive economic times or during world wars, that was the height of musicals in Hollywood.

The musical frequently subscribes to the "dreams do come true" philosophy, the romantic happy ending and the assurance that everything will be all right in the end. And what's wrong with a bit of optimism? But the dream for female characters in musicals is frequently limited to finding a man and abandoning her own personal dream in favor of his. Roles for women are becoming increasingly one-dimensional—victim/whore stereotypes—and women onstage are frequently denied their own identity or any complexity. Their function within the show is to allow the male story to progress. Does this tell women in the audience that their lives are irrelevant in comparison with men's lives, or that they are incomplete women if they do not have men by their sides? As Melanie La Barrie articulates, the absence of a woman's voice or influence in musical theatre is resulting in a particular kind of product.

> I mean, for a lot of people going to the theatre … it's about escapism, isn't it? And we don't have very many female writers. We don't have many women writers, so our voice is never from a primary source. Our voice is always imagined. It's what a male writer imagines a woman is like.

Rest assured, this book is not a self-pitying whine about how mistreated we women in musical theatre are, nor a vitriolic, separatist rant aimed at the men who currently dominate the industry. It is not even a call to arms for all thinking women to abandon musical theatre until equality and respect become commonplace in the genre. They'd have a long wait. And I'd be out of a job. (A number of interviewees did point out that I'd never work again should this book be published.) It is an attempt to ignite a debate about gender and musical theatre and explore reasons why women, even today, find it almost impossible to break through the protective barriers erected—however subconsciously—by the men dominating the industry. Anneke Harrison states,

> Take *Les Mis*, for example. The students are all great characters, they've all got names, they were all very well researched from the book, and that's fantastic. They've all got very individual looks, and they're all young, beautiful, idealistic young men. But the women are not named. It's Crone One, Crone Two. Whore One. Whore Two. And that, I find very distressing. I mean, even in the score … when I was working on the show I remember looking at it and there was an ensemble number and there was the female line, which was "girls," and there was the boys line, which was "men." I remember looking at it and thinking, "Why are the men called men, and the women are called girls?"

Focusing mainly on shows written since the second wave of feminism in the 1980s (although these shows were developed from a model established in the 1940s and 50s), this book will discuss a number of questions relevant to the issues surrounding gender and musical theatre. I will explore the changing face of the genre, the influence of the mega-musical and the effect the advances in stage technology have had on women's roles both on and off the stage. I will discuss the presence of the woman's voice in musical theatre and ask how authentic that voice can be if it is being produced by a man.

I will challenge the assertion that musical theatre offers great roles for women by asking what constitutes a "great role"—the number of songs the leading lady sings, or a contemporary portrayal of an independent, free-thinking woman? Is a show with a woman in the central character a feminist musical when the character she plays is defined by the rules of patriarchy? How likely is it that a role that can be reduced to a label—victim, whore, love interest—will contain the complexities of emotion that challenge any actor? Roles for men are rarely reduced to tags. The ubiquitous "victim song"—*Fifty Percent, Hopelessly Devoted to You, As Long as He Needs Me, He's No Good But I'm No Good Without Him*—will be discussed in terms of theories of patriarchal control and a view of women as inherently weaker than men. Within this, I discuss ways in which the genre reinforces a view that women's lives matter less than men's and question why female sacrifice—emotional or physical—is such a popular theme among the predominantly male writers of musicals.

Shows such as *Hairspray, Legally Blonde*, and *Funny Girl* will be discussed in terms of the theories of male gaze—art created for a viewer assumed to be male—and the objectification of women. Frequently, the costuming of female characters tells us more about how we are supposed to regard them than their lyrics do, and I will explore what the image of the leggy showgirl or blonde bombshell is really saying about women—or, indeed, about the male creators attitude towards women.

I debate why female sexuality in musicals is frequently depicted either as a threat (*Evita, Cabaret, Sweet Charity, Sunset Boulevard*), or an excuse for a comic number, when male sexuality is never a laughing matter.

Drawing on the feminist theory of difference—the normative being white, heterosexual, and male—I discuss the portrayal of women in musicals in terms of otherness and ask why, when political correctness rightly decries the portrayal of Native Americans in *Annie Get Your Gun,* Pacific Islanders in *South Pacific,* or black Americans in *Porgy and Bess* or *Showboat* as patronising and offensive, it does not similarly denounce the one-dimensional depiction of many female characters onstage?

The musical has always held an appeal to gay men—both as audience members and as practitioners within the business—and I debate whether the prevalence of gay men in the creation of shows results in female roles being influenced more by camp than reality. The acknowledged diva roles—Mamma Rose (*Gypsy*), Sally Adams (*Call Me Madam*), Dolly Levi (*Hello, Dolly!*), Auntie Mame (*Mame*), Reno Sweeney (*Anything Goes*)—often walk a fine line between actress and drag queen. Does the genre call for the larger-than-life leading lady, or is that what audiences have come to expect? Many female practitioners claim that the predominance of gay men on creative teams makes it even less likely that women will be hired, and I discuss the validity and consequences of this.

With producers increasingly reluctant to take a risk on a new musical, revivals of older hits are becoming commonplace. But many older shows were written at a time when attitudes towards traditional gender roles (and race) were firmly entrenched, and the shows reflected this. Should producers eschew these musicals when they hold historical significance within the canon, or restage them and run the risk of causing offence to a more enlightened audience? Do directors of revivals have a duty to update the show for a 21st-Century audience, or is citing the original source an acceptable way of presenting outdated attitudes towards gender? I debate whether or not it is possible to mount new productions of *Carousel,* with its tacit approval of domestic violence, or the inherently misogynistic *My Fair Lady* without at least acknowledging that such shows may be offensive to women in 2015.

In the final chapter I draw on suggestions made by the interviewees to discuss steps that could be taken to redress the gender imbalance in musical theatre, on and off the stage.

In Lerner and Loewe's *Camelot* (1960), Arthur struggles with the problem of "How to Handle a Woman." He is clearly under the impression that women require managing, or controlling, in a way that men do not. Men know how to deal with other men, but they have to learn how to handle women. Women have to submit to the handling. A wise man gives him the answer, "simply love her." Society has moved on in the 50-plus years since *Camelot* premiered, but the genre of musical theatre has not. This vision of a world where women are unquestioning and childlike, requiring nothing more than the love of a good man to be content, still pervades many of the shows we see today, and not just in revivals. When will the musical catch up with the rest of society? Is this image of a woman as something that has to be "handled" really a true reflection of the views of the men creating musical theatre today? If it is not, why do they persist in allowing it on the stage? My belief is that it never occurs to them to question it.

The question I find more interesting, is how this world of submissive women would change if women were creating it. Anneke Harrison notes,

> In all the shows I've done, the way women are portrayed … is really frustrating. And then you realize, well that's the male view of how women are, or how men would like them to be. Which I don't have a problem with, as long as we are honest about that. Just say, this is how men view women in the world, or how they want to represent them onstage.

1

Superboy and the Invisible Girl

The Lack of Women in Creative Positions

I think I bring something different into everything I do because I am a woman. I think my gender informs everything I do. Does it inform the way I direct? Absolutely. Does it inform the way I work with actors? Absolutely. Does it inform the material I am attracted to? Absolutely. But I think it's also very personal.

—Susan H. Schulman

The history of what we now define as the Broadway musical is unquestionably male. The acknowledged greats of the genre—Jerome Kern, Cole Porter, George Gershwin, Richard Rodgers and Oscar Hammerstein, Alan Jay Lerner and Frederick Loewe, Irving Berlin, Andrew Lloyd Webber, Hal Prince, Cameron Mackintosh, Claude-Michel Schöenberg and Alain Boublil, Bob Fosse, Jerome Robbins, Cy Feuer, George Abbott, Jerry Herman, John Kander and Fred Ebb, Michael Bennett, Stephen Sondheim—have one obvious thing in common. They are not female. Yet the musical as a form of entertainment has always held more appeal to women than to men. A study undertaken by the Broadway League, *The Demographics of the Broadway Audience 2010–2011*, reveals that almost two thirds of Broadway theatre attendees in that season were women. In real numbers, women accounted for 8.2 million admissions, whereas men accounted for 4.4 million.

But the lack of women practitioners in key creative roles means that other women are unconsciously supporting an industry that regards them purely as consumers. One could argue that similarly few women (excluding assembly-line workers) are involved in the invention and production of

15

domestic appliances, despite the fact that women are the primary users of the equipment, but can we assert with any certainty that a long queue of women with industrial design degrees are banging on James Dyson's[1] factory gates seeking their big break? What cannot be denied is that a number of capable and experienced creative women are finding the doors to musical theatre—both on Broadway and in the U.K.—locked and barred. In fact, it is now so rare to have women involved in the creation of a new musical that Wikipedia highlights as "unusual" the fact that the producer, director, and writer of *Mamma Mia!* (1999) were all female. There are women in senior management roles—associate or resident directors, choreographers, and musical directors—who maintain the show once the originators have departed, but not at the top level. The "broken ladder syndrome"[2]—the theatrical equivalent of the glass ceiling so prevalent in corporate board rooms—appears to be extremely successful in ensuring that creative women in musicals remain in regional/fringe theatre or Off-Broadway.

A quick glance at the credit lists from the golden days of MGM musicals reveals the names of two lyricists/librettists—Dorothy Fields and Betty Comden—cropping up regularly. Yes, it is only two, but these women were sustaining successful careers at the top tier of a notoriously fickle industry. Fields shared the 1936 Oscar for best original song with Jerome Kern for *The Way You Look Tonight* and had later writing partnerships with Cole Porter, Irving Berlin and Cy Coleman. Her pairing with the latter resulted in the Broadway musicals *Redhead* (which won the 1959 Best Musical Tony award), *Sweet Charity* (1966) and *Seesaw* (1973). Betty Comden, with her writing partner Adolph Green wrote screenplays for *Good News,* the Astaire/Rogers vehicle *The Berkleys of Broadway, On the Town* starring Gene Kelly and Frank Sinatra, and *Singin' in the Rain.*

On Broadway, the partnership of Comden and Green provided either book or lyrics (or both) for *Wonderful Town* (1953), *Bells Are Ringing* (1956), *Do-Re-Mi* (1961), *Subways Are for Sleeping* (1961), *Hallelujah Baby!* (1968), *Applause* (1970), and *Will Rogers Follies* (1991) and won a Tony for Best Book of a Musical in 1978 for *On the Twentieth Century.*

Women were also visible in Hollywood as choreographers during the golden age of the musical, most notably Agnes de Mille, best known for creating the dream ballet sequence for *Oklahoma!* in 1943. De Mille moved on to choreograph a number of musicals on Broadway—*Bloomer Girl* (1944), *Carousel* (1945), *Brigadoon* (1947), *Gentlemen Prefer Blondes* (1949), *Paint Your Wagon* (1951), and *110 in the Shade* (1963)—while creating new works for ballet companies across the U.S. In musical theatre, women have always been more conspicuous in the dance department than in any other (except possibly wardrobe—dressmaking being traditionally regarded as "women's work").

Female dancers with ambitions to choreograph often start out as the assistant to the male choreographer, some such as Graciela Danielle (*Pirates of Penzance* [1981], *Zorba the Greek* [1983], *The Rink* [1984], *Mystery of Edwin Drood* [1985], *Once On This Island* [1990], *Ragtime* [1998]) and Gillian Lynne (*Cats* [1981], *Phantom of the Opera* [1986], *Aspects of Love* [1990], *Gigi* [1999], *The Secret Garden* [2000], *Chitty Chitty Bang Bang* [2002]) making the successful transition to choreographers and, in their later years, directors. More recently, choreographers Susan Stroman (*Crazy for You* [1992], *Showboat* [1994], *Oklahoma!, Contact* [1999], *The Music Man* [2000]) and Kathleen Marshall—who started out as assistant to her brother Rob Marshall[3] on productions of *She Loves Me* [1993], *Damn Yankees* [1994], *Victor/Victoria* [1995], *Suessical* [2000]—have made similar moves from the role of choreographer to director. In 2001, Susan Stroman became the first woman to win two Tony awards on the same night for her direction and choreography on *The Producers*.

Female writers of musicals following the Fields/Comden footsteps include Marsha Norman (*The Secret Garden* [1991 Tony Award for Best Book of a Musical], *The Red Shoes* [1993], *The Color Purple* [2005]), Carol Bayer Sager (*They're Playing Our Song* [1979], *The Boy from Oz* [2003]), and Lynn Ahrens (*Lucky Stiff* [1988], *Once On This Island* [1990], *Ragtime* [1998], *Seussical* [2000], *A Man of No Importance* [2002], *Dessa Rose* [2005], *Rocky* [2014]). Women composers have fared less well. Lucy Simon (*The Secret Garden* [1991], *Dr. Zhivago* [2006]) and Jeanine Tesori (additional material for 2000 production of *Thoroughly Modern Millie, Violet* [1997], *Caroline or Change* [2004], *Shrek the Musical* [2008]) are the most prominent.

These eleven women are by no means the only representatives of past and present creative women on Broadway—I haven't even touched on the achievements of directors Julie Taymor (*The Lion King* [1997], *Spiderman Turn Off the Dark* [2011]) and Susan H. Schulman (*The Secret Garden, Violet*) or designers Susan Hilferty (costume design *Wicked* [2003], *Spring Awakening* [2007]) and Heidi Landesman—the first woman to win a Tony for scenic design of a musical for her work on *Big River* in 1985. Nor have I listed musical directors or orchestral arrangers, because this is not a book about lists. Notwithstanding the successes of the above women, the paucity of their number proves they are the exception to the rule. But if Betty Comden and Dorothy Fields were accepted 60 years ago, why are women today still facing an uphill battle to be admitted into the hallowed halls of musical theatre? Women who, without doubt, have the requisite talent and experience? Anneke Harrison observes:

> Yes, you do get the sense that you're in a male environment, but to be honest I don't notice that more in a rehearsal room any more than anywhere else where

I am in the world because most place you go, are. So it's sort of par for the course, in a way. And yes, I've been in room where you've got a female MD or stage manager, for example, but it's not very often you feel a female presence leading the room. Because the director is always male.

No doubt tradition plays its part—the genre has always been dominated by men—but it was not so long ago that a female politician would have been unthinkable. If Hillary Clinton, Condoleeza Rice or Margaret Thatcher were to provide us with their thoughts on this, their views would no doubt contain the words "progress" and "change." How refreshing if those same words could be applied to musical theatre. But as long as busloads of excited women continue to pour into theatres, why should producers feel the need to update their product and accommodate changing values? Who needs a conversation about female under-representation when the handful of men associated with the mega-musical and the jukebox musical are becoming millionaires, or billionaires, as in the case of Cameron Mackintosh?

It may well be the perception of musical theatre as trivial or superficial that excuses the genre from the probing self-examination that other art forms and strands of popular culture are subject to. Yet many practitioners and observers regard certain shows in the canon as high art. Ask Stephen Sondheim if he considers his works (*Company, Sweeney Todd, Into the Woods, Sunday in the Park with George*) frivolous distractions, and the answer is sure to be no. Did Jerome Robbins regard the musical as lighthearted entertainment when he created *West Side Story* or *Fiddler on the Roof?* Or Claude-Michel Schönberg and Alain Boublil when they penned *Les Misérables* or *Miss Saigon?* From the Gershwin brothers' *Porgy and Bess*[4] (1935) to *Memphis* (2009), writers of musicals have shown themselves willing to tackle subjects anything but escapist. The history of the musical reveals that, far from shying away from controversial issues, shows have confronted racial prejudice, depression, the Vietnam War, poverty, unemployment, AIDS, prostitution, gang warfare, religious wars, disability, immigration, political corruption, child labor, and even conjoined twins. So to dismiss the musical as irrelevant is to ignore the depth of the genre. If we accept that musicals tackle subjects of social and political concern, and have the power to influence an audience, then the genre cannot be immune to critical debate.

To return again to the paradox at the center of the contemporary musical: according to a 2010 research study conducted by Ipsos MORI for the Society of London Theatres:

Female visitors account for more than two thirds of theatre goers (68 percent). Those seeing a musical are more likely to be women (71 percent), whereas men are more likely to be seeing a play (38 percent) or an opera (47 percent).

Women are more likely to be visiting in a larger or organized group, with 81 percent of those in an organized group being women.

Women form the backbone of support for the industry, even when it presents them with the unthinkable—seven brothers kidnapping seven sisters in order to marry them[5]—as the basis for an evening's entertainment laden with macho dance routines and jokes about forcing her, whether she likes it or not. Would a female audience readily accept the stereotypical sacrificial women of *Les Misérables* or *Miss Saigon* (both currently enjoying revivals) on TV or film? Would they tolerate the hypersexualized women of *Rock of Ages* in a modern play? Why, then, are these values and representations received with a smile, applause even, when dressed up as musical theatre? Is there something inherent in the genre that exempts it from progressive values? Theatre critics are quick to pounce on caricatures in plays or films of gays/lesbians, or racial stereotyping, so why do they not similarly condemn the ultimate message of *Grease*—that to keep her man a girl has to dress in tight pants and comply with his demands for sex—as out of touch with a post-feminist society? Critics aside, why do women accept it? Are these the values we want our teenage daughters and nieces to absorb? Why do women continue to buy tickets for shows that, more often than not, present their sex as mindless, childlike, sexual objects, incapable of making their own decisions and utterly driven in their quest to find the right man? Are they really not aware of the underlying threat of patriarchal control over women at the heart of *Next to Normal* or *The Life*? Are we so inured to seeing women in musicals presented as scantily clad victims or dumb sex kittens that we don't pause to consider if the depiction of the female characters in *Rock of Ages* or the short-lived *Lysistrata Jones* is a respectful one? Or ask why all the women in *The Book of Mormon* are treated as a joke? Perhaps this is actually what we now expect of the genre in terms of female depiction, in the same way as we know exactly what we will get when we attend a "romcom" movie.

With so few women's stories making it to stage, and depictions of their sex that leave a lot to be desired, why do women continue to flock to musicals? Possibly, it is the romanticism at the heart of the genre that seduces them. The rousing wedding finale, or the ultimate "happy ever after" fantasy—often a stark contrast to the humdrum reality of a daily routine. An idealized version of true love is the driving force behind most musicals, and the search for it by the leading lady often forms the basis of the plot: the classic girl meets boy, girl loses boy, girls finds boy again formula so beloved of romantic fiction and chick flicks.

Perhaps many women go to musicals in order to place themselves at the center of the romantic attachment they see played out onstage, an attachment that may be lacking in their own lives. Or to have their private fantasy that someday their prince *will* come to be reaffirmed by the plot and characters onstage—"if it can happen to her, it can happen to me." But the romantic ideal becomes problematic when it calls upon women to surrender their independence and freedom, as is frequently the case in musical theatre scenarios. Susan H. Schulman says,

> I wouldn't call it just escapist. Look, any entertainment is an escape from your life because you go into someone else's world. But I don't want to use escapism as, "I want to run away from." I think musicals can empower as well, and I think the best musicals do both. They give you a sense that life is really worth living, that bad times can be overcome and that you have some power in that. Because good musicals deal with the central character overcoming some great obstacle. And having a propelling passion—being active in their own fate. And I think that all those things make you come away from musicals feeling better, feeling, "You know what? I'm not so helpless."

Many musicals have a physical community at the heart of their stories—*Oklahoma!, The Music Man, Brigadoon, The Witches of Eastwick, The Color Purple, Memphis*—and the town, or place, is as central to the action as the characters and their stories. Less tangible communities are presented in shows such as *A Chorus Line, Spring Awakening, Rent, Chicago, 42nd Street, Follies*—and perhaps it is the relationships at the center of these communities that strikes a chord with women—a feeling of togetherness, a family bond or shared experience. Attending a theatre is a communal experience—a group of people enter a building to witness and share in the same event.

Musicals take the shared experience one step farther—audiences are encouraged to clap along with the music, to dance in the aisles in *Mamma Mia!,* and even join the cast in the final number in the 2009 Broadway revival of *Hair* or the more recent *Strictly Ballroom.* This generates a feeling of community—an experience which is enjoyed and experienced as a collective, not as an individual. A communal experience unifies, and through audience participation the musical brings individuals together, allowing them to feel part of the whole.

Ian Bradley, in his book *You've Got to Have a Dream: The Message of the Musical,*[6] suggests that the collective emotional experience that occurs through communal singing, previously the domain of the church choir or football stands, is now being replicated by musical theatre—witness the popularity of singalong *Sound of Music,* or *Joseph.* Television soap operas, again with a predominantly female audience, also utilize the concept of the community to present stories that resonate with women and frequently appropriate the family values framework to expound a patriarchal viewpoint. The foundations of family and community serve to replicate the lives of the (female) viewers, reassuring them of the validity of their own choices. Subsequently, the soap opera becomes a hugely influential mouthpiece with which to reinforce a political ideology based on traditional gender role assignment and the division of labor. Musical theatre provides a similar vehicle to corroborate the values of patriarchy. Watching how other women behave and the values they adhere to can, over time, influence how the female viewer herself behaves, because it is what she sees around her. Female characters in soap operas or musicals rarely challenge the status quo, so the viewer—the audience—learns to accept that this is the way it is. And women attending theatre in a group of other women, 81 percent of group bookings, are even less likely to question what they see, since peer pressure is doubly persuasive.

But none of this really explains why contemporary women continue to pay a considerable amount of money to witness a depiction of womanhood onstage that may be at odds with their more enlightened beliefs. Possibly they are simply not as informed as I like to assume they are. Perhaps the liberal feminist finds the depiction of women in the musical too limiting for her taste and gets her cultural fix instead from art-house movies and "the women's play." The typical—if there is such a thing—suburban housewife may have no desire to be forced to think or have her belief system challenged on a fun night out with the girls. Just as war-weary women sighed dreamily over Fred and Ginger's celluloid tap routines, the musical possibly provides a much-needed sense of relief for exhausted "have it all" women, who happily abandon their feminist principles—if indeed they have any—in favor of a distracting night of feel-good fantasy. When we hear Rosemary sing of how happy she is to keep her husband's dinner warm in *How To Succeed in Business Without Really Trying*[7], we may not necessarily agree with the sentiment expressed, but it doesn't stop us enjoying the performer's rendition of the song.

While women may be the majority of the audience, the same cannot be said of their presence on creative teams or, as is increasingly the case, in the cast. Even shows with women as their central characters—*Legally Blonde, Matilda, Grey Gardens, Next to Normal, Sunset Boulevard*—are, more often than not, directed, choreographed, and created by men. This absence of women from the rehearsal room can be detrimental to the end product since only one point of view—the male one—is being taken into consideration. A woman's story directed or written by a man can never be the same as a woman's story created or realized by a woman. That is not to say that men should only direct musicals about men, and vice versa, but is a man really the person best equipped to relate stories that resonate more with women?

When a show such as *Next to Normal* for example, is built around a uniquely female experience—in this case, postnatal depression and the loss of a child—it is arguable that a woman is more likely to have a greater understanding of the issue. Consequently, a female director can lead an actress towards a deeper interpretation of the character, often based on a shared personal experience. Rebecca Luker observes,

> Because I play female characters, [a female director] ... really can relate more to the character I'm playing. We can both talk about what it would be like to be this woman. What she might be going through, which, you know, a male director could never know about, could never experience. I would love to work with more female directors, but there's just not enough of them.

If a truthful representation of the women depicted in *Gypsy, The Witches of Eastwick, Chicago, The Rink, A Little Night Music, The Life, Mame, Aspects of Love* is what producers are aiming to achieve, then why not engage a female director? The alternative—which producers now appear to be favoring—is to switch the focus back to men by telling men's stories or by simply eliminating women from the cast altogether. The musical theatre stages on both sides of the Atlantic are full of vibrant young men starring in *The Book of Mormon, Rocky, Spiderman, How to Succeed in Business, Billy Elliot, Kinky Boots, Jersey Boys,* and *Newsies.* When statistics show that men are the least likely group to attend a musical, how can this possibly make financial sense? Do women really need to see any more stories onstage where their sex is ignored or pushed aside in favor of men? Don't they get enough of that in real life?

Producers have repeatedly demonstrated their willingness to pander to the family market with the *Mary Poppins, Chitty Chitty Bang Bang, Shrek the Musical, The Little Mermaid, The Lion King, Beauty and the Beast, Aida, Aladdin* onslaught, shows that owe more to an eye on box office receipts than a desire to push the boundaries of the genre. The teen/young adult markets have also been unashamedly wooed with *Spring Awakening, Spiderman Turn Off the Dark, High School Musical, Thirteen,* and the casting of the non-singing, non-dancing Daniel Radcliffe in the 2011 revival of *How to Succeed in Business,* a blatant attempt to harness the Harry Potter fan base. So why are women left out in the cold? Does the female dollar not count, or are producers working on the assumption that women will go to a musical anyway, regardless of the subject matter? It is quite astounding that the phenomenal success of *Mamma Mia!* resulted in an excess of jukebox musicals, but not more shows aimed at the female audience. The sole exception was the 2012

London production of *Viva Forever!*[8] Created by *Mamma Mia!* producer Judy Craymer, the show was unashamedly designed to woo the middle-aged female audience with a female-centric plot and songs by the nineties pop band The Spice Girls.

But Ms. Craymer aside, producers seem to be missing a glaringly obvious point. Women actively demonstrate their eagerness to attend, on more than one occasion, a show with a story of female friendship at its heart, and no producer capitalizes on this with a second or third female-centric production. Why not, when there is clearly a market for it? Because they favor shows about men, or aimed at men. And a quick glance through the creative teams of current West End and, to a lesser degree, Broadway shows leaves us in no doubt that producers prefer shows created *by* men.

Only the fashion industry springs to mind as another example of an industry that treats its consumer with such flagrant disregard, promoting images of how a female *should* look by parading clothes that the average woman could never afford nor fit into. What the female consumer actually wants is less important than what the male designer, or director, wants to create.

Yet if the worldwide box office receipts of *Mamma Mia!* (or indeed *Wicked*) are anything to go by, the female musical theatre audience actively desires shows that present contemporary, strong females at the center of the story. Unfortunately this demand is rarely met, probably because most producers are men who either do not want to see a stories about women or who maintain a misguided belief that stories featuring strong, independent women at their core will not sell. And with so few women being given the opportunity to write scripts for musicals, it is hardly surprising that men's stories feature so prominently. What disturbs me more than the proliferation of male-centric shows is the fact that the female characters onstage are now so superficial that they border on caricature, if they are there at all. When Natalie in *Next to Normal* sings of "Superboy and the Invisible Girl," referring to the male as the infallible hero and the female as absent, she could well be referring to any area within contemporary musical theatre.

On the other hand, Susan Stroman says,

> I don't think it's a conscious decision to not hire women, I think it's more to do with men outnumbering women. There are some brilliantly talented female designers who directors, myself included, would love to work with, but because so few exist, it's tough finding one whose availability coincides with yours. But I think the imbalance is shifting.

When the "reimagined" production of *On a Clear Day*[9] opened on Broadway in December 2011, *New York Times* reviewer Ben Brantley noted:

The big difference is that Daisy is now David, a gay florist with commitment issues. Well, that's the first big difference, anyway. Daisy/David alter-ego, Melinda, is no longer a love-crossed English beauty from the 18th century but a feisty big-band singer from the early 1940s in search of a professional break. This transformation was even more troublesome to the "Clear Day" team than Daisy's sex change, since it meant coming up with songs that were more Benny Goodman than Thomas Arne.

Brantley clearly had no misgivings about the ethics of a leading role being taken away from a woman and given to a man. It is regarded as a minor detail compared to the style of music. The issue troubled *The Hollywood Reporter* critic David Rooney even less.

> Respect to director Michael Mayer and playwright Peter Parnell for their audacious attempt at reinventing a problematic musical in the Broadway revival of "On a Clear Day You Can See Forever" … Switching the gender of one point of the story's romantic triangle, the new team has turned it into "On a Queer Day.

Respect for what, exactly? Getting rid of another leading lady? Promoting a personal agenda?

No doubt he similarly salutes the *Book of Mormon* creators for dressing male cast members in drag instead of hiring women for the roles. But we don't know, as neither Rooney—nor any other critic for that matter—appeared to even notice. If they did, they did not consider it noteworthy enough to be remarked upon in print.

What would Brantley and Rooney's reactions be to the reintroduction of blackface to the Broadway stage in preference to employing African-American actors? Or to Patti Lupone announcing her intention to play Jean Valjean with a lesbian subtext? Extreme, I agree. But where are the voices raised in protest at this devaluation of women? An industry that once celebrated women onstage and indulged the female audience appears to be transforming itself into one in which women are deemed so irrelevant that they are replaced with ease by the "pretend female"—the gay man or the drag queen. And no one, least of all the critics, deems this worthy of comment. It is hard not to wonder if *On a Clear Day …* had been re-imagined by a female director and/or writer, would the character have remained Daisy, instead of mutating into David.

Musicals embrace the poetic point of view and relish sentiment. At the core of the genre is the conviction that a person can be so in love, or so overwhelmed by joy or sadness that the only way to fully convey the depth of the emotion they are experiencing is to sing or dance. Women, it could be argued, understand these emotions more than men, and they yearn to be transported by romance. They want to be moved to tears, and musical theatre traditionally provided this—this is a genre built on that love of heightened emotions, after all. But as men, and men's stories increasingly move to center stage, the sentiment, or the emotional heart of a show is gradually being eroded, replaced with cynical jokes and superficial characters. No one is going to *Rock of Ages, We Will Rock You* or *Xanadu* to experience elevated passion. Shows are beginning to wear a sarcastic sneer, and musicals that make fun of musicals are applauded as subversive.

Spamalot,[10] which won the 2004–2005 Tony award for Best Musical, started the sniggering by employing songs with titles such as *Twice in Every Show* and *The Song That Goes Like This* to seduce the audience into participating in the fundamental joke of the show—the parody of the structure and essence of the genre itself. Relying on audience recognition of the formulaic nature of older musicals, *The Drowsy Chaperone*[11] (2006 Tony Awards for Best Book and Best Score) continued the *Spamalot* gag with narrations and musical numbers designed to draw attention to the absurdity of the clichéd characters, comedic situations, and predictable songs so prevalent in shows (and Hollywood musicals) from the 30s and 40s. *The Book of Mormon* also falls into the "musicals mocking musicals" category—the pastiche reminders of shows such as *The Sound of Music, The Lion King,* and *Wicked* (among others) are conscious signals from the creators that they are aware they are making fun of the genre by utilizing it for their own purposes.

It seems to me that there is an underlying arrogance among the creators of these and similar shows, an attitude towards the genre that deems it second-rate and an indifference to the emotional core that formed the cornerstone of the traditional musical—a childish "anyone can do a musical" contempt. Anyone can *mock* a musical; it takes a Sondheim to redefine the parameters of the genre.

The number of Off-Broadway and U.K. Fringe productions that follow the title of the show with the words "The Musical"—*Jerry Springer: The Musical, Evil Dead: The Musical, Blockbuster: The Musical, Debbie Does Dallas: The Musical, 50 Shades!: The Musical, Pageant: The Musical*—indicates that the genre is no longer regarded as an art form, or to be treated with respect. But as Susan Stroman notes: "Before you can take a musical and turn it on its head, you have to have some knowledge of its history and respect for the genre—and that's what a lot of lesser works are missing."

The utilization of a form regarded as lowbrow immediately conveys the message that *Bat Boy: The Musical* for example, will lampoon the genre by taking an unlikely or ludicrous scenario and presenting it as a musical. *Bat Boy: The Play* would not have the same effect, because plays are seen as above the scorn and ridicule that musicals are subjected to. While *The Drowsy Chaperone* poked gentle fun at the genre, with obvious affection, *Spamalot* dripped with disdain. "Who could possibly like this stuff?" the show appeared to be asking. Well, we already know who likes this stuff: women.

So if the musical is now something to be scoffed at, what does that imply about the women (and men) who love it? Should they be reviled for not having higher aspirations? Even a brief skip through the cast recordings of any of the more trite or cynical shows such as *Spamalot, The Book of Mormon, Xanadu,* or *Bat Boy* leaves one in no doubt of the undercurrent of disdain for women pervading these shows. They use an undergraduate style of humor with chauvinistic foundations—*Avenue Q* has a character imaginatively named *Lucy the Slut*—and a masculine view of emotions as pathetic and the domain of the weaker sex. The removal of passion and sentiment from the musical is again, a mark of disrespect towards the audience—it is, after all, why the predominantly female audience is there. I am not suggesting every musical has to have the soaring melodrama of *Love Never Dies* but it would be a breath of fresh air among the crop of sarcastic parodies filled with caricatures currently on offer.

And perhaps that it is the real issue dominating contemporary musical theatre—a fashionable disregard throughout society for displays of emotion, or for anything that delves deeper than the surface. Virtual reality is preferable to a meaningful experience. Television shows featuring obese people losing weight or the daily machinations of a B-grade celebrity are easier to watch than thought-provoking dramas. Friendships are maintained through text messages and postings on Facebook, and online dating has removed the tedious inconvenience of having to actually meet with a potential suitor face to face to assess his or her credentials. It all adds up to the antithesis of everything musical theatre stands for—sweeping passions, elevated emotions and a great romance guaranteed to make the audience weep. *Spamalot* actually has a song—"The Song That Goes Like This"—which mocks that staple of musical theatre, the love ballad. Who would have thought we'd ever see the day when two characters singing of love in a musical was the cue for a derisive snort?

Wikipedia defines biological determinism as the "hypothesis that biological factors such as an organism's individual genes (as opposed to social or environmental factors) completely determine how a system behaves." This "nature versus nurture" debate has long been put forward as the explanation behind the assertion that men are more suited to power than women. Testosterone, apparently, endows men with innate qualities such as ambition, aggression, competitive spirit, and a lack of emotion, which makes them better candidates than women for politics, the judiciary, sport, the military: everything, really, except domesticity.

This notion is pervasive in the workplace and provides the perfect excuse to limit female advancement to managerial or leadership roles or to restrict their entry into certain male-dominated professions. In the field of science, for instance, an ability to detach emotionally is almost a prerequisite. The caring professions—aged care, nursing, teaching small children, social work—are seen as better suited to women's supposed innate nurturing skills and heightened capacity for empathy. In addition to empathy and nurturing, women are also credited with possessing diplomatic, communication, and negotiating skills, as well as being expert multitaskers—qualities acquired, no doubt, through daily interactions within a society predisposed to favor men. A woman juggling a full-time job and three children is bound to be expert in multitasking and negotiating.

Biological determinism also asserts that women are more sensitive to their emotions than men. In itself, this need not necessarily be a bad thing, but when the word "emotional" becomes interchangeable with "irrational"—as it frequently does—this reasoning becomes problematic for women. "Too emotional" becomes the major stumbling block to women's advancement in certain careers. But could this not be an advantage in the emotional world of the musical genre? Wendy Cavett:

> I'm a visceral and passionate conductor and I am emotional. And I would say that … I am more expressive than many male conductors would allow themselves to be. It's just a me thing. That's who I am and that's how I express myself musically. It also depends on the situation. There are times when it is appropriate and there are times when it is not. On this kind of show it can be appropriate because you want to give a lot of emotional juice. But there are times when if you are too emotional it reads as a lack of technique. And so you have to learn how to pull back.

If we define the job of a theatre director as that of a guide, or nurturer—someone who unifies a number of departments in pursuit of a common goal—then it follows that an ability to collaborate is essential, alongside the aforementioned female skills of negotiation, communication, and diplomacy. Collaboration may not be a biologically determined female quality, but few would disagree that women are better at it than men—particularly in the workforce, where men demonstrate a greater need to be in charge. If we also agree that women possess these skills and are more in tune with their emotions, then why aren't more women directing musical theatre, the one place where emotions are allowed—encouraged, even—to have free rein? "Too emotional" is often used in place of "weak," and the leadership required of the director of a musical has to be strong.

But this is assuming there is only one style of directing—a dictatorial school, where the director is the ultimate seat of power and the final word rests with him. A more inclusive style of directing can produce results that are just as successful, with none of the bad feelings and tantrums that dominate a rehearsal process run by a tyrannical, bullying director. Stroman offers,

> I think women are better listeners. We're not as quick to shut people down, which allows for ideas to be heard—and you never know where inspiration will come from. I feel like women instinctually take the time to really listen to what a person is saying, and that goes back to why it's important to treat everyone on a team with respect. There comes a point in your life when you understand the importance of how you treat people and it often means putting egos aside and working together to do what's best for the show—and I think that's something that comes easier to women.

Despite the qualities that make women eminently suitable for the director's role, producers remain reluctant to hire women. Perhaps stereotypical images of traditional femininity are at play here. A woman with power is considered unattractive and unfeminine. She is behaving like a man and therefore not a "real" woman—witness how quickly the phrase "career bitch" entered daily usage, and how high-ranking female politicians are judged more often on their clothes and success as a mother than on their political achievements. Few women in any sector of the workforce will deny there is a prejudice towards the authoritative female that is not perpetrated against a male in a position of power. Women have to be twice as good as their male counterparts to be considered on equal footing, and this is as true of musical theatre as it is of any other profession. Susan H. Schulman says, "I still think women are not allowed to fail as easily as men are. I think men are forgiven much more easily in commercial theatre for not having a hit than women are."

The idea of a woman holding a position of power in theatre—directing a musical—may simply offend traditional male beliefs. A number of musical theatre producers are of a generation which was not brought up to regard women as equal—particularly in the workplace.) Consequently, working alongside women operating on an equal level of authority is unlikely to be welcomed by a certain type and generation of men. It remains to be seen if the upcoming generation of male musical theatre producers have more enlightened attitudes. Current producers may also be influenced by the trend of new musicals to shy away from embracing emotion. If women are seen to be governed by their feelings, then "too emotional" becomes the perfect excuse for not employing a female director on a sentiment-free, so-called subversive musical. But what about the revivals of older shows, created long before emotion became a dirty word? If women really do have such a close relationship with heightened passion, wouldn't that make them the ideal directorial candidates for a new production of *Carousel* or *South Pacific*? It seems that the argument against female directors gets twisted to suit any scenario—too emotional for *Spamalot* but not detached enough to create a new *Follies*, and rarely even considered as a director for a show about women—*Wicked, Next to Normal, Legally Blonde, Sister Act,* or *Grey Gardens.*

Susan Stroman offers, "I feel we're better at it, to be honest. This is a field long dominated by men. That's changing—and there are a lot of women on the way up—but it's slow."

Way too slow. Producers continue to actively favor men over women when hiring directors for musicals. Yet back in 1989, writing in the *New York Times*, theatre critic Frank Rich commended director Susan H. Schulman for "forcing us to face Mr. Sondheim's music and the feelings it contains so intensely" in her production of *Sweeney Todd.*

In a later article on the same production,[12] Rich drew attention to the fact that a deeper exploration of the female characters onstage resulted in a more meaningful theatrical experience.

> I have usually been moved by "Sweeney Todd," but never in the way Ms. Schulman's rendering moved me. It is not that the director set out to create a feminist interpretation—which the text cannot support in any case—but that she gives equal weight to female characters who originally came off as stylized slatterns in a man's story. It may be simply that she sees the play's women more fully or has more compassion for them. Whatever the explanation, the balance of "Sweeney Todd" has subtly shifted.

The recent Spice Girls musical *Viva Forever!* appears to have been conceived as a woman's story, yet the saddest thing about it (apart from the reviews) was the fact that a show—dare I say product—that was shamelessly created to exploit women's love affair with the musical (and to harness their box office power), had a male director. A story that centered around women, with songs from the most successful girl band ever—the band, remember, who coined the battle cry "girl power"—had a man overseeing the entire production. What message does that give, both to female directors and to the women in the audience? And how disheartening that this message was delivered by another woman, producer Judy Craymer. If ever there was a case to be made for positive discrimination, *Viva Forever!* was it. I simply do not buy the excuse that there were no female candidates for the director's role. Or the old "best person for the job" claim. The best person to direct *Viva Forever!*

was a woman, even just to make the point that female directors of musicals do exist. *The Color Purple* on Broadway managed to find an entire creative team that reflected the themes of black empowerment espoused by the show and book. It is bitterly disappointing that *Viva Forever!* did not do the same.

Ms. Craymer may have spurned the sisterhood, but her business savvy in harnessing the music of The Spice Girls to appeal to women who adored the band twenty years ago appeared wise. *Viva Forever!* opened with a $4 million advance so it barely mattered what was onstage. All the director of the production had to do was point the actors in the right direction and run the tech. I can name a number of women directors who are more than capable of doing that and who might even—with their innate insight into the female mind—have directed a show that could have risen above reviews such as these:

It's clear that everyone involved wants this to be a women-affirming show: there are very few male parts and they're all cyphers. But, sadly, so are all the female parts. Viva and her friends are bland and indistinguishable; everyone else is a cliché. There's not much cockle-warming, despite the performers' best efforts. There is some glitz. But it says something when you find yourself scanning the audience for entertainment (there's Cilla! And Michael Caine!); when the most riveting plot point of the evening is whether or not Posh Spice will ever acknowledge the rest of her old band.—Miranda Sawyer, *The Observer*, Sunday, 16 December 2012

I'll tell you what I wanted, what I really, really wanted—I wanted this terrible show to stop. The producer Judy Craymer hit pay dirt with *Mamma Mia!*, which became a global smash hit. But that show was blessed with a witty and touching script by Catherine Johnson and a raft of perfect pop songs from Abba. So cashing in on the Spice Girls back catalogue must have seemed a nobrainer. In fact, it was a ghastly mistake."—Charles Spencer, *The Telegraph*, 12th December, 2012

"Somehow, though, the other members of Viva's band (spiritedly played by Dominique Provost-Chalkley, Lucy Phelps, Siobhan Athwal) get bafflingly sidelined. Sure, Girl Power reasserts itself when they swarm on near the end for a vibrant performance of "Wannabe." But a rousing celebration of individuality and rebellion feels a tad unearned as the climax to a show that's so lacking in any truly original or challenging spark of its own." Paul Taylor, The Independent, Tuesday, 11 December 2012

Perhaps the real problem around *Viva Forever!* was that it did not stem from a passionate desire to create a challenging new musical that would add depth to the genre by pushing boundaries and exploring the possibilities of the medium—as *Oklahoma!* and *West Side Story* did. Or most of Sondheim's works. *Viva Forever!* was clearly a money making exercise, designed to cash in on the *Mamma Mia!* audience and success. And if you are running a business, I understand that it needs to be financially successful in order to survive. But where is it written that financial success can only be achieved through a compromise of artistic standards and integrity? Ironic, really, that the conservative (with a capital and small c) British populace could elect a female prime minister, but a musical inspired by the Spice Girls failed to stay faithful to the band's original concept of Girl Power, even with a female producer.

My own unease with *Viva Forever!* is that the attitude at the heart of the show appeared to be grounded in a belief that women are so stupid they will go and see anything—that their passion for musical theatre renders them incapable of telling the difference between a good show and a bad one. The producers clearly understood that women are the mainstay of the musical theatre audience and created a product specifically designed to appeal to the female ticket buyer. I am all in favor of that; it's high time producers responded to the gender statistics that are glaringly obvious in audience demographic surveys. But it still has to be a good show. If the producers and creative team dumb the show down because they want to attract a female audience, the message is crystal clear: Musical theatre is lowbrow entertainment, patronized mainly by dumb air heads who don't know any better. Bless their hearts. Well, clearly the women who did attend *Viva Forever!* were savvy enough to recognize a terrible show and smart enough to realize they were being disrespected and treated like fools. They stopped buying tickets. The show closed after limping to a seven-month run, and with losses of $5 million (pounds) reported.

There is no doubt that the musical has changed almost beyond recognition in the last quarter-century. The genre is now Big Business, where production houses bear more resemblance to corporate institutions than centers of artistic excellence. Fears abound that while the genre may be "cool" among the younger generation again, it is dumbing down to accommodate the techno-savvy audience with a shorter attention span and a "seen it all before" attitude. Where have the sophisticated musicals gone? Where are the successors to Sondheim? To Jerome Robbins?

In 2010, David Camp in the *New York Times*[13] hoped, "The jazz-hands youth quake reaches its logical conclusion: a sustained resurgence of honest-to-goodness original shows, with original books, original music, original lyrics and no relation whatsoever to any pre-existing film, album, video game or comic book franchise." Sadly, we are still waiting. But the *Glee* generation cannot be held solely responsible for the collection of cartoons, uninspiring movies, and collections of greatest hits from long-forgotten bands currently masquerading as musical theatre. Traditionalists argue that the demise of the stylish, Sondheim-esque show began with the introduction of the mega-musical—productions that relied more on special effects and technology than good songs and a witty script.

The technical advances in sound, stage machinery, special effects and lighting in the last twenty-five years have allowed the musical to become more filmic, subsequently raising audience expectations. The industry response has been to produce shows owing more to Cirque du Soleil and rock concerts than to what the purists would term musical theatre. And as the shows grew bigger, so did the budgets. When *Spiderman: Turn Off the Dark* opened on Broadway after two years of delays, the final cost was reported as (U.S.) $75 million, which has to raise the issue of the musical pricing itself out of its own existence. Production costs have to be absorbed into ticket prices, and while audience members seem prepared to pay extra for what they consider an event or phenomenon, as opposed to a musical, they need the security of knowing what they are going to get before parting with their cash. Escalating costs demand guaranteed financial returns, and producers are increasingly fearful of risking an investment on a show that does not have immediate public recognition. Correspondingly, producers are even more reluctant to take a chance with new talent. But reverting to the same safe pair of hands means that the upcoming directors, writers, composers, and choreographers—many of whom are women—are finding it harder than ever to get a foot in the door. They are not helped, as Broadway general manager Nina Lannan suggests, by *"producers not wanting to put a thirty million dollar musical in the hands of a woman..."*

Men are still considered more capable than women when it comes to handling the pressure—the testosterone/biological determinism argument again. Beth Williams says,

> I think it's very natural for a group of successful men in the business to assume that the next group of successful people will be men because that's how it's always been. So if I'm in my 70s and the people I've worked with are all male, it's just natural for me to assume that the next generation down will all be male.

The rise of technology in musical theatre has had an adverse effect on women both on and off the stage. As in other professions involving mechanics or engineering, men dominate the field, and the backstage of a musical is no different. Particularly on Broadway, stagehands are almost exclusively male, and the perception that women directors—or designers for that matter—could not handle this dynamic continues to reign. Despite Julie Taymor's directorial triumph with *The Lion King*[14]—a show utilizing special effects onstage—the perception of theatre technology as a male domain is playing its own part in keeping women directors out of the now heavily automated musical. A belief that men are better than women at running the pressure-intense technical rehearsal period to schedule and have a greater understanding of the mechanics of a stage revolve or moving scenery still persists. Women deal with emotions, men deal with machinery. But women directors think otherwise. Susan H. Schulman:

> There are plenty of male directors who can't tech a big show and there are plenty of women who can't. And there are plenty of women who can. I really don't think it is truly gender specific. But I think the perception might be. But in truth, it's not true. I mean, just look at the wonderful women set designers and lighting designers. That's all technology.

The relatively recent phenomenon of the mega-musical—shows that have been turned into worldwide franchises and rely on technology in the form of automated sets and special effects—has also had an adverse effect on the women onstage. Far from placing female characters at the center of the action, female characters in mega-musicals tend to literally disappear, dwarfed by huge sets, male ensembles, and cumbersome costumes. *Phantom of the Opera* and *Wicked* both overwhelm the leading ladies with scenery and technological tricks, effectively denying them space.

The association of technology with men means that stories about men that require them to interact with the technology (the male revolutionaries on the barricade in *Les Misérables,* the soldiers in *Miss Saigon* boarding the helicopter, Spiderman flying) become prevalent. This has ramifications for women, as the traditional leading-lady roles are dismissed in favor of a featured set piece and the men who interact with it. The attention of the creators is focused more on the Phantom manoeuvring the boat than Christine sitting passively in front of him. Consequently, women's roles are relegated to the bottom of a long list of priorities, somewhere below the set, the costumes, and the men. Christine is so seldom offstage in *Phantom of the Opera* that it requires two performers to share the schedule of eight shows per week, yet the focus is always on the leading man. When he is not actually onstage, the other characters sing about him. *Les Misérables* reduces the women to bystanders watching the boys' revolution—the departure of the female ensemble from the barricades before the battle renders their contribution obsolete. The show may well be called *Miss Saigon*, but it is the Engineer who has the eleven o'clock number and is awarded the final bow. Women in the mega-musical—*Wicked* aside—are passive, the men proactive. Chris marries another woman, but it is his sorrow we are asked to empathize with at the end of *Miss Saigon*, not the sacrificial Kim's.

The mega-musical—and to a degree the jukebox musical—became responsible for the globalization of a particular kind of theatre, making certain musicals as ubiquitous worldwide as Starbucks or McDonald's. *Les Misérables* has been translated into 27 different languages and been seen in 38 countries. *Phantom of the Opera* is the highest-grossing entertainment event of all time, with worldwide box office takings of $5.1 billion—productions have played in 145 cities in 47 countries. Since its 1999 debut, over 42 million people have seen *Mamma Mia!* and the show has grossed $2 billion. *The Lion King* is now the highest-grossing Broadway show of all time, with box office takings of $853 million. The exporting of a show worldwide has turned certain musicals into a brand. Who can fail to associate the forlorn child's face in front of the Tricolor with *Les Misérables* or recognize the dancers in the cat's eyes as, well, *Cats.*

To further convince an audience that they were viewing an *experience,* logo-infested merchandise became a necessary part of the package. You've seen the show; now buy the baseball cap or key ring. A souvenir of the event became a necessity—prove to the neighbors you've seen *Spiderman* by drinking from the mug while ironing the T-shirt. The consumer now has a lasting reminder of what they have been told is the "theatrical event of the decade." When producers smelled the opportunity to commercially exploit the show even further, they achieved what had been assumed to be impossible. They transformed an art form into a product, traded like any other commodity and with a seemingly unending lifespan. The "now and forever" marketing tagline from *Cats* clearly wasn't the joke we thought it was at the time. Ironically, this universality may be reducing the "specialness" or "event" quality that was the goal. Geraldine Turner offers:

> When I was growing up you couldn't wait for the latest Broadway musical to come out. And you ran out and got the record to play it and there were new songs and you'd learn them and you couldn't wait for the show to come to Australia and you'd go and see it. Now people have to know the songs before they'll go. And producers know that too. So that's why it's safer and safer and safer and safer and safer.... Now you go to see Lion King the Movie. You take your kids ten times to it because they like it. You buy the DVD and they play it over and over and over again, a hundred times a day. You buy all the T-shirts when you go to the movie and you buy all the cups and buttons and everything. Then, a few years later they put the cartoon characters onstage— you already know the songs and now there are new T-shirts to buy and there are new mugs to buy and that's what Broadway has become and I find that a tragedy. It's a tragedy. There's nothing new. There's no audiences going to something going, "Oh, I want to hear a new song and feel that go into my body and love that new song." They want to know every song. They want to know the product. They want to know what they're going to see. They want to know that they've seen the cartoon version on the screen and now they're seeing real live people with lions' heads on. They want that.

The one thing there is no room for within the jukebox/mega-musical brand is a star. Once the initial excitement of who is playing the lead in the original production—Jonathan Pryce in the original *Miss Saigon* or Idina Menzel in *Wicked*—has died down, the stars are replaced from a seemingly endless pool of lesser-known performers. Occasionally a star will be brought back into the show later in the run to boost flagging box office receipts, but by and large, both the jukebox and the mega-musical do not rely on a household name to keep them running. Can anyone name the current star of the Broadway productions of *Jersey Boys* or *Spiderman*?

Following the launch in the U.K. in 2012 of *Viva Forever!*, British arts commentator David Lister[15] asked:

> Who are the performers in the show? Few will know or care. Like the director, they are not of major importance, at least at the launch stage. It's strange, as, with any other kind of theatre, actors and director are quite important. You'd be unlikely to buy tickets without knowing their identity. But with jukebox musicals, it's the jukebox that takes pride of place. That's not to be snobbish. I've seen most of the ones on in London, *Mamma Mia!*, *Jersey Boys*, *We Will Rock You*, and they are all highly enjoyable, though I couldn't name a single actor or actress in any. It's what's on the jukebox that counts.

The number of awards for technical excellence heaped on the various designers of *Cats*, *Les Misérables*, *Phantom of the Opera*, *The Lion King*, and *Wicked* compared to the number of awards garnered by the shows' performers is a good indication of where the focus of the mega musical lies. Who needs Ethel Merman when the sound designer can mix even the blandest voice so it carries to the back of the stalls? Who needs an experienced and respected musical theatre performer in the lead when the show itself has become the main attraction and can be replicated in multiple cities all over the world with look a like casts? Does the average ticket buyer actually know who is playing the *Phantom* twenty-six years down the line? Chances are, she is going for the experience of the show, regardless of who is in the cast. Consequently, the role of the performer becomes diminished by technology. Audiences are buying tickets to see Spiderman fly, not because they know the name of the actor playing Spiderman.

The ease with which new actors are slotted into the worldwide reproductions is a clear message to performers—you are not Mary Martin, Julie Andrews, Chita Rivera or Patti Lupone. You are replaceable. The show is the draw card. And the assembly-line techniques utilized when remounting these shows globally are light-years away from an organic, creative process where actors are encouraged to explore their characters and contribute ideas. This is about rehashing, not discovering. Fifteen years after the original production, does the new Nala in *The Lion King* really know what her motivation is, other than "that's what we've always done"? Actors, too, have become a commodity within the mega-musical. Harry Connick, Jr.'s name was emblazoned in lights above the theatre marquee when *On a Clear Day* played on Broadway, and the entire marketing campaign for *How to Succeed in Business* centered around Daniel Radcliffe. Would *The Boy from Oz* ever have made it to Broadway if Hugh Jackman's name had not been attached to it? But none of these shows fall into the mega-musical category, and all were relying on attributes other than technology to lure a crowd. But without a musical theatre star, composer/lyricist teams have no one to create shows for, or to be inspired by, and are no longer writing new musicals with a particular female performer in mind. Shows are now being created around the scenery, special effects, and bland pop hits from a former decade.

I'm not saying there is anything wrong with wanting to make a profit at the box office. No one produces a show in the hope of going bankrupt—except in *The Producers,* of course. The idea is to recoup the original investment, hopefully in order to stage another show and ensure the survival of the genre. The commercialization of the musical was deliberate—creating a worldwide, marketable brand doesn't happen by chance. The production houses of Cameron Mackintosh and Lloyd Webber realized there was money to be made from musical theatre, and they simply exploited the opportunity. There is nothing intrinsically wrong with that, except for the direction in which it inevitably pushed the genre. The musical reverted to the mass entertainment it was in the Golden Age, leaving the Sondheim aficionados and the musical theatre purists outraged at the misappropriation of what they considered to be their art form.

One could argue that change is inevitable in every artistic movement, and fluidity is imperative for any genre to move with the times. The sheer number of people attending musicals now who would never have done so before can only be a good thing for the form and theatre as a whole. Does the audience notice that the music of these techno-shows owes more to bland pseudo-pop than the traditional, distinctive sound of Broadway, and that the show's pace never varies, no matter what city the production is playing? As long as Spider-man and Elphaba fly on cue, the Phantom brings down the chandelier, and the cast replacements are ready to go, all is well in the world of the new musical.

But change is not synonymous with progress, and it is hard to see what exactly the mega-musical or shows such as *Spamalot, Xanadu, Shrek*, or *We Will Rock You* contribute to the artistic development of the genre, or to gender equality onstage. Financial gain seems to be the real driving force behind an excessive number of musicals in the last decade, not an appreciation or passion for the art form. And they are light-years away from the musicals of Jerry Herman or Kander and Ebb, which placed women downstage center in a spotlight all of their own. How many women can we name appearing in *Jersey Boys, Kinky Boots, The Book of Mormon,* or *Newsies?*

Musical theatre might well be aimed at women, but there is little evidence of a woman's voice throughout the genre: a uniquely female viewpoint that resonates with other women through recognition of a shared experience. It is unquestionably present in *Mamma Mia!,* due, no doubt, to the show being created by women. It is also visible in *The Secret Garden*—again a show with a female creative team. *Little Women* (2005) had a female lyricist (Mindi Dickstein) and director (Susan Schulman) and was adapted from the 1869 semi-autobiographical novel by Louisa May Alcott, in which the female voice is more of a shout than a whisper. *Violet* (1997 Off-Broadway, 2014 Broadway) had music by Jeanine Tesori and was based on the short story *The Ugliest Pilgrim* by Doris Betts. The show explores ideas around the construct of beauty—an issue resonating with most women. *Wicked* has female friendship as its driving theme, but pitifully few other musicals have a clear female voice that women in the audience can identify with. Wendy Cavett offers,

> I would say that the classic Broadway sound is not a female voice. That golden age, you know, Rodgers and Hammerstein, Lerner and Lowe and that chunk of material that happened between 1945 and 1965 that's such a specific, iconic sound. The orchestrations are very masculine, very brassy ... so I would say that is definitely a male sound. And then you get into the Hair, Jesus Christ Superstar ... the rock era, I would say that that is not necessarily male or female. You might say it was male but I think it was so connected to the political content ... what was going on in that era. So I think of our sound as being more politically and socially connected than gender connected.

The notion of the woman's voice in the arts is often dismissed with labels such as chick flick or chick lit—the implication being that if it is created with women in mind, it is not as serious or worthy as the "real thing," i.e., men's films, men's books. But as Frank Rich pointed out, when Susan H. Schulman injected her voice into *Sweeney Todd* and grounded the character of Mrs. Lovett in an emotional truth, rather than a stereotype or parody, it brought a new depth to the production. It is interesting to speculate what the addition of a female voice would bring to a production of *Evita, Gypsy,* or *My Fair Lady,* shows ostensibly about women, but written from a male perspective. Henry Higgins in *My Fair Lady* (1956) not only teaches Eliza how to speak, he teaches her how to *be* the woman he wants her to be. He literally supplants her voice with his own.

This is the same strategy, I would argue, employed by the male creators

of musicals when creating female characters—the women become the mouthpiece to express a male idea of how a woman thinks and behaves, or how
men *want* them to think and behave. The woman's voice is, in effect, silenced
and replaced with a male one. Is this a reflection of a wider view in society
of women's opinions being irrelevant? A rehearsal room with an all-male creative team is hardly likely to be a place where the woman's voice will be listened to. Just as a female dancer's body is controlled by a male choreographer,
or an artist possesses a woman's body by painting her nude, so the male director and writers of musical appropriate the woman's voice—both literally and
metaphorically—to promote their own agenda or beliefs.

How likely is it that a woman would write "What's the Use of Wondrin'"
from *Carousel* (1945), a song which defines a woman as belonging to a man
and encourages her total subservience to him, or "Peron's Latest Flame" from
Evita (1978), a song seething with misogyny and referring to Eva as a bitch
and a whore?

Both these examples demonstrate a view of women that is coming
unequivocally from a male perspective. And arguing that it is the *characters*
who are expressing this opinion does not, I'm afraid, let the writers off the
hook. What both of these examples also prove is that placing a woman at the
center of a musical does not necessarily mean that the resulting show will
have a woman's voice. How can it, when the show is written from a male
point of view? *Carousel* and *Evita* are, of course, 70 and 30 years old respectively, and detractors will be quick to point out that attitudes towards gender
have evolved since then. But have they?

Out of the ten shows that have won the Best Musical Tony award in the
last decade—*Kinky Boots, Once, The Book of Mormon, Memphis, Billy Elliot,
In the Heights, Spring Awakening, Jersey Boys, Spamalot* and *Avenue Q*—only
three of them had a woman on the creative team—less than a third. Small
wonder the female perspective is missing. A male director can never fully
understand the female perspective, because he has not experienced it. His
idea of how women react in certain situations, or how they negotiate their
place in society, is just that: an idea. When we add the robust male ego into
the mix, we are left with an interpretation that is blinkered, to say the least.

"Who cares?" you may cry. "It's just a musical." Well, it may not have
been noteworthy in the 1970s and '80s when the lack of any real direction
within the genre resulted in audiences looking elsewhere for their entertainment, reducing musical theatre to a subculture for the faithful few. But the
musical is back and more influential than ever. The thousands of teenage
girls who know all the songs from the TV series *Smash*, or who tweet and
blog online about *Wicked*, are enraptured with musical theatre—at the

moment. But when their feminist antennae start twitching (usually around the time they enter the workforce), they may gradually become more sensitive to the misogyny embedded within many contemporary shows, and all of a sudden, the musical will be less appealing—which adds up to empty seats. So, yes, the lack of a women's voice in musical theatre is worth debating, because ultimately, it could be the very thing that drives the audience away: the female audience, who are the majority of ticket buyers.

In *Mamma Mia!*, book writer Catherine Johnson gives the leading lady these lines of dialogue.

> DONNA: Don't you patronize me. I love doing it on my own—every morning I wake up and thank Christ I haven't got some middle-aged, menopausal man to bother me. I'm single. I'm free. And it's great.

Do we really need to ask why women have been flocking to this show for over a decade?

All of which brings me to the question at the heart of the issue—can women have a voice in musical theatre if they have no power and no status? Are shows that lay claim to the woman's voice—*Next to Normal, Wicked, The Life, Evita, Legally Blonde, Grey Gardens, Miss Saigon*—actually presenting a distorted version of that voice, due to the fact that the originators are men? It may be narrow-minded of me to suggest that there is a conspiracy among the current crop of producers to deliberately suppress a woman's voice—particularly as there is no proven reason why this prejudice would exist. Perhaps it is simpler than that. Perhaps we have all grown so used to seeing women presented onstage as the embodiment of how men see them that we no longer even recognize the distortion, let alone question why, just like the producers so accustomed to having a male creative team around them that it never occurs to them that there are women who could do the job just as well. Lucy Simon:

> I think men keep [women] out. I really do. I think they justify it by saying "oh, women can't handle the toughness … the tough decisions." Women are much more in the role of being the conciliator. Negotiator. And that's not a strong enough position for a director or composer, or the perception of what a creative person is in the theatre. However, as creators we are collaborators and that means something. We all work together. But if you have a male director, the male director will put his vision in place.

NOTES

1. English inventor of the Dual Cyclone vacuum cleaner and the ContraRotator washing machine.

2. Mary Jo Lodge , 2008, "The Rise of the Female Director/Choreographer on Broadway" in *Women in American Musical Theatre,* ed. Bud Coleman and Judith Sebasta (Jefferson, N.C.: McFarland), 221.

3. Nominated for an Academy Award for his direction of *Chicago* in 2002. He also directed the film version of *Nine* in 2009.

4. George Gershwin referred to *Porgy and Bess* as a "folk opera" and it was not until the 1976 production by Houston Grand Opera that the show became accepted as legitimate opera. A 2011 production at the American Repertory Theatre called it neither a musical nor an opera, but billed it as *The Gershwins' Porgy and Bess.*

5. *Seven Brides for Seven Brothers,* 1954.

6. Ian Bradley, 2004. *You've Got to Have a Dream: The Message of the Musical* (London: SCM Press).

7. Book by Abe Burrows, Jack Weinstock and Willie Gilbert; music by Frank Loesser.

8. Book by Jennifer Saunders; music and lyrics by The Spice Girls.

9. Reconceived and directed by Michael Mayer; new book by Peter Parnell.

10. Book and lyrics by Eric Idle; music by John Du Prez and Eric Idle.

11. Book by Bob Martin and Don McKellar; music and lyrics by Lisa Lambert and Greg Morrison.

12. "Critics Notebook: On Stage, the Feminist Message Takes on a Sly and Subtle Tone," *New York Times*, April 19, 1989.

13. "The Glee Generation," *New York Times,* June 13, 2010.

14. Taymor was also the original director and co-book writer on *Spiderman Turn Off the Dark* before being removed in March 2011 by the show's producers.

15. "Tell you what I want, what I really, really want: genuine musicals," *The Independent,* June 30, 2012.

2

Loving You Is
Not a Choice

Women as Martyrs
to Heterosexual Love

When you launch into song, your heart goes with it. In a musical,
you create a moment so emotional, so vitally important, it's impossible to speak—you have to sing. The moment is just filled with emotion and feeling. Women tend to be much more in touch with those
emotions than men, and I think we believe in the power of those
emotions more so than men. We believe these things can happen,
that you can love someone so much it makes you burst into song.
                                                            —Susan Stroman

As discussed in the previous chapter, the musical has traditionally been
grounded in romance and driven by the belief that "marry the man today"
is the mantra driving all women. Plot lines as far back as the golden era of
the Hollywood musical have been built around the central female character
finding the love of her life. How many shows end with a triumphant wedding
scene? Name almost any musical, and there will be a love duet contained
somewhere in it or a ballad about a broken heart sung by the leading lady.
The Drowsy Chaperone, which so accurately parodied the formulaic plot
line and structure of popular musicals of the 1930s, had all of the above in
Bride's Lament, Love Is Always Lovely in the End and the wedding finale *I
Do, I Do in the Sky.* The fact that audiences immediately recognized the
clichéd plot lines and characters as a gentle parody and laughed along demonstrates just how embedded the notion of romance is as the driving force of
the genre. Is it possible to imagine a musical without a love story? Even
the derisive *Book of Mormon* gives its own nod to romance with an—almost—

love duet, "Baptize Me," between Elder Cunningham and his Ugandan convert Nabulungi. I am not denying that love is the greatest story ever told, but what I find increasingly problematic with musicals is that when women are involved, it seems to be the *only* story ever told. Few female characters in musicals have careers or lives beyond their men, and few writers create roles for women beyond the context of romance. The driving thought behind this appears to be the belief that all women yearn for the love of a man and until they find it, they are incomplete. Sally Bowles in *Cabaret* describes herself as a "loser" because she is without a man and hopes that she has finally found one that will stay. Fair enough, given her history of broken relationships. But the main problem with a traditional interpretation of a romantic coupling is that it designates the female as passive. Women wait for love; men bring it.

By defining a man as the ultimate prize—the one competition all women want to win—the male is automatically elevated in status above the female. She becomes less important than the goal she is seeking. Consequently, her needs and desires take second place to his. Romance, for women, comes at a price—usually that of her personal freedom. This price may not have been considered too high in Jane Austen's day when a woman was unlikely to have an inspiring career to sacrifice for a husband, but women today have other options, and finding a balance between career and family, rather than sacrificing one for the other, is the choice favored by the majority of first-world women. Yet we rarely see this choice reflected onstage. By continuing to make an association between romance and female sacrifice—men are never required to give up anything for love—musicals persistently adhere to a point of view that designates men's lives of more significance than women's.

Most women in musicals are far too busy waiting for the right man to come along to have the time for a career, but for those who do there is the implicit understanding that the arrival of the masculine prize will put an end to any ambitions beyond the marriage contract. What more could a woman possibly want or need than a husband and two children? But the romance on offer to women in musicals is frequently more restrictive than empowering. In *Sunset Boulevard*, Artie assumes that the ambitious and smart Betty will no longer be working once they wed and announces his intention to move to the suburbs (it goes without saying that Betty was not included in this decision) where his plans involve Betty raising the kids and serving him beers as he reclines in a hammock in the garden. She will then, no doubt, join the ranks of educated, suburban housewives who stick their head into a gas oven just to escape the tedium. *Love Never Dies* only serves to convince us that Christine would have been better off having a glittering career at the opera than marrying the control freak Raoul. One can't help speculating if Diana in *Next to Normal* would be less depressed if she had a stimulating job and more interesting husband. And small wonder Donna hesitates in *Mamma Mia!* before accepting a marriage proposal from the nondescript Sam, subsequently relinquishing her emotional and financial independence. The male characters, quite simply, do not match up to the women they appear to believe they deserve.

Because musical theatre is built upon notions of romance and the all-encompassing female search for a husband, there is no place onstage for the single woman. She is either something to be feared or pitied. Lizzie, the lead character of *110 in the Shade*, is given a song titled *Old Maid* in which she outlines an empty existence filled with days of rearranging the furniture because there's nothing better to do. Labels such as "spinster" or "old maid" are far from complimentary, and the image of a lonely woman rearranging furniture to fill empty hours is not an appealing one. The message is clear—without a husband, there is little point to a woman's life. Don Black, lyricist on Andrew Lloyd Webber's *Aspects of Love* (1989), even gives leading lady Rose a song titled "Anything But Lonely" just to remind us that being alone is the ultimate female indignity. Rose also describes an empty life but takes it one step further by avowing there is no sense to life if she is alone. Fear of being single, or of the perceived social stigma attached to this status, compels women in musicals to lower their sights and accept whatever is on offer. But I'd be curious to know just how many contemporary single women with challenging careers would describe their lives today as "empty." Do Rose and Lizzie have no friends?

Interestingly, Don Black also penned the lyrics for Andrew Lloyd Webber's *Tell Me on a Sunday*, which premiered in London in 1982 as the second half of *Song and Dance*. *Tell Me on a Sunday* is a one-woman show, a song cycle that tells of the romantics liaisons between an English girl and her American paramours. Riveting stuff. It is also a show where the character played by the leading lady—the only person ever onstage—is not even given a name. That's how important she is to the evening's entertainment. When the show was staged on Broadway in 1985 starring Bernadette Peters, the character—apparently at Ms. Peter's insistence—had the name Emma bestowed upon her, but I doubt if anyone in the audience could remember it.

"The Girl" (not "woman," significantly) appears to have no job—how she affords the plane fare to the U.S. and pays for a New York apartment is never explained. All we ever learn about her is that she has a number of love affairs that end in tears—hers. Oh, and that she regularly writes home to Mum. She has no identity of her own; her view of herself is completely defined by the men she has sex with. The Girl has no earthly concept of independence, or career, or anything other than securing a man.

Is this really how Don Black and Andrew Lloyd Webber see women—as utterly obsessed with finding a man—even moving continents in order to snare one—because the shame of being single is too much to bear? Dare I suggest that both *Tell Me on a Sunday* and *Aspects of Love* are no more than lessons in male vanity, stemming from a belief that all women regard themselves as incomplete without a man? Perhaps it is what Black and Lloyd Webber prefer to believe, as they clearly cannot conceive of a single, happy, independent, and successful woman. Their other collaboration, *Sunset Boulevard,* is not a particularly positive view of women either, but no doubt they would blame the original material for that. Thankfully, Frank Rich in the *New York Times* proved to have a more enlightened perspective of women when he reviewed the 1985 Broadway production of *Tell Me on a Sunday*: "Empty material remains empty, no matter how talented those who perform it. Emma is a completely synthetic, not to mention insulting, creation whom no performer could redeem."

Indeed.

But Lloyd Webber and Don Black are not the only men in musicals penning this superficial, one-sided view of women's needs. In his show *Silk Stockings* (1955), Cole Porter asked, "Without love, what is a woman?" Citing these lyrics in his book *Something for the Boys: Musical Theatre and Gay Culture,* John M. Clum observes that women in musical theatre "exist to be loved by men; without love they are parodies of masculinity."[1] In other words, without a man, a woman is not a real woman. And, to be fair, there are women who subscribe to this belief. (I, personally, do not accept that they are the majority any longer, but I acknowledge that they exist.) Popular culture, with its pervasive images of heterosexual couples, confirms this conviction, telling us incessantly that women will be happier and more complete with a man, and a woman who deviates from this model will be relegated to the fringes of society. An entertainment genre that has its foundations based in a traditional definition of romance is hardly likely to disagree. Anneke Harrison states,

> I think that maybe the reason why women like these shows so much is because it gives them some kind of validation. They think if I'm important in this man's life, I will be treated well, I will be desired, I will be protected … and we are brought up to believe that that's important. So I think that maybe that's why women like musicals. Maybe that's why *Phantom of the Opera* has

such enormous appeal. Because this fragile singer is so sought after that this man will kill for her—chase her down to the ends of the earth because he wants her so badly. And being desirable to men is deemed incredibly important for women.

Romance is, of course, just another strand of escapist fantasies, fed to us since childhood through fairy tales. America has established a culture of optimism through Hollywood, Disney movies, and musical theatre for decades. Audiences are encouraged to believe that dreams do come true, that a happy ending awaits us all somewhere.

It makes perfect sense, then, that musical theatre is generally most popular during periods of economic depression or in war years, attracting audiences by offering a distraction from everyday financial concerns and societal pressures. The shows of the true masters of the genre—George and Ira Gershwin, Irving Berlin, Cole Porter, Noel Coward, Richard Rodgers and Lorenz Hart, George Abbott and George S. Kaufman—were at their most popular in the 1930s when America was reeling from the effects of the Great Depression. Musical theatre—and the glamour films from Hollywood—played an important role in reassuring a population that life would get better, that the disappearance of the American Dream was only temporary.

During the Second World War, musicals boosted morale and whipped up patriotic spirit with shows such as *On the Town*[2] depicting three sailors on shore leave in New York and Irving Berlin's *This Is the Army* (1942). The 1943 Hollywood version of the latter show featured Kate Smith singing Berlin's *God Bless America,* and following the terrorist attacks on New York and Washington, D.C., on September 11, 2001, Celine Dion's recording of the same song made it to number one in the charts—a clear indication of how musical theatre can reflect the current mood of a nation. This mirroring of prevailing societal concerns by musical theatre has been so accurate that Ian Bradley observes in *You've Got to Have a Dream: The Message of the Musical* that "it would be quite possible to write a cultural history of the United States and the United Kingdom over the last 60 years based on an analysis of the dominant musicals of successive decades."

To give a few examples, *Hair* (1967), *Pippin* (1972) and *Godspell* (1971) drew inspiration from the hippie counter-culture of the late 1960s; *Purlie* (1970) and *The Wiz* (1972) reflected a growing demand for a voice from African/Americans; *Falsettoland* (1990) and *Rent* (1994) featured characters with AIDS and the *Les Misérables* and *Phantom of the Opera* spectaculars reflected the excesses of the 1980s "greed is good" culture. So the ways in which women have been depicted by the musical offers a clue as to where society stood at the time with regard to gender roles. What conclusion, then, do we draw from the absence of women in *Jersey Boys, The Book of Mormon,* and *Kinky Boots*?

During the Second World War, women on both sides of the Atlantic gained immense satisfaction and financial independence from holding down jobs that had previously been denied to them, the absence of men making female entry into the workforce a necessity. Returning servicemen were alarmed by this apparent "masculinization" of women, and shows from the Golden Age of the Musical (1940–1960) subtly exhorted a return to traditional gender roles. This was echoed by another industry primarily concerned with women—fashion—which responded with the New Look—clothes for women that emphasized femininity with sweeping long skirts, fitted waists, and rounded shoulders. The New Look was the antithesis of the androgynous, practical clothes women had worn during the war and was designed to return women to their ornamental status. The musicals of the era reiterated the prevailing concern that the values embodied by the American Dream—marriage and family, the importance of community, women as homemaker/men as breadwinner, and the pioneering spirit—were under threat by female emancipation. The Rodgers and Hammerstein canon depicted women as homemakers and wives, and both *Oklahoma!* and *Carousel* emphasized the importance of community. *The Pajama Game* viewed the single working woman with suspicion, *Damn Yankees* portrayed the loyal wife at home as superior to the femme fatale, and *The Music Man* echoed the pioneering/community spirit. *Annie Get Your Gun, Kiss Me, Kate,* and *My Fair Lady* gave us strong women being "tamed."

All this was understandable when the historical context was a society fearful that women had been too liberated by a war and a desire to return to the stability of prewar values. Marriage and family were seen as the ultimate steadying influence, and popular culture reinstated this message through women's magazines, Hollywood, and the theatre—especially musical theatre. Almost 70 years later, Hollywood gives us female action heroes, and some women's magazines offer financial and employment advice, but musical theatre persists in presenting female characters onstage whose only desire is for heterosexual love. Of course there are many women who do indeed long for a husband and children and are completely fulfilled in this role, but it is no longer the *only* path open to them—as the musical seems to insist.

Melanie La Barrie suggest it's all about escapism:

> The fact is, that when people go to theatre there is a certain amount of escapism. It's not just fantasy, there's a certain, "I would like to see the world in the way that I imagine it" sort of thing. So therefore, "I want to see women in the way that I imagine they should be.

This idea that Ms. La Barrie submits, of wanting to see the world reflected in a particular way onstage, could answer my question about why so many women in the audience are willing to accept what I describe as gender stereotypes. Possibly they don't consider them stereotypes. Perhaps the majority of women do indeed want to see themselves portrayed solely within the structure of romance, because that is precisely their own escapist fantasy. Musical director Wendy Cavett asks, "Is there a type of woman who flocks to *Phantom*, as opposed to a type of woman who goes to another show?"

Perhaps the women who embrace the "romantic" shows cling on to the happy ending promised by the fairy tales, purely because the demands of women's lives today make a time when so little was expected of them look extremely attractive. No one onstage is juggling children, a career, a husband, a fitness regime, hosting lavish dinner parties, and upgrading to a bigger house all at the same time. And there is always the possibly that the majority of the female audience expect to see women portrayed only in relation to men because it is what they are accustomed to in their own lives. It is accurate reflection of how they are viewed by society and of how they view themselves. It also corresponds with the messages they absorb from popular culture and the media about the male/female role in society. To question this portrayal is to invite condemnation for nonconformity.

Women continue to go to musicals and ignore the misrepresentation of their sex onstage because the alternative—to stay away—denies them a fun night out. Romantic notions may indeed rule the lives of the majority of women in the audience—they flocked to *Little Women* and *The Secret Garden*—but is the all-consuming quest to find a man a real desire or a result of societal conditioning? While some women's magazines may have articles giving financial or employment advice, other popular weeklies still assume that all women are married or want to be. Toys aimed at little girls reinforce the homemaker role with miniature ovens, baking sets, and baby dolls that require feeding and changing. Teenage and fitness magazines stress the importance of looking good to attract a boyfriend. Single women are rarely portrayed positively on the small screen. The list goes on. So if women are determined not to be single, it could be a direct result of the societal influences they are subjected to from an early age. The musical is merely replicating the messages contained in magazines and on daytime television. This subsequently places the creators of musicals in a Catch–22 situation.

Writers position a romantic plot at the center of the show because they believe this is what the predominately female audience expects to see. If they do not get it, they will feel let down. At least, that is the supposition. How would we know if women would attend a show where the leading lady is not driven by a quest for a man until we see one?

The other interpretation of Ms. La Barrie's comment is that the predominantly male writers of musical theatre are presenting us with the world as *they* imagine it to be. And their imagination subscribes to the view of women being incomplete without a man. This idea is frequently taken one step further by writers portraying female characters being overpowered, or brought to life, by heterosexual love. Just as Snow White and Sleeping Beauty can only be awakened by the kiss of the handsome prince, women in musical theatre do not truly come to life until they find their men. In Merideth Wilson's *The Music Man* (1957), Marian sings of never having heard the bells ring until she kissed a man. Old Maid Lizzie in *110 in the Shade* is not only saved from her pathetic, lonely existence now that she has a man, she is suddenly beautiful as well.

These views of women as mere receptacles for male love are sadly not limited to shows from the pre-feminism era. The same interpretation is still in place in *Phantom of the Opera* (1986) and the turgid sequel *Love Never Dies* (2010), *Passion* (1994), *Legally Blonde* (2007), *Hairspray* (2002), and even in what Stacy Wolf[3] describes as a "feminist" musical, *Wicked* (2003). When they are not singing about how much they love their men, female characters sing about their longing for men, or how they feel less of a woman without one. When the wished-for man does make his appearance, he casts such a mystical spell over the woman that it renders her weak and ineffective in the face of his manly charisma. So powerful is his "love" that she surrenders all notion of self, taking up a secondary position behind the hypnotic and captivating male. Cue the excruciating Sandy from *Grease* (1971) who describes herself as "hopelessly devoted" to the mentally subnormal Danny Zuko. *Passion* manages to take this one step further, endowing Giorgio with such a hold over Fosca that he effectively controls her health. When informing Giorgio of the gravity of Fosca's illness, the doctor actually maintains that a few kind words from Giorgio will make her well. Fosca is so in thrall to Giorgio that his presence alone will succeed where medical intervention has failed. Oh, please. Do men really believe that they exert such power over women? That their sheer magnetism can miraculously cure a sick woman? The arrogance behind this thinking is actually laughable.

I'm not denying that many women grow in confidence when regularly complimented by a man. Or that "feeling loved" does wonders for their self-esteem. Certainly the opposite is true—constant putdowns and insults from a male partner erode a woman's sense of self. I will put forward, however, the argument that it is societal conditioning that makes women believe that their self-worth is reliant on a male opinion of how they look or behave. Women are conditioned to believe they are only beautiful, or clever, or thin, when a man says they are. The male sense of self-esteem is not tied up in a female opinion of him in the same way. Popular magazines exhort women to look good or employ sexual tricks to "please the man in your life"—as if nothing else is of any importance. Again, the underlying assumption is that a woman will have, or will want to have, a man in her life. The stigma of being single is not applied to men in the pervasive way it is applied to women. A woman who "can't get a man" is seen as lacking. She is an outcast. Well, maybe she doesn't want one. Maybe she, like Donna in *Mamma Mia!* is perfectly content on her own. But this is not an attitude reflected in musical theatre.

The notion put forward in *110 in the Shade* that Lizzie will blossom and become the real woman that she is suppressing with a marriage proposal from the sullen File is a reflection of the male ego. It flatters men to think that a woman will have greater confidence and sparkle in the reflected light of a man's love in a way she never has before. It reassures men of women's dependence on them—even for the occasional compliment. Actually, what Lizzie really needs to do is to stop keeping house for her father and controlling brothers who see her as little more than a servant, escape the suffocating town, and find a job that gives her financial independence and a sense of self-worth. But no one is writing those lyrics. Anneke Harrison muses,

> Something like Phantom—it's basically trashy, romantic fiction. This beautiful woman who is in the control of this hideous man who behaves utterly appallingly, who is violent, manipulative and aggressive—he kidnaps her, for God's sake—and at the end of it we're all supposed to go, "Oh, wouldn't it be great if she stayed with the Phantom." I mean, please.

Mamma Rose in *Gypsy*[4] (1959) allows the man she loves to walk away because her dreams for herself and her children are more important to her. In *Phantom of the Opera*, Christine gives up a promising career as an opera singer to marry the insipid Raoul. Interesting to debate which character is the stronger woman—the one who does what someone else wants her to do, or the one who does what *she* wants? Many women in the audience may well believe that Christine's choice is the braver one, for she puts her faith in love— possibly the most unpredictable of cornerstones to stake a future on. Yet this feeling of being powerless in the face of love again reaffirms a view of women as innately weaker than men. Women fall in love with men because they cannot help themselves. Fosca claims to Giorgio that loving him is not a choice. Yes, it is, just as walking away from his indifference is an alternative choice. But she appears to believe she has no control over her own emotions, even telling him he is the only reason she is still alive. Admittedly she is an invalid, but what a dull life she must lead if the swaggering, unresponsive Giorgio is her only reason for prolonging it. Men in musicals have the strength to resist love and abandon needy women whenever they choose, but women's genetic inability to do the same means they are destined to go through life falling in love with the wrong, read abusive, man. And it is precisely this passivity which defines most of the women in musical theatre. Once female characters have been "touched" by love, they willingly consent to their male lover's demands, regardless of their own needs.

Perhaps the men writing these roles secretly yearn for an obedient, compliant woman—she is certainly easier to handle than one with a personality. Whatever the answer, male writers appear to believe that being someone's wife and "belonging" to him is the happy ending the women in the audience dream about. But a happy ending for whom? For the prince who gets the beautiful and docile girl, or for the girl whose identity is no longer her own? Would we prefer to see Lizzie in *110 in the Shade* keeping house for the morose File, or out in the world exploring new possibilities? Why are female characters in musicals rarely presented with an option other than marriage? Because they are written mainly by men. And a woman at home with two children is far less threatening than a woman with ambition and a mind of her own.

Women martyring themselves for the love of a man—*Miss Saigon, Les Misérables, The Life, Passion, Once on This Island*—is a recurring theme in musicals (and opera). At the heart of the "noble sacrifice" theme is the familiar belief that women's lives are less important than men's and that a man exerts such a profound effect on a woman that she would rather die than contemplate life without him. Even if they do not go as far as to kill themselves, women will give up everything in their life that is important to them to emotionally support, or to win their man. Annie Oakley deliberately loses the finale shoot out in Irving Berlin's *Annie Get Your Gun* (1946) because to demonstrate her real prowess would lose her the object of her affection, Frank Butler. Ti Moune in *Once on this Island* offers her life to the Gods in order that her lover Daniel may live. She then wastes away watching him marry someone else. Eponine is happy to take a soldier's bullet because it enables her to die in the arms of Marius, and in *Passion,* we are told that Fosca has never recovered from being abandoned by her first husband and is literally willing herself to death.

Whatever happened to "hell hath no fury like a woman scorned"? A woman is more likely to engage in elaborate acts of revenge than lie down and pine to death because her husband has run off with a younger model. If the Phantom loves Christine as much as he professes he does, why doesn't he kill himself when he loses her? Ah, because then we'd be deprived of the thrilling sequel, *Love Never Dies.* Couldn't Kim in *Miss Saigon* turn the gun on Chris—the man who seduced and then abandoned her—rather than herself? Does Fosca really believe that love is the only way to living? Surely "living" involves moving on from the arrogant Giorgio—who, incidentally, does little to prevent her self-sacrifice—moving to Rome, and establishing an independent, more fulfilling existence. But that would be an affront to male vanity and to the belief that women never get over their encounter with men. Well, yes they do. Frequently, they thrive. Not in musical theatre, however, where the sacrificial woman is the basis for a good story and appeals to the ego of the narcissistic men in the audience who enjoy the reassurance of their superior status.

No doubt the creators of *Les Misérables* and *Miss Saigon*—Claude-Michel Schönberg and Alain Boublil—will cite the original sources[5] as justification for the self-sacrifice of Eponine and Kim. And who am I to say that it is more likely to be a reflection of their own personal views on the role of women? But in 2015, isn't the notion of the girl giving up everything—even her life— for her man becoming obsolete? Will we ever see a musical where the man sacrifices himself or his needs for his girlfriend, or, heaven forbid, looks after the children?

The sacrificial woman is also presented to us through the role of the mother whose personal needs matter less than those of her child (*Carousel, South Pacific, Miss Saigon, Blood Brothers, Ragtime, Next to Normal*). The musical clearly believes that women are born to be mothers, not leaders, and shows such as *The Sound of Music, South Pacific, Mame, Annie,* and *The Rink* present us with characters who find the real meaning of life with the introduction of a child into their homes. Playwright Willy Russell (*Educating Rita, Shirley Valentine*) has a reputation for penning strong, liberated women, but even he gives us this line of dialogue in *Blood Brothers* (1983).

> Mr. Lyons: Darling. Don't be so hard on the woman. She only wanted to hold the baby. All women like to hold babies, don't they?

Actually no, they don't. But the musical persists with its message that all women desire children, and if they don't, they should.

Childless women are classed as dangerous, as they are refusing to comply with the rules that designate motherhood and the family unit as the lynchpin of society and therefore must be punished—*Evita, Sunset Boulevard, Chicago, Cabaret.* This is, of course, a reflection of a pro-natalist society that backed up by the judiciary, the church, educational establishments, social security, and health institutions appears incapable of separating the word woman from the word mother.

In the Pulitzer Prize–winning *Next to Normal*, the central character of Diana is plagued with mental health issues due, we are told, to the death of a baby twenty years earlier. Unashamedly subscribing to theories of biological determinism—women are born to be mothers—Diana, we are told, has failed twice: the first time when her baby died, and the second because she has little connection with her teenage daughter who is on a voyage of self-discovery involving her mother's prescription drugs and non-stop nightclubbing. Diana blames herself for being a bad mother, based on the fact that she couldn't hold her baby in the hospital, and she is never presented to us as anything other than a parent, except wife, of course. But her failure, first and foremost, is as a mother. If the default setting for all women is assumed to be that of a mother, then Diana has also failed as a woman. What does that say about women who make a deliberate choice not to have children?

Next to Normal places the responsibility of child-rearing firmly on the shoulders of the mother—echoes of Billy Bigelow in *Carousel,* who intends to play games with his son, but not to parent him. Ellen in *Miss Saigon* endorses the belief that a child needs a mother more than a father when she declares it to be "impossible" to take a child from his mother, the mother being obligated to her child in a way that a father is not. When Ellen refuses to adopt Kim's son, Kim sees no option than to perform the ultimate sacrifice expected of any good mother and puts a pistol to her head. This is the "noble sacrifice" so beloved of melodrama, opera and musicals. A "good" woman, i.e., a mother, will put her child's needs before her own.

And while we're on the subject of motherhood, why do women in musicals regularly give birth to boys—*Miss Saigon, The Full Monty, Priscilla, Ragtime, Blood Brothers, Mame, Next to Normal*? How different would *Next to Normal* have been if the daughter had died and the son had survived? It feels that part of the problem is that it is the *son* who died. The son is the ideal. The daughter is what you get after you have had the son. When Mrs. Lyons in *Blood Brothers* fantasizes about having a child, it is a boy she sees playing in the garden, not a girl. How different would the story of *Blood Brothers* be if the twins at the heart of the story were girls? Why can't we imagine *Blood Sisters* packing the same punch? Or can we? In *Miss Saigon*, Ellen places unnecessary emphasis on the fact that Kim has borne Chris a son. Sarah in *Ragtime* stresses the significance of the sex of her child with the song *Your Daddy's Son.* In both cases, the baby himself seems to be of less relevance than the fact that he is a boy. Would substituting the word "child" for "son" carry the same connotations? The belief that the male child—the heir—is what everyone really wants is so entrenched in musicals that Billy Bigelow in *Carousel* sings an entire song about how terrible it would be to have a daughter. True, he revises his opinion by the end of the song, but then goes on to hit her, as he did his wife. At least a son would have hit him back, giving the women in the audience the opportunity to applaud.

Staying with Billy Bigelow for a moment, in 1999, *Time* magazine named *Carousel* the "Best Musical of the 20th Century," and Billy's *Soliloquy* is often regarded as the high point of the show. The song that separates the men from the boys.

In the song Billy describes how his son will be named after him, will look like him, will be tough as a tree, and will stand up for himself. Hell, he could even be president one day. The realization that Julie might give birth to a girl throws up issues of responsibility—not one of Billy Bigelow's strong points. Billy can throw a ball and bond with a son, but he has to parent a girl, implying she is incapable of looking after herself. He sees her in need of protection—ironically, although lost on him, from men exactly like him. Being a father to a girl will involve controlling his daughter in a way he would not have to do with a boy. Daughters, therefore, are a burden. This, from the "Best Musical of the 20th Century." Billy's assumption that the child will be named after him—Julie clearly has no say in what the child she has carried for nine months is named—gives a clue as to why a son is preferable to a father than a daughter. The father's name and self, to a degree, will continue. A son is *me,* Billy is saying. A daughter is someone else. Dino in *The Rink*[6] (1984) reiterates this when he turns his back on the daughter, Angel, he has not seen for years with the words, "I've got a family … two boys." The response from Angel's mother, Anna—"They all want sons"—indicates her sense of failure at having produced a daughter for Dino and not the longed-for son.

Are these images of the sacrificial or dependent woman, the docile submissive bride, and the mother cradling the male heir a true reflection of women today? When we go to a musical, can we honestly avow that the female characters onstage accurately portray the concerns and lives of contemporary women? With the growing demand for same-sex relationships to be officially recognized, women choosing careers over marriage, and an increasing number of women electing not to have children, the image of the devoted, passive wife or the lonely spinster pining for a man seems more than a little outdated and a pointless image to reinforce. By continuing to present these characters onstage, the musical as a genre is opening itself up to criticism from a wider public as being irrelevant and out of touch—an accusation increasingly hard to refute. And, yes, I do acknowledge that *Phantom of the Opera, Miss Saigon,* and *Les Misérables* are products of the eighties, but they are all still running either in their original form, or in revival in London, New York, and Australia, thereby, I believe, giving tacit permission to new or younger creators of musical to reproduce the same attitudes onstage.

Men's fear of women's strength causes them to portray women as the weaker sex, possibly in the hope that by telling a person something often enough, they will eventually come to believe it. Yet the evidence around us in society contradicts this view of women as feeble, delicate beings in need of male protection. We have female political leaders, women in the judiciary, female CEOs—admittedly too few of all of the above—yet female characters in musicals reflect none of these advances. Why don't we see powerful women in society reflected onstage? Where are the stay-at-home dads in musical theatre or the career women who are supported emotionally by their more liberal-minded husbands? Is this not a good story? There are men in society today who are feminist in their outlook, who adore smart, independent, and strong women and are happy—eager—to share the child-rearing responsibilities. True, they are not the majority, but couldn't we see one of them represented in a musical? Just once? Leo in *Parade*[7] (1998) recognizes the strength and determination in his wife Lucille and admits that he doesn't deserve her, but he is a lone voice in the misogynistic wilderness where most male characters are as vacuous and domineering as their women are passive. Apart from presenting us with a romantic ideal that is now outdated, this is not a truthful portrayal of the way men and women now negotiate their places in society.

There are two conclusions I can draw from this. The first, as I have already speculated, is that the writers/creators are depicting women in the way that they would *prefer* them to be, or indeed, as they regard them. The second conclusion refers back to Susan Faludi's book *Backlash*, in which she maintains that an increasing disregard for women, and women's needs, is a direct result of gains by the women's movement towards equality. Alarmed by the heightened status of women in society, particularly in the workforce and the family courts, men are fighting back by ferociously guarding their territory and reinforcing a stereotype of femininity and female passiveness that belongs more in the 1950s than the present day. The second conclusion would explain the absence of women from musical theatre creative teams— male producers are guarding their territory. Male writers play their part in the backlash by portraying women only in relation to men, or as simpleminded victims, or sex objects existing only for men's pleasure. This is how men want women to see themselves, because it subsequently makes them easier to control. Women who believe they have no power are not likely to speak up or to question the patriarchal status quo.

Perhaps I am making too much of this—it is only a musical, after all. But Geraldine Turner agrees:

> You know, it's usually men who make the decisions, usually men who produce the shows. There are women producers but not very many, not many female directors, or choreographers. So your question was, why aren't there more shows like *Wicked* and *Mamma Mia!* which have great role models for women. Well, that's not in men's interests really, is it? To have that. It's a male-dominated world.

Remember the, "Oh, but it's just a bit of fun justification? It's just a musical, it's harmless. Really? The sheer number of people now attending musicals or engaging in the genre through TV shows means that whatever message or value system is being reinforced by the musical gets through to a larger number of people than it would have done 30 years ago. Far from being harmless, the musical now has the power to influence the views of a great number of people, including—most worryingly—the impressionable, younger female generation. It is far from "a bit of fun" when teenage girls are being fed a message that they have no control over their lives, they are nothing without a man, and ultimately, what they think or feel is irrelevant.

If the creators of musical theatre were to use the excuse of responding to consumer demand as the reason they present women in a one-dimensional way onstage, the only way to disprove this claim would be for a broad-minded producer to stage a show that offered the opposite. Say, for instance, we had a musical centering around an independent career woman who turns her back on love and blazes a political trail ending up in the White House, who never sings a victim ballad or whines about how badly her man has treated her, and is an empowering role model for young girls in the audience. Would the women in the audience cheer the leading lady's achievements, or, influenced by a media that reinforces the homemaker role as most suitable for women, condemn her for daring to step outside traditional boundaries? Is the desire for heterosexual romance and compliant women so ingrained in ticket buyers that *Thelma and Louise: The Musical* would die a quick death at the box office, deemed too confronting for conservative out-of-towners? Having witnessed women in the movie theatre cheer the moment when Thelma and Louise take revenge on the lascivious truck driver, I suspect it would run for years.

The real problem in terms of the portrayal of women onstage is that the audience is not being offered anything other than the stereotype. I personally would love to buy a ticket to a musical that presented me with an independent, powerful woman who is not obsessed by the men in her life at the core of the story. But where would I find it? *Newsies? Jersey Boys? Kinky Boots?* In its absence, I will follow the hype and go to *The Book of Mormon* and spend an evening listening to jokes about female genital mutilation.

Women go to musicals that present their sex as less important, less intelligent, and inherently weaker than men because there is quite simply nothing else on offer. The irony of the women in *The Witches of Eastwick* realizing that they do not need a man to be complete is that it takes a man to reveal this to them. The show is actually upholding a (male) belief that women are incapable of thinking for themselves. In the end, it comes down to this. Lucy Simon's question:

> Do women want to see women as the way women portray them, or do they want to see women as men portray them?

To go some way towards answering Ms. Simon's question, we could take a glance at the worldwide *Mamma Mia!* box office receipts. Spectacular sets and special effects could partly account for the longevity of *Les Misérables, Phantom of the Opera, Wicked,* and *The Lion King,* but *Mamma Mia!* relies on the strength of the characters to win over the audience. And, of course, ABBA music, which always held more appeal to women than men—unless they were gay. Women recognize the authentic female voice in *Mamma Mia!* because it resonates with them in a way that a male voice impersonating a woman does not. Wendy Cavett, current musical director of *Mamma Mia!* on Broadway, suggests that the women onstage in the show are attractive to the female audience because the characters are more truthful representations of women *as they see themselves*, not as men see them:

> They love seeing women represented in a strong way. They love that these women are not overly sexualized ... represented in ways that ... that they are just trying to get laid. They have sexual histories but their sexual histories have come out of their own appetite ... it didn't come out of being an object. And I think that's really empowering for women to see that.

Empowering is not a word that could be applied to *Miss Saigon* which includes a situation so beloved of straight men, that of two women fighting over him. In the New York production, the song "Now That I've Seen Her" replaced the cringe-worthy original "It's Her or Me"—a clichéd declaration of war from the second wife to the first. Both songs reiterate the belief that a woman will do anything to keep her man, especially when faced with a rival. I suppose we should be grateful that "It's Her or Me" was eventually removed from the show—it's just a shame it wasn't replaced with "You Take Him, I Deserve Better." And yes, I do think it's relevant that *Miss Saigon* was written by two straight men.

When creating *Dr. Zhivago,* composer Lucy Simon met with opposition from male members of the creative team when she proposed a scene that reflected a particularly female experience:

> There's a scene in the book where Lara goes to help Tonya deliver her baby. It's not … it's just mentioned—"I helped Tonya in her confinement." It's not drawn in any way in the Pasternak. But in the play, I wanted to make that a meeting. But the people who really wanted to make that happen and who created the song "It Comes as No Surprise/I Feel Him Closer" were the men. [The director] and [the bookwriter] wanted to see what would happen when a mistress and a wife came face to face.… And that wouldn't have been my choice of scenes to do. I wanted Tonya giving birth and Lara helping her.

Helping her husband's mistress in her hour of need says more about the strength of Lara's character than having her passively accept the threat to her marriage over a shared library book. And the latter is—from a woman's point of view—highly unlikely. It is all too easy to speculate as to why two straight men would want to have a scene where a mistress and wife come face to face and form a friendship. Dare I call it the ultimate male fantasy?

In *The Sound of Music*, Liesl is presented to us in Act One as smart, defiant, and determined to pursue what she wants. In act two she is told to go as soon as a boy calls for her. A product of the times in which it was written, or an insight into the characters of Rodgers and Hammerstein? It seems incongruous that we turn to Disney—the originator of the "someday my prince will come" dream—to find strong-willed, free-thinking, intelligent women in musicals. True, they all get married in the end—and I am not saying there is anything wrong with that—but at least Belle in *Beauty and the Beast*[8] (1994) spurns the macho muscle man in favor of someone more inspiring. This is possibly due to the fact that the book writer was female and may have held more enlightened views on women's needs and wants.

That is not to say that Rodgers and Hammerstein did not give us some magnificent, strong women—they did. As did Kander and Ebb, Stephen Sondheim, and Jerry Herman. But the men creating musicals today prefer to define women by their weakness, not their strength. Diana from *Next to Normal* is the perfect example. Until more women composers and book writers are involved in the creation of a new show, it is impossible to know if gender does have an effect on how the characters are drawn. While men may see Kim's sacrifice in *Miss Saigon* as the right and proper thing to do, women may view it as a touch melodramatic—she is perfectly capable of living a fulfilled life without the self-obsessed Chris. Does it follow, then, that if more women were involved in creating new musicals we would see more realistic female characters whose actions better reflect contemporary womanhood? Susan Stroman answers,

It's hard to say. It's not like an exact formula exists for creating a hit musical. If it did, we'd all be using it! At the moment I'm working on a new piece with Lynn Ahrens and Stephen Flaherty based on the girl who was the model for Degas's sculpture "Little Dancer Aged Fourteen." The story follows her struggles with the Paris Opera Ballet and how few options were available to women making a living for themselves or who wanted any type of independence. And I'm sure Lynn and I bring a point of view to the work that an all-male creative team might not. Still, there just aren't many female book writers for musicals.

Susan Stroman is not the first person to bring up the fact that the lack of women book writers has an adverse effect on the resulting product. But they certainly exist—as Rebecca Luker confirms. "The BMI[9] workshop is full of as many women as men. There's a lot of women in there. Are they just not getting the same opportunities, for whatever the reason?"

Indeed, the BMI homepage includes photographs of women. Not as many as of men, but women are there. So where are they in the industry? Until they manage to break through the barrier and be considered as equals alongside their male counterparts, the depiction of women onstage will continue to reflect a male perspective. General Manager Nina Lannan is aware of the importance of a woman's influence in the creation of a new musical—especially one based around gender politics.

We're going to be working on a new musical of *Tootsie* … and so I went back and watched the movie two weeks ago and then I watched all of the interviews. And there were interviews with Dustin Hoffman, Sidney Pollack … and they were talking so much about Elaine May. And how Elaine May helped them to get a woman's perspective into *Tootsie*—how she really helped with cracking the character of the girlfriend … how they needed that woman's point of view.… And I was struck by how important Elaine May was to that script—not just for the comedy, but as a woman. I know that (the producer) is in the process of building a creative team for the show and I want to talk to him and say—hire a woman—somewhere!

Just as the genre has changed over the past two decades, so too has the audience for the musical. Musical theatre is now considered mass entertainment—witness the box office receipts for *We Will Rock You* or *Jersey Boys*—as opposed to an art form. Where the genre once catered to a sophisticated, informed purist—the Sondheim devotee—the musical is now classed as populist. The number of musicals taking animated, or previously successful, films as their source material, or the jukebox musical, attests to this. Bear in mind we are in a society now where reality television shows are classed as documentaries, and soap operas as drama. The entertainment industry is now, more than ever, pandering to the lowest common denominator and the musical is no different. Producers want to make money—lots of it—and shows that require an audience to think, or that challenge the accepted norms (either in terms of storyline or structure) are considered too risky.

Directed by Susan Stroman, *The Scottsboro Boys*[10] (2010) retold the true story of nine black teenagers falsely accused of rape in 1931. Despite critical acclaim—Elisabeth Vincentelli in the *New York Post* called it "A masterwork, both daring and highly entertaining"—and 12 Tony Award nominations, the show managed only an eight-week run on Broadway. This could be attributed to the confronting subject matter—as Elisabeth Vincentelli pointed out, "'The Scottsboro Boys' is a hard sell in a Times Square dominated by escapist fluff" and later, that the show is "grimly thought-provoking." A further indication that this musical was a departure from the more usual light distractions came from online reviewer Elyse Sommer[11] who noted, "For all the singing and dancing, this is not a cheerful story, nor does it have sexy ladies or a romantic element. But neither is it the overly familiar standard fare geared to the tourist trade." And perhaps that was the problem—a reluctance on the part of Broadway musical theatre patrons—mainly tourists—to attend a show requiring a deeper level of emotional engagement than, say, *The Addams Family*.

Prior to *The Scottsboro Boys,* in 2006, Broadway saw the premiere of the musical adaptation of *Grey Gardens*[12]—the 1975 seminal documentary by the Maysles brothers, Albert and David, about the lives of Edith Ewing Bouvier Beale ("Big Edie") and her daughter Edith Bouvier Beale ("Little Edie").

The critics were more effusive with their praise for leading lady Christine Ebersole (who won the Tony Award for Best Performance by a Leading Actress in a Musical) than for the show itself, but there was little doubt that here was a show which at least attempted to redefine the boundaries of the genre. Despite its ten Tony Award nominations, *Grey Gardens* lasted only eight months on Broadway, another victim, possibly, of the preference of new musical theatre patrons for mindless distractions over shows that challenge. Perhaps *Grey Gardens,* with its depiction of two lonely and abandoned women living in squalor, was—like *The Scottsboro Boys*—simply too confronting for an audience seeking an escapist fantasy. *Mary Poppins*, which opened in the same month as *Grey Gardens,* was still running six years later.

Nina Lannan suggests that the changing audience demographic is partly responsible for the proliferation of lightweight musicals currently dominating Broadway.

> Let's remember you don't have people going to see a Broadway show every week. It's not like the fifties when people would attend theatre frequently and theatre events were cocktail hour conversation.... Broadway has now a major tourist audience. Whether that's domestic tourists or international, it's a tourist audience. So together with the infrequent attendance of local audi-

ences, you can see that there may be a trend to write and create work that is mainstream—that has the broadest appeal. And then think about women directors and writers and how they may fit into mainstream entertainment—it's usually rare to find them.

I could also posit here that the current ticket prices on Broadway ensure that few enthusiasts are able to attend theatre as frequently as they may want to. Consequently, the informed dialogue, the "cocktail hour conversation," has disappeared. The well-versed audience with sophisticated taste and a desire to be challenged intellectually or emotionally has given way to a patron who attends rarely, probably on a special occasion, and simply wants to be entertained, which is fair enough. But creators of contemporary musical theatre appear to be under the impression that unless women onstage conform to a sexual or emotional stereotype, the audience will not consider it entertainment.

And, as has already been established, there are more men involved in the creation of musical theater than women.

This could account for the fact that the thinking woman onstage is not something that would ever be considered as appealing to the masses. It does not appeal to the men creating the shows; subsequently, they *assume* it would not appeal to the men in the audience, and creating entertainment for men is always the primary concern, regardless of the fact that the majority of ticket holders are women. By claiming they are pandering to audience expectations, the producer/writer/director enables the vicious cycle to continue. They provide mindless entertainment with stereotypical female characters, claiming it is what the public wants, and the audience applauds it because it is what they have come to expect. It is a chicken and egg situation, but which comes first—the lowering of expectations, or the dumbing down? And within the dumbing-down category, I include the return to the depiction of women as caricatures or sex objects when we were once offered *Mame* and *Gypsy*.

The claim by producers that the tastes of an out-of-town audience are less than discerning can only stand up as an argument when audiences have been offered something else and refused. *Scottsboro Boys* and *Grey Gardens* were never intended for a mass audience, and using their perceived failure on Broadway as a justification to continue to stage shows that are driven by box office returns rather than artistic excellence is narrow-minded at the very least. It's like offering sushi to someone who has only tasted McDonald's. Surely there is a happy medium somewhere between *Scottsboro Boys* and *Rock of Ages: The Color Purple,* for example, or *Dirty Rotten Scoundrels*[13] (2005).

Admittedly, *Grey Gardens* and *Scottsboro Boys* were possibly too extreme for an inexperienced audience seeking an evening of mindless distraction, but there are people who want to be challenged by musical theatre and who appreciate thought-provoking works. The two should not, and did not used to be, mutually exclusive. And within this happy medium there must be, I believe, a place for shows which depict women in a more realistic manner and reflect the changing attitudes towards gender roles in contemporary society. Even the most inexperienced theatre goer would agree that Miss Celie in *The Color Purple* is a more positive portrayal of women than the pseudo pole dancers in *Rock of Ages.* While female (and male) audience members may not actually go as far to complain about the latter, I doubt if they would rush out to buy a ticket for their impressionable daughters. So women in the audience have their role to play in this too, by demanding that their needs and desires are met, and that real women with issues that contemporary women can identify and sympathize with are up there onstage. By continuing to tolerate, even enthusiastically applaud, shows such as *Rock of Ages, Next to Normal,* or *On a Clear Day*, women are inadvertently colluding in maintaining the status quo. They are condoning a depiction of women that pleases and entertains men. Anneke Harrison asks:

> Why don't women kick up a huge fuss and say this is unacceptable? I do not know. Is it that horrible thing of the snake eating its own tail? You know, men want women to be this way, so they portray them like that onstage, so those are the role models women see so they then perpetrate that? I don't know.

I am not, by any means, making a plea to women to stop attending musicals—I love the genre as much as they do and have a personal stake in its survival. I am requesting only that they question what they see, and ask where it is coming from. Is the voice a genuine female one, or is it a male one, substituting his point of view for ours? Do we really view ourselves as compliant and subservient victims? Or is this how men view us? More to the point, what can we do to change this misrepresentation onstage?

Notes

1. John M. Clum, 1999, *Something for the Boys: Musical Theatre and Gay Culture,* (New York: St Martin's Press), 87.

2. Book by Dorothy and Herbert Fields; music and lyrics by Irving Berlin.

3. Stacy Ellen Wolf, 2010, *Changed for Good: A Feminist History of the Broadway Musical,* (New York: Oxford University Press).

4. Book by Arthur Laurents; music By Jule Styne, lyrics by Stephen Sondheim.

5. "Les Miserables" 1862 by Victor Hugo; "Madame Butterfly" 1904 opera by Giacomo Puccini.

6. Book by Terrence McNally; lyrics by Fred Ebb; music by John Kander.

7. Book by Alfred Uhry; music and lyrics by Jason Robert Brown.

8. Book by Linda Woolverton; lyrics by Howard Ashman and Tim Rice; music by Alan Menken.

9. Created in 1961, the BMI workshop offers an opportunity for writers and composers of musical theatre to hone their craft under the tutelage of respected professionals. Female graduates include Susan Birkenhead—*Jelly's Last Jam; Triumph of Love;* Lynn Ahrens—*Ragtime; Once on This Island; A Man of No Importance,* and Carol Hall—*The Best Little Whorehouse in Texas.*

10. Book by David Thompson; lyrics by Fred Ebb; music by John Kander.

11. CurtainUp: www.curtainup.com/scottsboroboys.html.

12. Book by Doug Wright; lyrics by Michael Korie, music by Scott Frankel.

13. Book by Jeffrey Lane; lyrics and music and by David Yazbek.

3

He's No Good, but I'm No Good Without Him

Great Roles for Women?

When Cameron Mackintosh started, and the Frenchmen[1] who wrote all those musicals—they started writing really strong men's roles and the women's roles ... they're good, they have a couple of nice songs, but they're not as ... kind of interesting as the roles pre feminism for women in musicals. Where the focus was on the woman in musical theatre and not on the man.

—Geraldine Turner

The lack of a woman's voice in musical theatre is ironic given that more women than men have earned their star status through leading roles in musicals and remain associated with certain characters in popular psyche. Who can imagine *The Sound of Music* without Julie Andrews? *Funny Girl* without Barbra Streisand? But those leading female roles that defined a particular show have all but disappeared, replaced with musicals where the plot revolves around a man, or men. Women have been relegated to the sidelines, playing the dumb blonde or the love interest—although the last type is nothing new. Writers of musicals appear to have great difficulty seeing beyond the Madonna/Whore paradigm, with female characters who display any streak of independence falling into the latter category and the passive, love interest girl/woman in the former. The result—as we saw in the previous chapter—are female characters who lack both individuality and complexity. Yet the musical is frequently credited as offering "great roles" for women.

This may well have been correct when Jerry Herman and Kander and Ebb were creating shows, and few women would turn down the opportunity to play Mame, Dolly Levi, or either Velma or Roxie in *Chicago*. But where are the other great roles? And how are we defining "great"? If roles are judged simply on stage time and the number of songs the leading lady gets to sing, then yes, the women's roles in *Wicked, Next to Normal, Nine, Tell Me on a Sunday, Oliver!,* and *Little Shop of Horrors* could be considered great. But if we are looking for a realistic depiction of a female that reflects contemporary values, then the claim is a fallacy. When musicals place a woman at the center of the action, the power that should result from this is often dissipated by the imposition of a character that is grounded in a stereotype. The actress may be onstage in almost every scene and have all the big numbers, but she is portraying either a dependent, childlike victim or a scheming, manipulative whore—with the big-breasted, squeaky-voiced bimbo and the fat-girl comic relief somewhere in between.

The question of what makes a role "great" for a woman really depends on who the individuals are who are having the discussion. The writer believes he has created a great role simply because the central character is female. The actress gets to sing the big ballad and be the main focus of the story instead of appearing in a couple of scenes where she flirts with the supporting male character. Or the questioning audience member is troubled by the recurring image of women as sex objects, victims, or irrelevant.

No point inviting a critic to join the debate—as we have already seen, they clearly don't care how women are portrayed.

A great role can only emerge when female characters are endowed with the same complexity and powerful status that is awarded to male characters. But it is almost impossible to demonstrate female strength when the context is heterosexual romance. From the Bible to the marriage ceremony, women are told to obey their husbands, or—in the words of the new Anglican service—submit to them. The fact that men are not given the same instruction automatically elevates their status above that of their female partners. Regardless of how many books on female empowerment contemporary women devour, the prevailing attitude in society continues to designate the female as subordinate to the male. Men lead, women follow or offer unconditional support. Girls learn at an alarmingly early age that what the boy wants is more important than what she desires and that securing a man is of the utmost importance. How many men consider themselves incomplete or their lives as meaningless because they are without a female partner? Women are trained (often by their mothers) to tolerate men's abusive behavior and to accept their infidelities as part of their lot in life. More enlightened attitudes do exist, but they are rarely on display on the musical theatre stage, where romance for women frequently equals suffering. If we accept that the musical does reflect prevailing beliefs in contemporary society, then how can women play anything other than minor roles, when that is how their place is defined in most other areas?

Before I am howled down by protesting voices invoking *Sweeney Todd, Evita, Mamma Mia!* and *Wicked,* let me clarify one thing. Yes, I agree, there are leading roles for women in contemporary musical theatre, but frequently their function is to allow the male story to progress. Is *Miss Saigon* about Kim or about the Engineer? Are the women in *The Witches of Eastwick* the focus of the show, or is it Darryl van Horne? Norma Desmond's story in *Sunset Boulevard* is told to us from Joe Gillis's point of view, not Norma's. The few shows that do have a woman at heart of the story frequently present us with an unsympathetic portrait or a stereotypical one. So where exactly are these "great roles for women"?

In *Nine,*[2] perhaps? With so many plots of musicals revolving around men, female performers were thrilled when this show, with a cast of twenty-one women and one man, premiered on Broadway in 1982. And at first glance they had a right to be. But a closer inspection of *Nine* reveals that the 21 women are only ever seen in relation to Guido, the leading man. It is his journey we go on, not theirs. It is his breakdown—a result of his many sexual liaisons—that we are asked to sympathize with, not the women he has been unfaithful to. The characters of Luisa, Carla, and Claudia are admittedly given their own songs, but they sing about Guido or for his entertainment. Claudia appears not even to have her own identity, so completely has she been consumed by her lover Guido.

Despite the fact that Guido has at least two other women on the go and Claudia has a successful film career, she credits him with making her complete. She is effectively denying herself an identity. *Nine* elevates the male to almost god-like status, with Guido enthroned on his pedestal and his harem waiting patiently at his feet. The fact that the women might have their own tale to tell appears immaterial, and none of the female characters are endowed with any real complexity. (In the musical writers' defense, the show is adapted from Federico Fellini's 1963 film *8½,* which Fellini described as autobiographical. The women in the original film are drawn in the same way.) True to the genre, *Nine* centers around romance and subscribes to the belief that women suffer for love in ways that men do not.

The women each love Guido alone; he loves himself and a number of different women. The female characters are aware of his true nature and tolerate his behavior, thereby inadvertently becoming victims. *Nine* unashamedly panders to the male ego, presenting the Guido as the flame around which the female moths flutter, no doubt to fight for the honor of being burned alive. Don't misunderstand me; there are wonderful moments in this show and beautiful music, and it is thrilling to see a stage dominated by women instead of men. But the female roles are one-dimensional and clearly written from a male point of view.

Fifteen years after *Nine* had taken its final bow, the Broadway premiere of *The Life*[3] in 1997 again promised meaty roles for female performers in a show exploring the underbelly of the streets around Times Square. How disappointing, then, to watch the hideous assortment of clichés paraded in front of the audience, in what is undeniably a male view of the world of pimps and prostitutes. The character of Sonja sings of "Gettin' Too Old for the Oldest Profession"—a song designed to raise a laugh, but for a woman who relies on her looks and body to make a living, this is a serious concern. Later, she is revealed as in her mid-thirties—hardly old. Perhaps the lyric was intended as a wry comment on men preferring younger women. Sonja also has lyrics describing prostitution as "fun," and when she counts up how many men she has had sex with she estimates it is over 15,000. I could be wrong, but I suspect we'd be hard pressed to find any woman living on the streets who defines turning tricks as "fun." The implication is crystal clear—this is a choice, not a necessity. Sonja enjoys being a hooker. Why tell us how many men Sonja has had sex with unless we are being asked to judge her lifestyle and condemn her as a lost cause to depravity? Would a female writer be less harsh in her condemnation?

Well, yes, as proven 20 years earlier by Carol Hall in her musical *The Best Little Whorehouse in Texas*[4] (1978). The Texas brothel where this show is set—presided over by Miss Mona—is unmistakably a woman's world, and at least the girls here give an impression of having some control over their lives. Undeniably, it is the *Pretty Woman* version of prostitution, but the women are a far cry from the drug-addicted victims who populate *The Life*. And unlike the pimps in *The Life,* Miss Mona is not exploiting her girls—she runs a business, and the girls are there to make money—their own money. While Miss Mona's rules may seem more reminiscent of a girls' boarding school than a high-class brothel—no lying late in bed, no chewing gum, no chatting for hours on the phone, no kissing on the mouth—Miss Mona protects her girls. There is always the argument that prostitution, like pornography, can never be anything other than exploitative, but at least these girls have someone looking out for them. Miss Mona is far from the long-suffering victim so beloved of musicals. When she loses everything, including the man she loves, she shrugs and gets on with life. Not for her the tragic ballad bemoaning how life and her man done her bad, but she'll stay anyway. Miss Mona takes the time to encourage self-confidence in her girls, exhorting them to find dignity in their lives. The song, "Girl, You're a Woman" is a celebration of womanhood and the innate strength of women—albeit with a few clichéd smatterings; it was pre-second wave feminism, after all. The main difference between *The Life* and *The Best Little Whorehouse in Texas* is that in the latter, we see a complex female character holding the reins of power. Dare I use the dreaded "f" word? Could we call Miss Mona a feminist?

Despite the fact that the women in *Best Little Whorehouse* are prostitutes—not the most empowering of professions—the show imparts a more positive message about being an individual and taking control of your life than many musicals that claim to be about strong women. The irony is that it takes a show about hookers living in a Texas brothel to impart that message.

While *The Best Little Whorehouse* can be criticized for presenting a sugar coated interpretation of the lives of female prostitutes, *The Life* offers the opposite extreme—women with no control, no choices, and subjected to daily violence from the men around them. Perhaps the creators of *The Life* were attempting to elicit sympathy for the women onstage by presenting them as the victims of abusive, controlling men, but it is difficult to be sympathetic towards anyone who appears to be choosing their dire circumstances, which is what the writers seem to be saying through songs such as "A Lovely Day to Be Out of Jail," "It's My Body" and "The Hookers' Ball." The lead character in *The Life*—Queen—is so completely reliant on her lover, Fleetwood, that in reality, the only thing that is preventing her from leaving him is herself—echoes of the women in *Nine,* who are so dependent on Guido's affection they are effectively incapacitated, and of the dance hall hostesses in *Sweet Charity*[5] (1966), who understand that there is something better than the life they are living, but never actually leave. (Interestingly, Cy Coleman wrote the music for *Sweet Charity* and *The Life*—both shows about women selling their bodies and exhibiting passive, victim-like tendencies.)

The prevailing view of women in *The Life* is outlined by the hustler Memphis in a particularly unpleasant song, "Don't Take Much," in which he describes how easy it is to control women, particularly when you understand—as he does—that no really means yes. What Memphis tells the audience through this song is that women are so stupid, so gullible, and so dependent on men that they can be coerced into doing anything. The trouble is that none of the female characters around him do anything to contradict this opinion. They do allow themselves to be manipulated and put up little resistance to the male control over their lives. It is therefore impossible for us to view them as anything other than compliant and willing participants in a cycle of abuse. Consequently, the real issue at the heart of *The Life* is that we are asked to pity these women, not because of the circumstances they are in, but because their innate weaknesses *as women* renders them open to abuse. They can't help living up to their victim status, because they are biologically determined to do so.

Which leads me to wonder how the actresses felt playing these tragic, exploited under-dogs every night? Probably they felt very much like their characters—that they had no choice. They needed the money and had to agree with whatever the men on the creative team wanted. Most likely they did what many other female performers in musical theatre do—swallow their protestations at the clichéd representation of women onstage in order to keep their jobs. Who would they complain to, anyway? Cy Coleman?

What's fulfilling for a performer playing a one-dimensional, clichéd victim? There's certainly nothing uplifting about watching one. And yes, I am well aware that these characters are not real and that the performers are only pretending to be victims. But couldn't they pretend to be less obsessed by men and have some control in their lives? Better that we take our daughters and nieces to *Legally Blonde: The Musical* where even the "dumb blonde," accessories-obsessed Elle Woods presents a more positive role model.

Not only is she accepted into Harvard University, she graduates top of her class. True, she ruins it by proposing to Emmett in the final scene, but at least she'll have her law degree to fall back on when the marriage breaks up.

As is becoming apparent, when a feminist reading is applied to musicals, the texts are revealed as sadly lacking in respect or regard for women. The same can be said for the female roles. On the surface, some roles may appear to be the lynchpins of their shows, but a closer female-driven scrutiny reveals the roles as subscribing to patriarchal values and actually subverting the initial image of a strong woman. Anneke Harrison observes:

> Even in something like Miss Saigon—it's the title role, Miss Saigon—it's about a woman. The whole show was supposedly inspired by a photograph of a woman giving away her child, and yet the character in the show has her life controlled by men at every step of the way. Her only choice in the end, to get what she wants, is to destroy herself. I find that really exasperating.

Evita is another classic example. The diva role of Eva Peron is undoubtedly a huge challenge for any performer to take on, but can it really be classed as a positive image of a woman onstage? The real life Eva Peron was corrupt, ruthless, and ambitious—no one denies that. But so was her husband. Yet the musical endows only Eva with these qualities. Juan Peron is depicted as little more than a cowardly pawn, and the lyrics in "Goodnight and Thank You" clearly intimate that Eva slept her way to the top. We are never told how exactly Peron arrived at his position of superiority or how he removed opposition to his dictatorial regime. By drawing attention to Eva's sexuality and her willingness to use it, the show condemns her more for her feminine wiles than for her abuse of political power. At the heart of *Evita* is a condemnatory, male voice urging the audience to dislike her. We are not supposed to be impressed by a woman who gets what she wants, especially when sexual manipulation is involved.

That *Evita* is a depiction of a woman in power viewed through a male lens is nowhere more palpable than in the closing scene, when lyricist Tim Rice effectively has Eva apologize in "Lament" for not living a more demure life. The idea of Eva Peron apologizing for anything is questionable, and the sense of judgment on her behavior implicit in "Lament" appears to be the real reason for the song. Eva does not deny that she loved the glory and all the trappings that her position as the president's wife brought her, but the audience is left wondering if she had lived a quieter life of conformity, would cancer have ravaged her so young? Interestingly, when *Evita* was made into a film in 1996,[6] a new song was added for Eva to sing to her husband from her hospital bed. "You Must Love Me" (which won the 1996 Oscar for best song) appeared to be an attempt by Rice and Lloyd Webber to soften the character of Eva Peron, but having her plead for the love of a man who admits to others he has used her to maintain his political position completely undermines the strength of her character. It is out of step with the woman we have been watching stop at nothing to get what she wants for the last two hours. The powerful woman is reduced to a pathetic shell, begging for male reassurance that she is loved. "You Must Love Me" could also have been an attempt to inject some romance into a central couple whose symbiotic relationship had, in the show, little to do with love. Subsequent stage productions of *Evita* have included the song in act two.

Desiree in Sondheim's *A Little Night Music* (1973) is another role that lays claim to the "great" label. She has the show-stopping dialogue and sings "Send in the Clowns." So it seems almost churlish to point out that the only reason Frederick returns to her is because he has been abandoned by his much younger wife. That Desiree is relegated to his second choice is often overlooked in the general enthusiasm for the role among female performers.

Why quibble with Frederick's motivation when the rest of the show has Desiree firmly in the driver's seat? Well, because Desiree's unquestioning acceptance of Frederick undermines our belief in her as a strong woman.

The search for a great role is hampered by the fact that female characters in musicals tend to come with labels attached. It's almost impossible to bring any complexity or emotional depth to a tag line. The ingénue—Christine in *Phantom*, Maria in *West Side Story*, Laurey in *Oklahoma!*, Cosette in *Les Misérables*. The love interest—Rosemary in *How to Succeed*, Sarah Brown in *Guys and Dolls,* Anne in *La Cage Aux Folles.* The victim—Effie in *Dreamgirls,* Nancy in *Oliver!,* the entire female cast of *The Life,* Ti Moune in *Once on This Island,* Bea in *Ballroom,* Sally in *Follies,* Wendla in *Spring Awakening,* Kim in *Miss Saigon,* Eponine and Fantine in *Les Misérables*; it's hard to know where to stop with this category. Maria in *West Side Story,* the Mistress in *Evita,* Mabel in *Mack and Mabel,* Bertrande in *Martin Guerre,* Diana in *Next to Normal,* Claudia et al. in *Nine*; ... You get the point.

Then there's the bimbo, the "character" role (overweight or old), the femme fatale, the sex kitten. Male roles fall into far fewer classifications: usually the leading man, the bad guy, and the comic relief. Men, it would appear, are far more difficult to categorize due to their superior complexity. Then there are the "bad" girls, which usually means deviant. Another definition would be "women with a bit of backbone" who don't conform to patriarchal expectations—Eva Peron, Velma and Roxie in *Chicago,* Sally Bowles in *Cabaret,* the three women in *Witches of Eastwick,* Queenie in *The Wild Party.* And if they're not bad, they're bound to be mad (read menopausal): Norma Desmond in *Sunset Boulevard,* Mamma Rose in *Gypsy,* Little Edie in *Grey Gardens.*

In the "mad" category, the latest so-called great role is that of Diana in *Next to Normal.* Alice Ripley won the 2009 Tony award for Best Performance by a Leading Actress in a Musical and undoubtedly savored the opportunity to play such a complicated character. *Next to Normal* was awarded the 2010 Pulitzer Prize for Drama (only the eighth musical to be honored) and was widely praised for utilizing the musical form to tackle the subject of mental illness. As the show opens, we learn that Diana has been diagnosed as a "bipolar depressive with delusional episodes" brought on by the death of her infant son 16 years ago. The musical follows her through various stages of treatment, and although the writers place Diana at the center of the show, it is the men around her—the all-knowing doctor and the well-meaning husband—who make her decisions for her.

Critic Ben Brantley[7] assumed the show would resonate more with women than men.

> Mr. Yorkey's script will also seem familiar to anyone who has watched the Lifetime channel's inspirational dramas about mothers and daughters on the brink of sanity. (Since Lifetime is "television for women," the fathers and sons tend to suffer on the sidelines.)

Mirroring the dismissive "television for women" label, *Next to Normal* places itself in the "theatre for women" category by building the show around a female lead and purporting to deal with "women's issues" (depression is still widely regarded as more common in women than men, possibly due to the fact that more women sufferers than men actually seek treatment.) Yet the show was created entirely by men, and the patriarchal voice at the core of the show pervades almost every scene. Not once in the show does anyone wonder if it is in fact the situation itself that is making Diana depressed— stuck with a dull husband, non-communicative daughter, and no career. When she sings of how she misses the mountains, she is not talking figuratively. It is a metaphor for the life she could have had, if she had not become pregnant while in college and abandoned her degree (while her husband continued his) to become a mother. She even says she misses her life, but no one around her appears to be listening. They are too busy reshaping Diana into the good wife and mother they want her to be—that, apparently, will solve the problem. When Diana does finally leave the family home, Dan's subsequent lyrics apportion blame and paint Diana as the selfish half of the marriage for abandoning him. He is the martyr for sticking by her.

It cannot be denied that in terms of both a vocal and an acting challenge, Diana is a great role for a female performer. But let's be honest here: *Next to Normal* is a male view of female depression, and the writers appear to be stuck in theories from the 1950s in terms of the causes and treatment of mental illness among women. Drawing a connection—however tenuous— between female "madness" and hormones is insultingly passé, and the male voice driving the show deems the suffering of Diana's husband, Dan, as greater than hers. Diana masquerades as the heart of the show, but it is in fact Dan who is the pivot. It may claim to be Diana's story, but it is told from her husband's point of view. A female lyricist would perhaps have led us to a deeper understanding of the sufferings of the female patient rather than focusing our attention on how her husband copes. A female doctor onstage may have alleviated some of my misgivings about two men discussing electric shock treatment for a woman, requiring her husband's permission, without including her in the discussion. A great role should empower both the actress playing it and the women in the audience experiencing it. I'm not sure what is empowering about either playing or watching a woman characterized by her weaknesses instead of her strengths. Rebecca Luker opines:

> The great musicals, I think, are the ones where the woman defies the stereotype, and the great writers write those women. You know, they don't make them complete victims or complete sex goddesses—or whatever they are. Madonna/Whore, you know. And I think the great musicals are the ones that are more complicated than that, that don't put (women) in a box.

Putting women in a box, or ignoring them, has sadly become the norm in the majority of new musicals. And yet the more complex roles do exist. Mamma Rose in *Gypsy* (1959) is often regarded as the Hamlet or Lear of musical theatre and has been played by the true legends of the genre—Ethel Merman, Bernadette Peters, Angela Lansbury, and Patti Lupone. In the *New York Times* in 1974, critic Clive Barnes described Mamma Rose as "possibly one of the few truly complex characters in the American musical."[8] Almost 30 years later Frank Rich considered the show "one of the most enduring creations of the American theater."[9] It is the one role every musical theatre actress longs to play: a feisty, strong woman in control of her life, who never gives up or laments her current existence. And she gets two of the most memorable songs in musical theatre—"Everything's Comin' Up Roses" and "Rose's Turn."

Before *Gypsy,* there were two previous shows created as vehicles for Ethel Merman—*Annie Get Your Gun* in 1946 and *Call Me Madam*[10] in 1950. Merman's bold, brassy voice alone indicated that here was no shrinking violet, and the actress herself was renowned for her no-nonsense, straight-talking style. Little wonder, then, that the roles created for her reflected this, putting her firmly center-stage and as far away from the victim stereotype as possible. No one messed with Merman. Or Mamma Rose, Annie Oakley, or Sally Adams.

Composer/lyricist Jerry Herman built two hugely successful shows around larger-than-life leading ladies: *Hello, Dolly!*[11] in 1964 and *Mame*[12] in 1966. The popularity of these and previous "diva" shows was so high that they were all made into films—*Call Me Madam* in 1953 with Ethel Merman reprising her role as Sally Adams, *Gypsy* in 1962 with Rosalind Russell, *Hello, Dolly!* in 1969 with Barbra Streisand, and *Mame* in 1974 with Lucille Ball. Sadly, those gutsy leading roles for women have all but disappeared, replaced with the needy Mary in *Jesus Christ Superstar,* the sacrificial Kim and Ti Moune, the intellectually stunted Clara in *Light in the Piazza,*[13] the simpering Christine or Cosette, and, possibly worst of all, Sandy in *Grease.* The strong leading roles in contemporary musicals are primarily for men.

So, did composer/lyricist teams stop writing for female stars because the stars were no longer there, or had the stars disappeared because the roles no longer made them into stars? Rodgers and Hammerstein wrote *The Sound of Music* for Mary Martin and *The King and I* for Gertrude Lawrence. Gwen Verdon was the inspiration for *Sweet Charity* and *Chicago.* And without Liza Minnelli and Chita Rivera, *The Act, The Rink, Kiss of the Spiderwoman, Flora the Red Menace*, and *The Visit* may never have materialized. Susan Stroman says,

> Well, I think those composers have gone too. Kander and Ebb were there for Liza and Chita. Jerry Herman was there for everybody. Those kinds of composers are gone, and we aren't creating new ones. Sondheim certainly celebrates Bobby in *Company,* or he celebrates the two boys in *Merrily We Roll*

Along, or he celebrates Sweeney in *Sweeney Todd*, but those celebrations are more about the everyman. Sondheim did really set the tone for the modern musical, and I think younger generations follow his lead. But they've written away from Jerry Herman, or Kander and Ebb, or Bock and Harnick. There are fewer roles for women because those parts aren't being written like they used to.

Which has to beg the question, why? The lack of "bigger than life" female performers can only partly explain the disappearance of the feisty leading lady. It has to come down to the writers and their reluctance to create roles for women. Perhaps the new generation of (male) composers, lyricists and book writers are less aware of women and what women bring to the musical theatre stage than their predecessors. Perhaps they simply don't care. Their focus and attention is clearly on men and men's stories. And by using the excuse that female performers of the caliber of Ethel Merman, Chita Rivera, Mary Martin and Liza Minnelli no longer exist, we actually place contemporary performers in another catch–22 situation. If the leading roles are no longer there for them to perform and to gain experience through performing, they cannot establish the star status necessary before a composer/writer will be inspired enough to create a show for them.

The men who wrote the celebratory shows for women may have gone, but there are new and successful writers in their place. What would happen if one of those writers teamed up with an up-and-coming leading lady and created a show especially for her? Would we see the re-emergence of the indomitable, wise-cracking champion at the center of a the plot, belting out the big numbers and tap-dancing her way down a grand staircase? It may not be so simple, offers Susan H. Schulman:

> Now they bring stars from elsewhere to be in musicals—from film and television. So I think a true, home-grown musical theatre star like Sutton Foster is rare. Or Kelli O'Hara. Those are rare nowadays. Or Idina Menzel. I don't know how *If/Then* was written. I don't know if it was written for her or not, but it certainly seemed like it was. I mean, she fit that musical beautifully. And I think Kelli O'Hara fit *Bridges of Madison County* beautifully too. So I think you can specifically write for people in mind, and I think that writers often do write for people in mind. They don't always get them.

There is always the possibility that the new writer/composers have no desire to write for women, and indeed, nobody is saying that creating a diva musical is a prerequisite for entry into the world of musical theatre. It just seems a shame, given the status this type of show once held within the genre. But one fact does stand out. Jerry Herman, John Kander, and Fred Ebb were gay men of a certain generation: a generation who possibly appreciated—

needed, even—the support of female allies more than the current generation. And perhaps the genre itself has moved so far away from the traditional definitions of musical theatre that this type of show has now passed its sell-by date. Certainly the arrival of the sung-through musical tolled a death knell for musical comedy—the traditional vehicle for the bold, brassy leading lady. Geraldine Turner says:

> Well, all those early shows that Ethel Merman did, all the Irving Berlin shows, *Annie Get Your Gun, Call Me Madam* … when I grew up, they were the roles I wanted to do. And I was waiting to get old enough to do them, because they were strong women. Even though they were prefeminism and … there was a different way of doing things in the fifties and sixties—women were portrayed in a totally different way. But they were still strong roles. But unfortunately when I got to the age when I should be playing all those roles, those roles had disappeared from the repertoire, and there was the Les Mis and the Phantoms … and all that happened and I think that … actually the focus of musical has moved from women to men, with the British musical taking over.

Whatever the reason, it is sad to think that a genre that once admired and feted the leading lady now relies on drag queens and gags about female genital mutilation to raise a laugh. Where are the strong, positive role models of women in musicals for teen girls to emulate? Turner continues:

> That's the good thing about Wicked, let's not forget that. That they're great role models for young girls.… The weird green girl gets the guy. You don't have to be the pretty blonde one. You can be strong, and stand up for what you believe and still succeed in life. All those underlying messages of that show, are really good messages for young women. That's why it's run so long. Well, apart from the Harry Potter thing going on in it. You know, they go to witch school together.…

Which leads me to ask, is a great role *model* the same as a great role?

When *Wicked* premiered on Broadway in 2003, it garnered mainly negative reviews for its reliance on technological tricks and unimpressive score—"Bland, easy listening, Broadway pop mode," wrote Charles Isherwood in *Variety*. Notwithstanding negative reviews, *Wicked* has gone on to become the highest-grossing musical in theatre history and is praised by author Stacey Wolf[14] for its message of "girl power." "Girl Power" was a phrase popularized by the British girl band The Spice Girls in the 1990s. Purporting to stand for female empowerment, the phrase was incorporated into the *Oxford English Dictionary* in 2001 with the definition: "Power exercised by girls; spec. a self-reliant attitude among girls and young women manifested in ambition, assertiveness, and individualism."

Laughable really, when we consider the breast implants and near-starvation diets employed by members of *The Spice Girls* to conform to a male definition of the perfect female body.

In terms of stage time, yes, *Wicked* revolves around two women who are barely offstage, but can Glinda and Elphaba really lay claim to being empowering role models when they are fulfilling every stereotype—the cute one is good, the ugly one bad—and they spend most of the show fighting for the same boy? What is liberating for the girls watching when the two leading female characters see their futures only in terms of men—either the Wizard or Fiyero? Where is this ambition, assertiveness, and individualism supposedly embodied in "girl power"? Undeniably, allowing two women to control the story onstage imparts a more positive message to little girls in the audience than the one they absorb when they see themselves represented as eye candy or love interest. But are they great roles? I'm not convinced. If *Wicked* really is the feminist musical Stacey Wolf claims it is, then surely the two women would go off on their own and find careers.

No one can blame a female performer for being so thrilled at the prospect of headlining a new production that she chooses not to question the depiction and motivation of the character she is being asked to play. There are so few roles for women in musicals that for a performer to turn down the opportunity to play Nancy in yet another revival of *Oliver!* for example, on the grounds of the demeaning stereotype being at odds with her feminist principles, would be considered madness. I'm not suggesting she should—many divorced Catholic women still attend mass, after all. And what female performer wouldn't want to tackle a role that gives her the opportunity to display both her singing ability and acting prowess at their best? The actress playing Nancy doesn't have to agree with the dubious lyrics in order to sing them well. And she still gets the show-stopping ballad "As Long As He Needs Me."

The trouble is that nothing Bill Sykes says or does throughout the entire show indicates that he needs Nancy in any way, shape, or form. She is deluding herself, and women in the audience in 2015 cannot possibly be unaware of this or believe that she is doing the right thing by staying with a man who beats her, ignores her, humiliates, and then kills her. So who does this caricature of womanhood appeal to? I can only guess and say it is welcomed by the hardy few traditionalists who refuse to accept that times have changed and who may, in a nostalgic sense, enjoy a depiction of women as subservient and pliable. Fortunately, I don't know these people.

The female victim is a staple of the musical theatre canon. They can be any age and come from all walks of life, but they have one thing in common:

they are all universally disempowered by their dependency on the men in their lives.

He can be selfish and indifferent, he can physically and emotionally abuse her as much as he likes, and her only reaction will be to sing about how much she loves him. This song is the ubiquitous victim song, so beloved by the creators of musicals. On the surface, it is the big ballad sung by the leading lady, usually in Act Two. Underneath, it is a song which reinforces the male conceit that a woman cannot survive without the love of a man, regardless of how badly he treats her. Songs such as "Loving You Is Not a Choice," "A Boy Like That," "I Know Him So Well," "On My Own," "I Still Believe," and "What's the Use of Wondrin'" are only the beginning of the sacrificial or abused wife/girlfriend ballads that have at their heart a resignation and acceptance from the character that this is her lot and she is powerless to change it. Like Nancy, nursing a black eye and belting out "As Long As He Needs Me" to the back of the stalls, the characters singing these songs display masochistic tendencies, and an apparent belief that true love can only ever be real if pain and suffering are involved.

How do you play against the victim type if you're playing Queen in *The Life,* a character who brings a whole new depth to the word victim. I'm not sure where exactly any actress would discover the inner strength of someone who defines herself so completely by her man. She may as well have "I don't know, ask him" tattooed across her forehead. "He's No Good" along with "As Long As He Needs Me," "Fifty Percent," "You Must Love Me," "Unusual Way," and the excruciating "How Many Tears" from *Martin Guerre* all subscribe to the "this is what I deserve" philosophy. The women appear to have such low self-esteem that they will put up with anything and be grateful for it, because—in their eyes—they're lucky to have found any man at all.

Queenie in *The Wild Party* is, like Nancy and Queen, another victim so in thrall to her abusive partner that she cannot bring herself to leave. She talks about it, sings lyrics about growing and walking out the door. So why doesn't she do it? What, apart from herself, is stopping her from changing? She too, has masochistic tendencies and gains some enjoyment from her physical humiliation and pain at the hands of Burrs.

But even that is not quite as bad as the whining Fosca in *Passion* who, when reminiscing about her first husband, remarks that his dangerous and violent nature "excited her." Really? James Lapine and Stephen Sondheim subscribe to the chauvinistic "they love it" school of defense? How disappointing. I've yet to find a single woman who enjoys being beaten up by her male lover, but maybe I move in the wrong circles. Yes, there are women who stay in abusive relationships or who continually attract abusive men. The reasons behind that are and multi-faceted and far more complex than Quee-nie, Nancy, or Fosca demonstrate. And if we have to see women suffering domestic abuse onstage (what happened to musicals being a frivolous dis-traction?) could we at least have it presented to us from a woman's point of view rather than from a man who assumes he knows how a woman in that position feels? He doesn't.

Why do the men who write these songs refuse to entertain the idea that a woman can be single, strong, and happy? Does that not make her a believ-able character? It worked fairly successfully for *Mamma Mia!* Two billion dollars worldwide would suggest to me that women have no desire to see powerless, female victims onstage. Nor do they write them, incidentally.

Geraldine Turner has her own thoughts on the victim song, starting with every drag queen's favorite, the torturous "Fifty Percent" from *Ballroom* (1978).[15]

> It's actually stating up front that I'm only half a person without this person. And I like to iron his shirts and … oh please. I don't think I ever want to sing that song. I don't think "As Long As He Need Me" quite goes there. She's say-ing she wants to be needed, not that she's nothing without him. Which is what "Fifty Percent" is saying. And "Time Heals Everything" from Mack and Mabel is saying … I mean it's a fabulous song but … time heals everything but loving you. I'll always love you … that's not true. Of course you get healed from lov-ing someone.

What are young women in the audience supposed to make of these songs? That a woman's lot is to endure pain, and while you can sing about how bad you feel, you don't actually have the power within you to do anything to change it. Or that these women are heroines for battling on in a misguided attempt to keep their undeserving men? Hopefully, women in the audience are more enlightened these days and would hand Nancy or Queen the number of the nearest women's shelter. MTV infantilizes women by dressing them in baby-doll negligees and school uniforms to make them seem less threatening, the musical gives them the victim song. Perhaps defining women as victims gives the male ego the boost it desires, but is this really how men view women in 2015? I'd be surprised if it is.

I'd also be surprised if the majority of women who go to these shows define themselves as victims. But perhaps they are too busy cheering the skills of the performer playing Effie in *Dreamgirls*[16] (1981) when she delivers the show-stopping "And I'm Telling You, I'm Not Going" to hear the subtext of dependency in the lyrics. At least Mrs. Johnstone in *Blood Brothers* (1983) is spared the humiliation of the "poor me" song—and she actually would be entitled to it, given the hand of cards that she has been dealt in life. But the character has been written from a place of great respect and admiration. Willy Russell has clearly encountered this type of woman—the working-class survivor who has no option but to get on with life. Could the stoicism and humor in the character of Mrs. Johnstone have anything to do with the fact that when the show closed in the West End in 2013, it had run for 24 years?

The closest Donna in *Mamma Mia!* ever comes to feeling sorry for herself is when her daughter is about to leave home and Donna sings "Slipping Through My Fingers." She never complains of her struggle as a lone parent nor describes her single life as empty. She surrounds herself with female friends, opens a bottle of cheap wine, and gets on with doing what needs to be done. Could the strength and resilience of this leading lady partly account for the show's 13-year—and counting—run in the West End?

What is it about these two shows, I wonder, that entices women back into the same theatre time and time again? It really doesn't require brain surgery to work it out. The women in the audience recognize the resilience displayed by Donna and Mrs. Johnstone, and they like what they see. Women do not want to see female victims onstage. It's not how they view themselves. Why is that so hard for male producers, writers, composers, and directors to understand?

Possibly it's because the idea of a woman in control of a story, or the creation of that story, challenges men's view of themselves as the rightful possessors of power. A show that depicts a strong woman successfully surviving on her own is not the message many men want women to absorb. They might get ideas in their pretty little heads. And a show created by women leaves men out in the cold.

In *The Color Purple*[17] (2005), the character of Miss Celie transcends the abuse at the hands of the men around her to find inner strength and financial independence. When I was present at a performance of the show, the audience stood to applaud Miss Celie's lyrics in the affirming "I'm Here." Miss Celie's assertion that she "is here" can also be interpreted as "I matter." Or "I am not invisible." Perhaps this, along with pride in the character's accomplishments, was the real reason behind the standing ovation. Women in the audience were responding to a validation of their own personal beliefs in themselves as powerful and relevant human beings.

Donna, Mrs. Johnstone, and Miss Celie are realistic and complex characters who the women in the audience can identify with. Chances are, the experiences they see the women go through onstage mirror their own lives. So are these three roles "great" ones for female performers? Do these characters empower both the actress and the female audience member? Without question. Does *Jersey Boys,* with the only memorable exception to the practically all-male cast a drug-dependent daughter? *Miss Saigon* (currently in revival in London) where the women are either prostitutes, or self-sacrificing? *Rocky*—a show about male aggression disguised as sport? *Kinky Boots* or *Hedwig and the Angry Inch*—shows that don't actually need real women onstage, since the male imitation is so much better?

I find it depressing. What I find even more depressing is that I seem to be the only one who finds it depressing or even notices. When I do point it out, I am the separatist harridan ranting in the corner. Buy her a drink and change the subject. Or worse, the, "Oh, I know. But it's a *musical...*" But Melanie La Barrie says,

> If I choose to go and see a musical it tends to be because there is a strong female in it. I'd see something like *Caroline* or *Change.* That sort of thing ... I remember seeing *Evita* with Elena Roger and being completely blown away. I know that Evita is a controversial historical figure but I was completely blown away by somebody who was completely in charge of herself. Not just a character who is in charge of her life story, but to see an actress onstage being so in charge of herself and her craft.... And I'm in a musical that is led by four young, strong women—you know, the Matildas are young and strong women. So I tend to surround myself—in terms of the material I consume and the material I am a part of—with strong women.

My search for the great female roles led me to ponder the existence of the feminist musical and to ask if there even is such a thing. Can it exist when so many of the female roles reflect patriarchal values? The Encarta dictionary defines feminism as a "belief in the need to secure rights and opportunities for women equal to those of men, or a commitment to securing these."

A feminist musical, then (and I need to make it clear here that I am using the word "feminist" as defined by Encarta and not in place of "separatist"—a word appropriated by men for their own advantage to demonize the women's movement), would have to have women onstage as individuals i.e., not defined by their relationship to men. They would have to be strong, feisty women who persevere and who find their own power throughout the show. The show would also have an equal number of women on the creative team. That's a tall order. However, when *The Secret Garden* premiered in New York in 1991, much was made of the fact that the show had an all-female creative team[18] and was led by director Susan H. Schulman and producer Heidi Landesman. The show was adapted from the 1911 novel by Frances Hodgson Burnett, which features a determined little girl as the central character and an assortment of women (and boys) in the background supporting her journey of empowerment. The female voice in this show—onstage and off—resounded triumphantly.

We hardly need to question *Mamma Mia's* feminist credentials—a female book writer, producer, and director, and a show that unashamedly celebrates female strength and friendship, or those of *The Color Purple*—three women were part of the creative team, the show was co-produced by Oprah Winfrey, and it had a female musical director. The 2005 musical adaptation of Louisa May Alcott's 1869 novel *Little Women* would also fall into the feminist musical bracket: five female protagonists and two women—lyricist Mindi Dickstein and director Susan H. Schulman—on the creative team.

Composer Jeanine Tesori's *Violet,* which premiered Off-Broadway at Playwrights Horizons in 1997 (and is, at the time of writing, enjoying a hugely successful revival at the Roundabout Theatre, New York, starring Sutton Foster) was again directed by Susan H. Schulman with choreography by Kathleen Marshall. The show was adapted from a short story by Doris Betts—*The Ugliest Pilgrim*—and follows Violet, a young disfigured woman, on a bus journey across three states in the hope of being healed. Like *The Secret Garden, The Color Purple* and *Little Women, Violet* can cite the original source material as its feminist cornerstone. The woman's voice in all those original stories is more of a bellow than a whisper.

So if the creators of new musicals are at a loss to understand how strong, independent women think or how to portray a female character beyond the Madonna/whore paradigm, perhaps they should spend an afternoon browsing the shelves of their local library. There they will encounter printed gems such as *The Secret Life of Bees* (2002) by Sue Monk Kidd, *Fried Green Tomatoes at the Whistlestop Café* (1987) by Fannie Flagg, *Divine Secrets of the Ya Ya Sisterhood* (1996) by Rebecca Wells, *Small Island* (2003) by Andrea Levy, and, if they are truly daring, *The Women's Room* (1977) by Marilyn French. All of these, in fact any book shortlisted for the Orange Prize for Fiction,[19] would give the female audience a more uplifting and satisfying musical than *The Book of Mormon* or yet another revival of *My Fair Lady.*

It could be argued that *Legally Blonde: The Musical* gives an empowering message to young girls about the importance of education over a boyfriend, but it is difficult to call it feminist, when the leading character defines herself by her ex-lover and by her hair color. And such a pity there were no actual women on the creative team to assist in telling this story about other women. Could we call *The Rink* a feminist musical? Or *Cabaret* (1966)? Possibly. If new productions had women on the creative team. Both shows have strong minded, female protagonists and not a victim song in sight. (I prefer to think of "Maybe This Time" as a song of hopeful yearning!) Come to think of it,

Angel and Anna from *The Rink*, and Sally Bowles from *Cabaret* can join the ranks of the great roles category. Thank you, John Kander and Fred Ebb.

Kander and Ebb also gave us such memorable female protagonists as Velma Kelly and Roxie Hart in *Chicago,* Tess Harding in *Woman of the Year,* and the headstrong Flora Mezaros in *Flora the Red Menace*—a woman who gives up her boyfriend in favor of politics. Add that to the list of great roles, and award an honorary knighthood to both John Kander and the late Fred Ebb for services to women in musical theatre. Seven out of the ten roles making the "great" cut were created by these two men. Is there really no one out there prepared to take up this baton or a producer willing to hand it on to a woman?

Which brings us back again to the woman's voice.

The musicals that I am classing as feminist had female characters driving the story, but as *Nine, Sweet Charity,* and *The Life* prove, boosting gender equality in the cast numbers is only empowering if the women are playing complex and truthful characters. There may be more female performers onstage—and subsequently more jobs for women—but who benefits if they are playing bimbo or victim clichés? Do the provocatively attired female characters in *Rock of Ages* and *Chicago* empower women in the audience or merely corroborate a male fantasy of women as sexually available?

The main statement imparted by the cheerleading girls in the short-lived 2011 show *Lysistrata Jones*[20] (like *Next to Normal,* this show also had an all-male creative team) is one of female power being intrinsically linked with sexuality. Perhaps young women in this post-feminist age really do believe that female power lies within sex, and taking control of their sexuality instead of designating the responsibility to men allows them to believe they have won equality. But reducing female-ness to sex or body image is playing directly into the hands of the patriarchy by upholding a male view of women as primarily sexual objects. Is withholding sex from their basketball-playing boyfriends until they win a game—as demonstrated by the girls in *Lysistrata Jones*—really the embodiment of the ambition, assertiveness, and individualism that makes up the definition of "girl power"? A demonstration of true power would involve the girls starting their own college basketball team and being more successful than their boyfriends. Although that, no doubt, would be the end of their relationships.

I am optimistic that one of the reasons behind the dismal failure of *Lysistrata Jones* was due to female ticket buyers expressing their disapproval at being portrayed only as a sexual subtext to a male story, that lyrics such as those from "Lay Low" with their sinister no means-yes undertones hopefully served only to offend more enlightened women. And if the excuse of original source material is going to be thrown up again as the reason behind the plot line, then I have a very simple answer. Find different source material. We don't want to see submissive, controlled women. Probably the three-week run of the show had more to do with the lack of a star name, an unpronounceable title, and an unknown creative team than feminist sensibilities, but I remain hopeful.

The glaringly obvious feature of the feminist musicals is that women were involved in the creation of the show. This resulted in strong, realistic female roles, written with empathy and understanding, i.e., the sound of the woman's voice. But, as we have seen, these musicals are few and far between. All too often what we are presented with onstage is confirmation of women's perceived weaknesses instead of an affirmation of their strengths. That strength may well be the determination displayed by Maria Von Trapp in *The Sound of Music*—a woman who goes after what she desires, secures it and then leads her new family to safety.

She does not conform to the rules, and she is far from the abused victim. Maria Von Trapp makes choices, takes action and awakens love in a man. Even the Mother Abbess shows more determination and integrity than the women in *Wicked*.

We have seen what can be achieved—*Mamma Mia!, Blood Brothers, Violet, Little Women, The Secret Garden, The Color Purple*—when women have a voice. And we have seen how audiences respond. But until that same audience protests at seeing the opposite extreme and actually votes with their feet (as they clearly did with *Viva Forever!*) these stereotypical female characters will continue to dominate musical theatre. And for whatever reasons, producers appear to be unable to join the dots that connect the audience and the story onstage with box-office success. Let me spell it out. Why is *Mamma Mia!* a worldwide smash hit? Because it is created by women, for women. And the women creating it know what the women in the audience—*the majority*—want to see. Anneke Harrison evaluates the show's appeal:

> If you take the example of *Mamma Mia!*, a show completely controlled by women … that lovely bedroom scene where they were just being women and having fun. And yes, they are talking about men but they're being real about it. It's quite lovely. I'm not sure how that scene would be with a male writer or director. Women together behave differently when men are not in the room, so to create that specific female scene requires female input. That's why those scenes work so well, because they are genuine female friendships onstage. And what's lacking in most musicals is the authenticity of those relationships.

If the critics would only question the depiction of women onstage the way they do with racial or sexual stereotyping, producers and creators might sit up and take notice. Theatre critics wield considerable influence and could easily open up a debate about the lack of female roles with any depth or complexity in current musicals. The fact that they do not—and bear in mind the most influential critics are male—means one of two things. They either don't notice, or they don't care. Until they do either of these things, the musical will continue to present an image of women as obsessed with finding a man, pitiable (or dangerous) without one, sacrificial of her own needs, and possessing no identity—assuming, of course, there are any women in the show at all. The feisty depictions of womanhood depicted in *Mame, Gypsy, Hello, Dolly!, The Rink, Cabaret,* or *Call Me Madam* are, by and large, relics of the past, replaced by a string of mad or power-crazed bitches, pathetic, dependent victims, or vacuous bimbos—not, by any stretch of the imagination, great roles for women. Rebecca Luker hopes,

> You know, that audience for Wicked, they're girls who blog and who tweet, and maybe that will be the thing that changes these women's roles ... the teen generation of today will certainly grow up to be women who aren't just going to want to see victim roles, aren't just going to want to see you know ... a limited version of what a woman is.... Maybe there is a lost generation in there of women, and maybe they are waking up now to write more women's stories.

Let's hope so.

NOTES

1. Alain Boublil, Claude Michel Schoenberg (*Les Misérables, Miss Saigon, Martin Guerre*).
2. Book by Arthur Kopit; lyrics and music by Maury Yeston.
3. Book by David Newman, Ira Gasman and Cy Coleman; lyrics by Ira Gasman; music by Cy Coleman.
4. Book by Larry L. King and Peter Masterson; lyrics and music by Carol Hall.
5. Book by Neil Simon; lyrics by Dorothy Fields; music Cy Coleman.
6. Directed by Alan Parker.
7. *New York Times,* February 14, 2008.
8. "Gypsy Bounces Back with Zest and Lilt," *New York Times,* September 24, 1974.
9. "Gypsy: Then, Now and Always," *New York Times,* May 4 2003.
10. Book by Howard Lindsay and Russel Crouse; lyrics and music by Irving Berlin.
11. Book by Michael Stewart; lyrics and music by Jerry Herman.
12. Book by Jerome Lawrence and Robert Edwin Lee; lyrics and music by Jerry Herman.
13. Book by Craig Lucas; lyrics and music by Adam Guettel.
14. Stacy Ellen Wolf, 2010, *Changed for Good: A Feminist History of the Broadway Musical* (New York: Oxford University Press).
15. Book by Jerome Kass; lyrics by Alan and Marilyn Bergman; music by Billy Goldenberg.
16. Book and lyrics by Tom Eyen; music by Henry Krieger.

17. Book by Marsha Norman; lyrics and music by Brenda Russell, Allee Willis and Stephen Bray.

18. Book and lyrics by Marsha Norman; music by Lucy Simon; scenic design by Heidi Landesman; costume design by Theoni Aldredge; lighting design by Tharron Musser.

19. Launched in 1996, the Orange Prize celebrates excellence, originality and accessibility in women's writing. Previous winners have included Rose Tremain, Zadie Smith, Andrea Levy, Chimamanda Ngozi Adiche, Lionel Shriver, Ann Pachett, and Kate Grenville.

20. Book by Douglas Carter Beane; music by Lewis Flinn.

4

If a Girl Isn't Pretty

Male Gaze and the Musical

I was thinking about the shows I've done recently. It's interesting the way the women are costumed. Because we love to go to the theatre to set up an ideal. Or we go to the theatre to see an ideal set up onstage in front of us. Some kind of human condition. Some kind of hyper reality, if you like. So I was looking at it and I thought ... *We Will Rock You, Rent, Saigon, Les Mis* ... so many of the women are dressed basically to look sexy. It's their role. It's the responsibility of women to look appealing. To look hot. And to look sexy.

—Anneke Harrison

In his 1972 book *Ways of Seeing,* John Berger states, "Men look at women. Women watch themselves being looked at."[1] From an early age, women become accustomed to being looked at by men—every young woman dreads the walk past the building site. French psychoanalyst Jacques Lacan (1901–1981) is credited with defining the anxious state that comes with the awareness that one can be viewed as the "Gaze." Lacan contended that the anxious state arises from a realization by the person being viewed of their loss of power and status. The gaze effectively reduces them to an object. The young woman walking past the building site dreads the experience because she is uncomfortably aware that she is being viewed primarily as a sexual object. Feminist theory redefines this as the male gaze.

Film theorist Laura Mulvey first introduced the concept of male gaze in her essay "Visual Pleasure and Narrative Cinema"[2] and argued that the language of film spoke primarily to the heterosexual male by reducing the woman onscreen to an object of desire. Lingering shots of a woman's body or her moist lips, for example, encourage the male viewer to collude in the (male) gaze of the camera. In the same way, artists painting nude women are doing so with the assumption that other men will share their personal pleasure in the naked female form. Feminist theory asserts that the male gaze expresses an unequal power relationship between the man and the woman—the viewer and the viewed. The man imposes his gaze, reducing the woman to an object, whether the woman desires it or not. The naked woman in the oil painting has no control over the men looking at her—she is displayed purely for their enjoyment.

What does this have to do with musical theatre? Well, I would argue that the costuming of many female characters onstage frequently subscribes to theories of male gaze. The women are often dressed in a way that is designed to appeal to the heterosexual male—micro-miniskirts, see through shirts, tiny shorts, figure-hugging pants, high heels, corsets designed to push up the breasts. The irony of this—need I say it?—is that the audience directing their gaze onto these women is predominantly other women or gay men. The majority of both groups are unlikely to appreciate women dressed as sexual objects. Any straight men in the audience are in the minority, and yet the costuming of female characters is designed to appeal directly to them. It is intended, perhaps, to give the men something to fantasize over while they appease their wives by accompanying them to a musical.

John Berger goes on to say: "Men survey women before treating them. Consequently how a woman appears to a man can determine how she will be treated."

The first impression—what we initially see—has an immediate impact on how we subsequently judge a person. Race, weight, and age all contribute to this, as does the way a person is dressed. This last factor has particular relevance for women, as assumptions are made based on a woman's appearance in a way that they are not with men.

The way women are dressed onstage is a conscious effort by the director to influence our initial impression of the character and make us view her in a certain way. A good example of this is found in *Chicago*, where the lyrics sung by the "merry murderesses" indicate that these are women of action. True, their actions have been to murder their cheating or controlling men, but the fact that the 1996 Broadway revival is still running 17 years after it opened suggests that many women do not find this idea entirely unpalatable. The "Cell Block Tango" celebrates the fact that the women have taken responsibility for their situations, instead of sitting around looking pretty and waiting for a man to change it. Yet the strength of these characters as women is completely undermined by their costumes. They are dressed as male fantasies, with see-through mesh dresses revealing their lingerie, tiny skirts, and black, figure hugging lycra. These characters are presented to us first and foremost as sexual objects. Regardless of their actions or the lyrics they sing, it is impossible for any audience member not to make the association between the way these women are dressed and their sexual availability. The implication is clear. Women who use sex to get what they want are only one step away from prostitutes—hence the costumes—and will come to a bad end.

Decades before the revival of *Chicago* came along, the women in *Sweet Charity* set the precedent for drawing a direct line between the way women are dressed onstage and their sexual availability. Before the dance-hall hostesses have sung a single lyric of "Big Spender," the audience knows exactly who and what they are. Dressed in revealing dresses and fishnet stockings and draped over the dance barre in sexually suggestive poses, the visuals tell us everything we need to know. These women are available.

When women are costumed onstage as sex objects, then that is what the men in the audience will assume they are. They are responding instinctively to the image they are being given. Sexualizing women is another form of patriarchal control. Reducing a woman to little more than her sexual allure robs her of any power she may have gained from her achievements—witness how often and effectively it is used against female politicians or sportswomen. Deriding the female gold medalist as too muscular to get a man draws attention away from her winning performance. Theatre performers have little or no say in the costumes they are given to wear and subsequently cannot control the image their characters are presenting to the audience. A woman in a department store can choose whether or not to buy clothing that draws attention to her sexuality. The female performers in *Rock of Ages* have no such choice. The female characters in *Chicago* or *Sweet Charity* are perhaps poor examples to use, as these characters are already sexualized by their actions or professions. But what exactly are we being told about the characters in *West Side Story* when Maria appears wearing a remodeled Communion dress and Anita is in a low-cut dress that exposes her underwear when she dances? Maria is the Madonna, Anita the whore, metaphorically speaking.

Dressing women in a sexualized manner also conforms to the power theories of male gaze. One half of the population exists for the pleasure of the other half, and the former is powerless to change this imbalance. Women onstage experience what I term the double gaze. Not only are they subjected to the gaze of the men in the audience, they are also initially objectified by the gaze from the men around them onstage.

In "The Heat Is On in Saigon" the male characters overtly objectify the girls (already diminished by being dressed in bikinis) by choosing the most appealing out of the group. Appealing is taken to mean sexy—these girls are prostitutes, after all. The attitude of the men onstage towards the women reinforces to the men in the audience that it is acceptable to view these women in a certain way. The male audience members are given permission from the stage to collude in the gaze.

If we were to remove the lyrics and dialogue from the scene, the audience would still immediately understand the power dynamics between the male and female characters because of the manner in which the men onstage regard the women. Of course, the male performers onstage are playing characters— I am not saying the performers themselves are objectifying their female colleagues—and they are interpreting their characters in accordance to the direction they have been given. The gaze, therefore, both onstage and from the audience, is ultimately controlled by the director. And he may not be above objectifying his performers.

This inequality of power at the heart of male gaze was apparent in the Broadway production of *Spring Awakening*[3] (2006), where director Michael Mayer had Wendla bare her breasts while having sex, but her male lover, Melchior, remain clothed. In the Australian premiere of *Dr. Zhivago*[4] (2011) directed by Des MacAnuff, Lara sang *When the Music Played* dressed in her underwear, while, again, her husband remained fully clothed. In addition, nude images of Lara were projected onto a large screen behind her—a moment referred to by critic Deborah Jones in *The Australian* as "soft porn." In both these examples, the women onstage were literally stripped of any power by male directors. As characters, Wendla and Lara were reduced to passive sexual objects. As actors, the young women were placed in an extremely vulnerable position, one they were unlikely to have the confidence to challenge in rehearsal. Their nakedness onstage had little to do with advancing the story and more to do with pleasing the male eye, either that of the men in the audience or the directors themselves.

Theatre critics Vicky Frost and Cameron Woodhead both raised misgivings about the blatant sexualization of the female ensemble in the Australian premiere (supposedly prior to Broadway) of *King Kong: The Musical* in 2013.

> The female chorus—problematically perpetually in their knickers—pop up for some great numbers, such as a sassy, syncopated version of "I Wanna Be Loved by You" and "Special FX," in which Anne is serenaded by dominatrices in PVC corsets and suspenders, their fake boobs bobbing [Vicky Frost, theguardian.com, June 17, 2013].

> The use of tits and arse, in particular, can feel utterly gratuitous.... In a story that condemns the crass exploitation of an animal for entertainment, the portrayal of women is troubling [Cameron Woodhead, *The Age* and *Sydney Morning Herald*, June 15, 2013].

What is even more troubling is that this show had a female producer, Carmen Pavlovic. Did she really not notice that the female ensemble spent most of the show in their underwear? And did it really not occur to her that this image was demeaning to her own sex? Or even that the female ticket buyer may find it so offensive that it prevents her enjoyment of any other aspect of the show?

Unsurprisingly, *Mamma Mia!* escapes the male gaze accusation. The leading lady wears denim work clothes, and her friends are dressed in flowing skirts or linen pants. It is the younger men in the show who provide the visual sexual stimulation—regularly removing their shirts and dancing bare-chested. Is this the female gaze at play? The antithesis of this was on show in *Dirty Dancing* (2006), where the character of Penny is unnecessarily costumed in skin-tight lycra shorts and high heels. The director or designer may argue that Penny is a dance instructor and naturally would be dressed in lycra, but next to her pupil—dancing in jeans and a T-shirt—her costume appears to have been designed more to appeal to the straight men in the audience than to service the story. Rebecca Caine notes:

> Cosette is not an easy role because it's so cardboard cutout. She is the romantic interest, to the point that the people don't like her because Eponine gets all the sympathy. And I don't blame people for thinking, "go with Eponine." Particularly as Eponine has always been … she's presented as really rather gorgeous. Whereas if you read the book, she should be something that he barely looks at. She should have bad teeth and be covered in mud; she's something you shake off your shoe. But she's not like that in the show. And in the movie they had her do her big number practically in a wet T-shirt—all that rain pumping down on her. But, sex sells. And it sells more than ever now. I think it's hilarious on Broadway now that it's like the sizzling-hot cast of *Les Misérables*. I mean, it's about dispossessed people in the nineteenth century. It's not about sex!

Women in the audience are so accustomed to being the subject of the male gaze that they learn to regard other women in a similar manner. By accepting the sexualized costuming of female characters and allowing the actions of male performers onstage to influence judgments they as audience members make, women inadvertently collude in the male gaze. (This could also possibly apply to the female director and choreographer of *Rock of Ages*[5] and the female costume designer of *Chicago*.[6] Or perhaps they were under pressure from male producers.) Despite that fact that women are in the majority, a resigned acceptance from the female audience that what they are seeing is what men want to see, takes precedence over what the women themselves would prefer to see. This again is the imbalance of power contained within the structure of the male gaze. What women—performers included—want, i.e., not to be looked at or objectified, is rarely taken into account.

When the men in Frank Loesser's *The Most Happy Fella* (1956) sing of their enjoyment at watching the passing parade of girls on the street in *Standing on the Corner*, they are acknowledging that men look at women and women cannot stop them. While the lyrics appear innocent, a feminist reading of "giving all the girls the eye" reveals the lyrics as a sexual threat from the predatory, voyeuristic male. None of the men singing pause to consider how the women feel when they know they're being watched. All women are aware of the fine line running between being watched and being leered at, but the men in this song appear to be completely oblivious of it. Either that, or they simply don't care, secure in the knowledge that they—as the watchers—hold the reins of power.

In *Legally Blonde: The Musical* there is again an acknowledgement of the fact that men watch women, but the song "Bend and Snap" could be seen as an attempt by the girls to subvert the gaze by playing up to it. By overtly using their sexuality, the girls attempt to take back some of the control denied them through being objectified. They manipulate the gaze by deliberately presenting the image they know the men want to see and by taking advantage of the inevitable male reaction. Personally, I'm not convinced that bending over in front of a man in order to cajole him into buying a drink can be defined as power, but at least the characters in *Legally Blonde* appear to have some control over the gaze being directed towards them onstage and are not passively accepting their designated role of viewed object.

Again, if "Bend and Snap" was performed without the dialogue and lyrics, the underlying message of the scene is patently clear through the visual imagery—women are defined by their sexuality and exist for men's enjoyment. It is, however, a more enjoyable number to experience as an audience member than watching four men standing on a street corner leering at women. Wendy Cavett notes:

> If it's popular theatre, it's geared towards the population, and our population still is based on how your body looks, and how do you look to a guy, and are you hot or not. You know, there are all sorts of messages like that out there.

When the plot line of so many musicals revolves around the quest by the leading lady to find a man—reinforced by a subtext that deems it crucial for her to do so—then the way she looks becomes a fundamental component in her success. In order to secure the love of a man, a woman must conform to the societal construct of beauty. The more beautiful a woman is, the greater her chances are of being "chosen." Beauty pageants—under pressure from the women's movement, which deemed a contest in which a woman was valued purely for her physical appearance as degrading—have had to adapt in recent years, placing more emphasis on a contestant's charity work, public speaking abilities, and education. But there is no hiding the fact that the women are being judged first and foremost on their appearances, and crowning the successful candidate—giving her the title of Beauty *Queen*—elevates her status above that of the other women.

In the musical *Passion,* Fosca is described as "an ugly, sickly woman," and her lack of beauty is referred to constantly by other characters. On hearing a scream from Fosca's bedroom, one soldier quips that someone has just hung a mirror in her room. Her cousin the colonel points out that unattractive women are gullible and suggests that an ugly woman is so desperate for love she will believe anything a man tells her. Fosca herself seems obsessed by her plainness, referring to herself as repellent and comparing herself to a dog. But how is the beauty that eludes Fosca being defined—and more to the point, by whom? In *Beauty and the Beast* we are given a similar moral story—that it is what is inside that truly counts—but the "ugliness" of the beast is apparent the minute we see him. In the production shots of the original production of *Passion,* Fosca is costumed to look less confident in her sexuality than her rival Clara, but she is hardly unattractive. She is not covered in weeping acne, nor in possession of protruding teeth, piggy eyes, and a bulbous nose. We assume she does not smell—the soldiers would have made a joke about it. So what exactly is "ugly" referring to? Her age? Her dress sense? The way she does her hair? Fosca herself attributes her obsessive behavior to her looks, claiming her bad behavior is a result of her appearance. Are we supposed to deduce from this that pretty blondes with perfect teeth and shining hair are also endowed with superior morals and ethics? News to me.

Fosca's stalking tendencies and penchant for manipulation do not affect her appearance, but the musical would have us believe it is Fosca's looks alone that condemn her to a lifetime of longing. Her revelation in the closing scene that she is "someone to be loved" is a result of Giorgio being man enough to overcome his distaste and make love to her. She subsequently dies happy, believing herself to be beautiful. Giorgio is depicted as some kind of saint for finding it within himself to love such a hideous creature, and his realization that she loves him in a way no other woman ever has comes a little late, given that she has practically willed herself to death. But at the end of the show I am still unclear as to what it is that causes Fosca to be derided as "ugly." The other female character in the show, Clara, is dressed in revealing corsets and spends much of the show in Giorgio's arms (or bed). So the message is clear—what makes women beautiful is their sexual allure, and without beauty, women are worthless. In whose eyes, I wonder?

It's depressing to think that this affirmation of a societal construct of "beauty" as being paramount to a woman's success and happiness in life was brought to us from the same minds that gave us the groundbreaking *Into the Woods* and *Sunday in the Park with George.*

Isn't true beauty subjective? In the eye of the beholder? Or is that the exact point *Passion* believes it is making, and I missed it because I am a moderately attractive woman and therefore bound to be stupid and unable to follow the plot of a "sophisticated" musical?

Violet is set a century later than *Passion* but the same preoccupation with beauty is an essential component of the story. But Violet is different from Fosca in that she has an unsightly scar across her face—a result of a childhood accident—that causes her to class herself as unattractive. She has saved for two years to pay for a trip to see a televangelist who she believes can bring about a miracle and remove her scar. Violet knows she cannot currently be classed as pretty and dreams of looking like the movies stars she gazes at in her fan magazines. Unlike Fosca, however, Violet's fixation on her appearance is perfectly understandable given the context of a prominent facial scar. Violet is not seeking the removal of the scar solely to find a husband; she believes her life will be better if the scar is not her defining characteristic. Given the reaction from other characters—both the Bus Driver and the Old Lady express shock when they first encounter her—it is hardly surprising that Violet wants the scar to disappear. Her life would be much easier.

Both these shows have their foundations in a societal construct of beauty that tells us it is necessary for women to look a certain way in order to be successful in life. Violet wants to attain the unrealistic perfection she sees in her film magazines. Fosca believes she is undeserving of love because she is not conventionally beautiful. The other characters around the women in both shows confirm this. Sadly, these musicals reflect a contemporary prevailing attitude towards women and their appearances. Violet is influenced by movie magazines in the same way as women today are manipulated by pervasive messages from social media, billboard advertisements, TV commercials, films, and the multi-billion-dollar cosmetics industry into believing they have to conform to a designated look and live up to an unrealistic image.

The fashion industry has been increasingly criticized for favoring unnaturally thin (and underage) women to market their product, thereby encouraging impressionable young girls to emulate the waif-like, androgynous catwalk models. Hollywood, the music industry, and yes, musical theatre are little better, reinforcing an image of conventional beauty as young, glamorous, and thin. Brooke Wyndham's lyrics in *Legally Blonde: The Musical* reveal the contemporary conviction that a woman's appearance alone dictates her success in life. And success, according to Brooke, is defined as fitting into a size 2 pair of jeans. The character of Brooke Wyndham is intended to be ironic, and the show itself is satirizing society's obsession with appearance. But within the wider musical theatre genre, appearance is everything. When directors refer to "the look" of a show they are not just discussing the set and costumes. They include the performers in this generalization, and "the look" is particularly relevant for female performers. Christine Toy Johnson notes:

> When I was younger, I didn't get cast as what I call the white man's vision of what an Asian woman should be, because I was always taller and curvier and just didn't fit that whole lotus blossom kind of thing. So I didn't do any of those roles. But as I've got older, I'm playing everyone's mother, and it seems to be OK with everyone that the mother is taller and curvier, so I don't get as stereotyped.

The creator's vision for the look of the show also has a negative effect on non-white actors. Despite the fact that Western society is multi-racial, popular culture seldom reflects this. Asian or black women are rarely considered for leading roles in musicals unless the script specifically calls for it—*Sister Act, Jelly's Last Jam, The King and I, Miss Saigon, Memphis*. West Indian/U.K. performer Melanie La Barrie observes: "I would never be a Mary Poppins or whatever. There are so many of those roles that aren't open to me."

While directors or producers can argue that historically or socially it makes no sense that a particular character is played by a black or Asian woman, often the decision has more to do with the aesthetic of the show. The all-important look would be unbalanced. Detractors can point out that Asian actress Lea Salonga has played Eponine[7] in *Les Misérables*, and African/American actress Audra McDonald has taken leading roles in both *Carousel* and *110 in the Shade*, but I suspect the star status of both of those performers outweighed any concerns about audience acceptance.

Audiences are becoming more accustomed to seeing mixed-race ensembles in musicals in the U.S. The leading roles still have a long way to go before they are cast purely on merit and not skin tone, but progress—slower in the U.K. than in the U.S. (and virtually absent in Australia)—is being made. Due to the fact that an audience member forms an initial judgment of a character based on a visual interpretation, the race of an actress becomes an issue when she is the only non-white performer. As the 2007 Roundabout Theatre Company production of *110 in the Shade* irrefutably proved, when the entire cast is made up of an even balance of white and non-white performers, the issues ceases to exist. Visually, we immediately absorb a message of equality. Johnson adds:

> You're not going into a newsreel or a documentary film. You're going to a place where people sing and dance. It's not literal. So I do think that when you have a situation like *110 in the Shade* with a mixed-race family and you don't talk about it at all … a couple of things can happen. The audience can go "Huh, OK. Well, maybe his wife was African American. Or maybe she's … whatever." But now I'm watching the story. And I think it happens that fast. You probably have a kind of reaction like this; then it doesn't matter because you're in the story.

Women onstage have an added pressure to conform to the construct of beauty because a paying customer wants and expects the heightened reality that musical theatre offers, not the mundane. The women in the audience, the thinking goes, should want to *be* the glamorous woman they see onstage. The men in the audience should want to have sex with her. As the character of Eddie in *Funny Girl*[8] (1964) tells us in "If a Girl Isn't Pretty," if a man is going to lay out money on a theatre ticket, the woman he sees onstage had better offer him something he doesn't see at home. Other characters in *Funny Girl* repeatedly tell leading lady Fanny Brice that she will never triumph onstage because she is not conventionally pretty. Part of this is ascribed to her "Jewish-ness" but also to the idea that a woman onstage must glitter like a diamond and be a particular body shape. Fanny does not conform to this look, and subsequently the only way she can achieve success is as a comedienne. Funny girls don't need to be attractive or thin. Fanny's first step towards stardom occurs when she subverts the image of the glowing bride in the dubiously titled "His Love Makes You Beautiful" number by appearing onstage as a heavily pregnant bride. While her defiant act delights the audience, Fanny is making a point about being judged on her looks. Her mission appears to be to prove that talent and brains are more important.

Eddie's observations in *Funny Girl* about women onstage are echoed in *A Chorus Line*[9] (1975)—a show focusing on a group of dancers auditioning for a musical. The characters are so acutely aware of how they are expected to look in order to be deemed passable onstage that when Connie Wong is asked what she will do when she can no longer dance for a living, she answers, "I can finally go off my diet." The song "Dance Ten, Looks Three" leaves us in no doubt that these women are cognizant of the fact that they will be judged more on their looks than their talent. So pernicious is this attitude that the character Val has cosmetic surgery to enlarge her breasts, thereby enhancing her job prospects. While Val may well be a character expressing an opinion, it would be interesting to do a survey among ensemble members in musicals to discover just how many young women—and men—are currently starving themselves, employing cosmetic surgeons, pumping weights, and taking steroids to conform to the unrealistic body shape favored by producers, choreographers, and directors when creating "the look" of the show. Anneke Harrison notes:

> And there are attractive men up onstage as well, so yes, it's the responsibility of male characters to look sexy and appealing. But they also need to be in command of the story, making decisions, driving the plot. That's the male characters' role. For women, if they look attractive, job done. They don't have to do anything else. The problem is that they are only ever looked at in that perspective. Which then informs, down the line, their role in society. If we hold theatre up as a reflection of how we live in society, then that's how we perpetuate that myth, that a woman's job is to be appealing—to be decorative in a male world.

Anyone who has ever been present in an audition for a musical will be able to tell you who the first candidates are to be cut: the heavy girls. Not because they can't dance, sing or act, but because if no role has been written specifically for a woman of size, there is no place onstage for an ensemble member who is overweight. Musicals are escapism, remember? And escapism is not reality. Too bad if the majority of women in Western society are not a size zero, the skinny girl is what the audience will see onstage. What she actually says onstage matters less than the visual image she projects—beauty, as defined by body size. The prevalence of eating disorders among young women in musicals, particularly dancers, shows just how dangerous the imposition of this construct of beauty can become. Producers might protest that audiences are used to seeing the glamorous, slender dancer onstage and will not readily accept an image that goes against that. These are the same producers who often still insert the "fat clause"—restricting an actor's weight—into certain performer's contracts, a clear indication that they too have fixed ideas of how women should look. I have yet to hear of a male performer with a fat clause in his musical theatre contract.

When larger women do appear onstage in the musical, their designated role is that of the comic relief. Fat women are figures of fun, something to be laughed at, and their departure from the accepted template of beauty is emphasized even further by having the lone large woman surrounded onstage by an ensemble of women who do adhere to societal definitions of beauty. The fat woman as a joke is taken one step further when she is endowed—as she often is in the musical—with a voracious sexual appetite. The idea of a fat woman wanting sex—and any man wanting to have sex with a woman who is overweight—is considered so ridiculous that it is a cue for a song. The character of Gooch in *Mame* is usually played by a larger woman, and "Gooch's Song" in Act Two is designed to make the audience laugh at the now pregnant character. If Gooch were not played by an overweight woman, the visual gag that the audience enters into would not work, because there is nothing for the audience to laugh at. It is purely because she is fat that she is a figure of fun.

Nicely Nicely in *Guys and Dolls* is usually played by a larger man, but his show stopping number "Sit Down, You're Rockin' the Boat" has nothing to do with his sexual appetite, nor are we being encouraged to laugh at him. His size does not prevent us from taking the character seriously in the way it does with larger women onstage. Madame Thenardier in *Les Misérables* seems to have evolved—if that is the right word—into the "fat" role. It wasn't regarded that way when the show first opened, and perhaps it is a result of the producer or director wanting to inject some humor into the production. Rebecca Caine observes, "Well, Madame Thenardier ... she should be really scary, but her weight shouldn't have anything to do with it. She should be funny and terrifying. But now she's the panto, the light relief."

Given that the producer and director are male, it was probably inevitable that the character selected for the fat/funny label would be female. Even *Mamma Mia!* engages in the notion of fat women possessing rampant sexual desire. The act two number "Take a Chance on Me" is designed to raise a laugh when the "fat friend" Rosie attempts to seduce the reluctant Bill. His relief when the arrival of other guests spares him the indignity of actually having to respond to Rosie's advances is clear. As too is the message we are being given—no man wants a fat woman. This preys on women's insecurities about not being attractive enough to secure a husband and imparts a more disturbing message to women in the audience—fat women need to control themselves, in more ways than one. It also serves as a reminder to the women watching from the audience that if they do not conform to the beauty ideal, they will be laughed at. And ridicule—as anyone who has ever experienced it, knows—has at its core condemnation.

Hairspray is a show which challenges preconceived ideas about the way a woman should look by placing "pleasantly plump" Tracy Turnblad at the heart of the story. Her quest for TV stardom and the love of heartthrob Link are both initially thwarted by her size, but her integrity and open-minded approach wins her both in the end. Link manages to overcome his reservations about Tracy's size, and the public votes her the winner of the televised Miss Teenage Hairspray competition. The subplot of the growing demand by black Americans for integration underlines the central theme of the show:

that judging someone purely on their looks is narrow-minded, at the very least. Tracy cannot get on TV because she is too fat; Li'l Inez is rejected for being black. This show attempts to subvert the stereotypical image of beauty by placing characters who do not conform to the slim, white and passive ideal of femininity at the center of the story. The acceptance of difference is reinforced visually by the coupling of Tracy and Link—big girl, slim boy— and Penny and Seaweed—white girl, black boy. Songs such as "Big, Blonde and Beautiful," "Without Love" and "You're Timeless to Me" reinforce this visual message by reiterating the theme of accepting someone for who he is, not how he looks.

In Naomi Wolf's seminal 1990 book *The Beauty Myth*, she discusses the connection drawn between women's weight and their sexual appetites.

"Fat is not just fertility in women, but desire. Researchers at Michael Reese hospital in Chicago found that plumper women desired sex more often than thinner women. To ask women to become unnaturally thin is to ask them to relinquish their sexuality" (p. 158).

So while there is evidence to support the belief that overweight women have a healthier sexual appetite than underweight women, there is nothing to explain the attitude towards heavier women as figures of fun.

Many Eastern cultures celebrate the curvy, womanly form as more desirable than the angular one. It is only in the West that we have designated women of a larger size—and I am not referring to obesity here, but a healthy dress size of 12 or 14—as unattractive. A girl in a pair of extra-small jeans will get her man before the woman in the medium sized ones will. This pervasive notion sold to us by the media and popular culture could be interpreted as another form of patriarchal control.

For centuries, men have demonstrated a fear of women's apparent sexual power and have sought ways in which to repress it. Some organized religions, for example, operate from a patriarchal standpoint and impose rules on women designed to control their sexual activity—no sex before marriage, covering up flesh, chaperoning of young women on dates, forbidding birth control, forcing arranged marriages and denying access to abortion. The rules, it goes without saying, are not applied to men. Encouraging women to be thin—read underweight—is an insidious way of curbing natural female sexuality, as anorexic and bulimic women frequently report a loss of sexual appetite among their symptoms. This allows men to uphold their view of themselves as sexually more powerful within a society that glorifies virility as an indication of manhood. A woman who enjoys sex and actively seeks it out is viewed as trespassing on male territory, as sexual desire is considered attractive only in men.

Every teenage girl is aware of this double standard—a girl who has lots of sexual partners is a slut, a boy who does the same is a stud. The latter is something to be admired, the former something to be despised. In the case of the larger woman, the threat posed to men by the sexual female is dissipated by turning her into a joke and thereby wearing away at her self-esteem. Onstage, thinner women take up less space, physically and metaphorically. Next to the pumped-up leading man, the visual image of the tiny woman standing beside him reminds us of her insignificance. She does not deserve the same amount of space as her male counterpart simply because she is female. Her physical frailty also serves to enhance the patriarchal message exuded by the men around her. Without the characters uttering a word, we understand merely from looking that the woman is weaker than the man.

Aside from the fat character with the insatiable appetite, female sexuality is something writers of musicals appear at a loss to know how to handle. This could be a result of the fact that many of the writers are gay men, and their experience of a woman as a sexual being is extremely limited. The woman with a sexual appetite is—like the fat woman—a joke, an excuse for songs such as "Whatever Lola Wants" (*Damn Yankees*), "I Cain't Say No" (*Oklahoma!*), "Naughty Baby" (*Crazy for You*), "A Call from the Vatican" (*Nine*), "When You've Got it, Flaunt It" (*The Producers*). These songs are designed to encourage the audience to laugh at the preposterous notion of a woman taking control of a sexual situation—very often the man onstage who is the focus of her attention is flustered and unable to handle the overt sexual implications, because the correct and acceptable situation would have the roles reversed. Needless to say, the women are dressed to emphasize their supposed wantonness—Carla in *Nine* is lolling on a bed clad only in a sheet as she sings down the phone to Guido; Lola wears a corset and stockings.

The alternative viewing of female sexuality by the musical is that of a threat. Perhaps men regard women's perceived sexual power as dangerous because it undermines their own—hence the desire to control it, or punish women who display it. Eva Peron, Norma Desmond, Sally Bowles, and the lead characters in *Chicago* and *Witches of Eastwick* are all women who are not afraid to engage with sexuality. More than that, these women use it to get what they want or to control a relationship with a man.

It therefore follows they must be seen to be punished, as they are not conforming to the dependent, compliant role of womanhood prescribed to them by a patriarchal society. The anger from the men in *Evita* is not purely because they perceive they have been made to look fools; it stems from the fact they have been made to look foolish by a woman who has taken control of a sexual situation. These musicals appear to be telling the women that if they insist on flaunting their sexuality (as a man does), they should expect retribution. Eva Peron ends up dead, Norma Desmond mad, Sally Bowles and the women in *Witches of Eastwick* are left alone, and the women in *Chicago* serve hefty prison sentences. If men don't like women who are overweight, they dislike women who show a streak of independence even more. It comes as no surprise to discover that none of these shows were written by women.

Naomi Wolf also notes: "Youth and (until recently) virginity have been 'beautiful' in women since they stand for experiential and sexual ignorance. Ageing in women is 'unbeautiful' since women grow more powerful with time" (*The Beauty Myth*, p. 4).

The older woman in musical theatre generally escapes the ridicule directed at the overweight woman or the woman who enjoys sex, because older women are not considered sexual. (The one exception is *The Producers*[10] where the notion of older women being sexually insatiable is fodder for an entire musical number.) Within the beauty ideal, the affirmation that only young women are considered attractive is prevalent—how many catwalk models are over 40? Older men enhance their status by winning the coveted prize of the younger woman. Mature women with young men are considered ridiculous or desperate. In the 1993 Lloyd Webber/Don Black spectacle *Sunset Boulevard,* the salesman Manfred has little respect for the relationship between Joe Gillis and the older, wealthier Norma Desmond, but it does not prevent him from exhorting Joe to make the most of it by spending Norma's money.

Naomi Wolf's assertion that women grow more powerful with time is true for some women, but for those who define themselves—or who have been defined by others—by their appearance or sexuality, aging deprives them of any sense of power they may have previously experienced. But if we assume it is true that women really do grow more powerful with age, it explains a very noticeable shift in the casting of musicals in recent years. Rebecca Caine notes:

> All the older roles are now being cast with younger women. And the roles that I used to play, now they want twenty year olds. They … don't want experience. So these girls now, if they're lucky, they can get one or two of those roles in before they're 25 and then they're out. Likewise, voice type has changed and become so light and so Disneyfied that they sound like little girls now. They want this sort of juvenile sound.… So the roles that were traditionally for older women are being cast with younger women and the young female roles, they're getting really young women to do.

Younger women, however liberated and self-assured, are less likely to speak up—to "cause trouble"—than a more experienced actress. They are also at the beginnings of their careers and more likely to accept the minimum wage.

The girls in *Legally Blonde: The Musical* are well aware of the perils of aging when they warn of the dangers of looking your age—your husband will stray. This may be tongue in cheek, but it serves as a reminder of just how far we are influenced by the pervasive images of beauty and the correlation those images make between attractiveness and youth. The girls' lyrics also hint at the common fear among women of being abandoned by their male partners for younger women.

This is underlined further by the visual image onstage—a cast dominated by young girls, all except one conforming to the societal construct of beauty. The one who does not is lesbian. Clichéd? Really?

In *Sunset Boulevard,* Hollywood legend Norma Desmond prepares for her onscreen comeback with a rigorous diet and exercise regime, urged on by a team of masseurs and beauticians from the "no pain, no gain" school of thought. Much is made of the fact that Norma is now 50 years old and considered past her sell-by date by an industry that relies on the youth of its stars to attract an audience. The implication is that older women are neither beautiful nor desirable. Ironically, it is the male character of Joe Gillis who points out to Norma that there is "nothing wrong with being fifty." But in an industry where looks are everything, there is plenty that is wrong with looking mature. Far from being empowered by age, Norma Desmond has had all sense of power—which she previously derived from her career—removed by men who now deem her unattractive. Echoes here of "I'm getting too old for the oldest profession" from *The Life,* or *A Chorus Line,* where the female auditionees repeatedly dodge questions about their ages.

The star female roles in *Mame, Hello, Dolly!, Anything Goes, Gypsy,* and *Call Me Madam* are curiously asexual, probably due to the fact that they are generally played by women in their forties or older—experience being a prerequisite for anyone taking on these giants. The characters in question may want husbands, but there is no suggestion that they are looking for sex. They are dressed in a way that tells us they are glamorous, but nothing about their costuming indicates these are women with sexual desires. Full-length evening dresses, sequins galore, smart daywear, hats and gloves all indicate that these are mature women whose minds are fixed on things higher than sex. Yes, these shows are set in a particular period, but the plunging necklines and tiny skirts are still in evidence on the younger female cast members. The costume designers may have been of the opinion that it is inappropriate to dress mature women in a sexualized way (is it ever appropriate to dress women as sexual objects?), but the deliberate denial of a mature woman's sexual energy by dressing her in "matronly" designs gives a clear message about male attitudes towards women over 40. They are not regarded as sexual beings. Young girls, and young female bodies, are the sexual trophies that men crave.

A woman who shows little interest in how she looks, or refuses to style herself in a particular way is regarded with suspicion, at best, outright hostility, at worst. She is not conforming to societal rules that state it is a woman's *duty* to look good, to make herself pretty for the enjoyment of men. And perhaps that is the real problem. By refusing to participate in the construct of beauty, a woman is seen to be rejecting the need to attract a male partner. By not wearing high heels and lipstick or dressing for male approval, she is rebelling against a society that tells women it is imperative to have men. The mutinous woman's natural face and practical clothes are a signal that she can survive perfectly well on her own. This not only offends the male ego, it also succeeds in making other women feel uncomfortable. Their slavish adherence to the demands of the beauty ideal renders them unable to understand any woman who would deliberately deviate from it. It is as if their choice is being questioned. In order to be accepted by other women and society, the mascara-free deviant has to submit to the indignities of the makeover. The fact that this makeover takes place at the hands of other women is particularly disconcerting. Under the guise of "sisterhood," one girl transforms another into yet another replica of the faceless bimbo so desired by straight men. Perhaps this is what the Spice Girls meant by Girl Power? By banding together we can *all* be what men want us to be. Forget Equal Rights. Let's go shopping together for push-up bras and stilettos.

The makeover scene or song is a favorite of the musical. We see the plain/ugly/asexual girl transformed into the bombshell. It hardly needs a genius to interpret that message: looks are everything. Glinda in *Wicked* can do nothing about Elphaba's green skin, but she can show her the right way to dress and how to fix her hair in order to be popular. Glinda believes that unless Elphaba looks like the other girls, they will not accept her into their group, and her makeover of Elphaba is designed to make her fit in. Elphaba's skin color, Glinda believes, will prevent her from being a real contender in the marriage battle because in Glinda's eyes, it all comes down to how you look. And Elphaba looks odd. The creators will no doubt argue that the fact that Elphaba does get the sought-after man in the end is a message of triumph over the narrow-mindedness of racism. I remain unconvinced.

In *Legally Blonde*, hairdresser Paulette is given a makeover—of sorts—in the "Bend and Snap" number when she is taught by the girls how to use her body to entice a man. This, according to the sisterhood (and the Spice Girls) is power. When Baby in *Dirty Dancing* appears with a new hairdo (why do makeovers always involve hair dye?) and a figure-hugging frock, Johnny is suddenly interested. Baby's new look also miraculously enables her to be a better dancer, thereby earning Johnny's respect as well as his sexual interest. It's just a shame no one thought to include an adult name in their makeover plans. It's pretty impossible to take seriously a grown woman who allows herself to be called Baby. I'm surprised she doesn't wear fairy wings.

New girl Shy in *Best Little Whorehouse* is given more appropriate clothes and a hairdo (again!) by the regular prostitutes to encourage her to make more of herself, i.e., look pretty for the men. Admittedly, Shy is joining a brothel, where she has to look good in order to earn a living, but the lyrics from the other girls again stress the importance of looking the same as everyone else in order to fit in with a group. This is echoed by the other makeover scene in *Legally Blonde,* when Elle buys Emmett the clothes that will make him socially acceptable. Emmett's comment that he "looks like Warner," i.e., any other preppy lawyer, is an indication of how successful his transformation has been. Elle has removed his identity and replaced it with the one *she* wants to see. The show may subvert the usual gender roles, but the message remains the same. In order to be successful, one's appearance must conform to what is considered acceptable. Even (drag queen) Edna Turnblad in *Hairspray* cannot escape being taken shopping by her daughter Tracy and "transformed" by new clothes. Looking good is feeling good. If your self-esteem is low, a quick visit to the beauty salon or department store will make everything all right again.

The moral of the makeover is so clear as to be transparent—looking good will make all your problems disappear. Because, according to the musical, then you'll find a man and therefore become a complete woman. This takes as its starting point the assumption that a woman who is plain (or overweight, or old) is unhappy or unfulfilled and in need of "help." That help, on the excess of TV makeover shows currently dominating our screens, involves weight loss, plastic surgery, orthodontic treatment, liposuction, face peels, hair extensions, new clothes and lots of makeup. And nine times out of ten, the experts performing this transformative work—at the behest of the sisterhood—are men, sculpting women's bodies and faces into the image *they* prefer. The subject of the makeover is convinced by the sisterhood that she has a duty—not just to herself but to her husband and children—to make the best of herself. Her marriage will be happier, her children will be better-behaved, and her sex life is bound to improve. No doubt she'll also move to a bigger house and be promoted at work as a reward for undergoing the pain of a facelift in order to become a better person.

I'm being facetious, but the makeover scene in musicals is not as far removed from the extreme versions as it might appear.

The most disturbing makeover on a musical theatre stage has to be that of Sandy in *Grease.* Sandy's fresh-faced image has caused both her and her boyfriend, Danny, to be ridiculed throughout the show. Under pressure from Danny and her high school colleagues, Sandy realizes she has to abandon the identity she has chosen for herself and adopt the look favored by the other girls. After Sandy's transformation, what we are presented with is a girl who is now undeniably sexually available. Gone are the bobby socks, the wide skirts, the hair band, replaced with skin tight pants, permed hair, heavy makeup, and a low-cut T-shirt. Sandy has conformed and Danny likes her now, mainly because her *look* holds the promise of sex. But by giving up her individuality she has discarded the very thing that made her unique in the first place: her difference. She no longer stands out. She has become just another girl who dresses to please her boyfriend, regardless of what she herself wants to wear. What is particularly worrying about the image she now presents is that Sandy has ended up being sexualized, as opposed to becoming sexually empowered. The creators of the show have reduced the character to a look. Prior to this, Sandy had a personality. Now she has become a sexual object, subjected to the gaze—welcomed or not—of the men around her.

Norma Desmond endures a bit of pain in her quest for a youthful figure. Sandy transforms her look for Danny, not for herself. Lizzie in *110 in the Shade* abandons her morals along with her hairpins, as does Gooch in *Mame.* At the heart of the claim that looking good equals with feeling good is sexuality. The more men display an interest in a woman, the more emancipated and powerful she will feel. The moral of beauty being in the eye of the beholder is twisted out of recognition by these so-called liberating makeovers. The woman—the object of the male gaze—drastically alters her appearance and often her personality to fit in with what the perpetrator of the gaze prefers. I struggle to understand what is either liberating or powerful for women about that. Yet the message that women should suppress their identities, or abandon their individuality to acquiesce to what a man prefers her to be is still pervasive in society. Men appear to retain the right of ownership of women's bodies, and their "look"—airbrushing away any signs of personality, in order to create the cute, unthreatening Barbie doll.

But women have to take responsibility for their part in allowing this to happen. Why do they agree to lose weight because "my husband says I'm too fat"? Or get a new hair color because the boyfriend prefers blondes? Why do women buy tickets for musicals that dress women as sexual objects, laugh at the fat girl, and emphasize an unrealistic ideal of how women should look?

Woman should be booing furiously at the "transformation" of Sandy and Baby and questioning the producers as to why the women in *Rock of Ages* are dressed like pole dancers when the men in the same show do not look like male strippers. Maybe the reason we do not is that we are so used to seeing the stereotypical image of women onstage that we are no longer even aware that it is a stereotype. Or perhaps we are so conditioned into believing that man are imperative to our happiness that we fail to realize it is a societal construct imposed upon us. Only that could explain why the female audience at *Dirty Dancing* is thrilled that a smart, strong young woman would suppress her personality in order to land the spectacularly dumb Johnny Castle. She's got a man! Yay!!

But at least we now know where Sondheim and Lapine went wrong with *Passion*. If Clara had shown Fosca how to apply lipstick and concealer, taken her for a color rinse, then bought her a few push-up bras, Giorgio would have married her without question.

The view that female beauty and brains are rarely twinned is rampant throughout Western culture—the "dumb blonde" is a concept we are all familiar with. Blonde hair has long been considered more attractive than dark hair—especially when coupled with blue eyes—and popular culture, particularly advertising, adheres to this premise. Men may well find blonde women more attractive precisely because of the association of fair hair with a lack of intellect—few men truly want to be challenged by a smart woman. Blondes are also perceived as sexually unrestrained—the "blonde bombshell" image and marketing of Marilyn Monroe being the prime example.

Director and choreographer Busby Berkeley fully understood the appeal of blonde women to men and staged extravagant Hollywood musical numbers featuring scores of faceless, young, platinum-haired women. The girls are paraded in front of the camera, lines of leggy chorines one after the other, until the effect is almost overwhelming. But these women are merely faces and bodies; they embody a "look." They never speak because thoughts in their head would indicate a brain or a personality, and the whole point of a chorus line of girls is to suppress individuality. The girls in Berkeley musical numbers are attractive to men because they are a collective and therefore characterless. The image of the glamorous showgirl—high heels, tall feathered headdresses, sparkling leotards—is designed to convey a message of women as ornamental.

The association between glamor and sexual availability makes the showgirl the perfect male fantasy—she is both silent and sexual. The male gaze inherent in a line-up of showgirls reminds the women that they are subordinate to the men viewing them. They exist only for their pleasure and are worth little beyond how they look. In *The Producers,* the character of Max Bialystock reiterates the clichéd male connection between beauty/glamour and sexual prowess when he tries to persuade Leo to join him in a fraudulent scheme by promising "beautiful girls/wearing nothing but pearls." It is precisely this male vision of utopia that is embedded in the showgirl line-up: not one girl, but many.

Roscoe in Sondheim's *Follies* (1971) sings of "beautiful girls"—note the plural. Mack in *Mack and Mabel* (1974) describes how girls onscreen are boring unless there are hundreds of them. One girl has to be given consideration as a fellow human being; dozens of faceless ingénues can be dismissed as a thing. The final number from *A Chorus Line* makes a statement about the faceless ensemble perfectly in time with one another, no individual personality, a single unit. But the number *One* also tells us about the image of the woman who is being celebrated. We do not see the leading lady the chorus line is praising because we do not need to. We know exactly the woman we are expected to imagine, as we have seen her so many times before—the glamorous, leggy showgirl, center stage. The "singular sensation."

Interestingly, when a chorus of boys surround a leading lady and praise her in song—"Hello Dolly," "When Mabel Comes in the Room," or "Mame," for example, it tends not to be sexual. But when an ensemble of girls surround a man—"Can't Be Bothered Now" (*Crazy for You*[11]), "I Wanna Be a Producer" (*The Producers*), or "The American Dream" (*Miss Saigon*)—it enhances his virility. The girls all seemingly adore him and therefore long to have sex with him, but by elevating the male sexual status, the girls diminish their own. The image of a man surrounded by scantily clad, faceless, worshipping women tells us he is the prize. The women support this image by seemingly competing for his affection.

If we were left in any doubt as to what men in a musical look for in a woman, we only have to turn to the sailors in the Rodgers and Hammerstein classic *South Pacific* (1949) and listen to the lyrics of "Nothing Like a Dame." The song even admits that it doesn't matter if a girl isn't smart; intellect is not what the men are looking for. The song gives a good impression of celebrating women, but in fact, the men are extolling only one virtue: her sex appeal. Well, at least the sailors are honest about it.

Musical theatre subscribes to the notion of a dumb woman being more attractive to men than a smart one. Marian in *The Music Man* is regarded with suspicion because she reads—ditto Belle in *Beauty and the Beast*. Betty in *Sunset Boulevard* is clearly smarter than Artie, which is exactly why he will stop her from working—she might be more successful than he is. In *110 in the Shade*, Lizzie's brother actually tells her to "act dumb" and "flirt more."

Elle Woods in *Legally Blonde: The Musical* deliberately dumbs down to boost Warner's ego. It's depressing that women view themselves as more attractive to men when they are stupid, but that is exactly the message men have been giving them for centuries.

To quote the indomitable, late Joan Rivers: "No man put his hand up a woman's skirt looking for a library card."

As previously discussed, the musical tells us that a woman's foremost aim in life is to find a man and that without one she is less than a woman. When a woman does find her man-she is often transformed physically—the emotional make-over. The love of a good man makes a less than average woman beautiful. In *100 in the Shade* much is made of the fact that the lead character Lizzie is considered "plain" by members of her family and the wider community. Her enduring spinsterhood is attributed to this fact and she is exhorted to take the first man who asks her. But Lizzie does find a man willing to kiss her, and the act physically changes her. She is transformed and no longer plain. Quite astonishing, really, the power men in musical theatre appear to possess over women. Lizzie is "beautiful" because a man loves her—or even professes to.

The song "In Buddy's Eyes" from *Follies* reiterates this idea. Sally sings of how she is both young and beautiful in the eyes of her husband. Buddy only needs to look at Sally with what she takes to be admiration, and she believes she is beautiful. Self-confidence counts for nothing here; it's what Buddy thinks that counts. Countess Aurelia in Jerry Herman's *Dear World* (1969) also endows her male lover with the power to make her beautiful just by looking and goes one step further by claiming that his love was so strong that it enabled her to do anything. It's hard not to yawn.

It returns us to the earlier discussion about a woman needing to be complimented by a man in order to feel good about herself. The idea that a woman *becomes* beautiful because a man says she is, is simply an extension of that. What it never acknowledges is that the woman in question actually has the power within her to transform herself. No man—or anyone for that matter—controls someone's self-esteem. But *Follies, Legally Blonde, Grease, 110 in the Shade* and *Dear World*—to name but a few—are telling women that a man is the catalyst they need for transformation. If Sally believes that she is beautiful only if Buddy tells her she is, well, that's her problem. It's just a shame she cannot believe it herself without involving him. The greater pity is the emphasis she places on her physical appearance. What about substituting words such as smart, truthful, honest, powerful, kind, strong, generous, empathetic, instead of "beautiful"? Aren't these all greater assets than an appealing face and straight teeth?

Not only do men in musicals have the ability to make women happy and content, but that their love is so overwhelming it can transform any woman into a beauty (except Fosca, who appears to be a lost cause.) The spectacular conceit behind this thinking would be laughable if the underlying message was not based around issues of patriarchal control and power. A woman concedes all control over how she looks to a man, endowing him with the ability to make her more attractive with just one kiss. It is light-years away from the more empowering message delivered by Miss Celie in *The Color Purple* about beauty emanating from within. When the character of Shug Avery acclaims Miss Celie's worth, she defines beauty as an intrinsic quality, the essence of someone. This conviction that beauty is more than face value is also stated in *Violet*. Violet's father cites strength and an ability to look deeper than the surface as more important than looks.

Yet the visual definition of beauty is constantly given more weight than the innate. The only ugliness evident in Fosca is in her self-absorbed personality, but we are asked to condemn her for her looks alone. In another Lloyd Webber/Don Black collaboration, *Aspects of Love*, (1989) Rose's lyrics in "Anything but Lonely" indicate that she believes that any power she has emanates from her face and her body, not her brain or her earning ability. She needs a man—any man—to tell her "how good she looks" in order to feel better about herself. Bear in mind that this is a woman who has a hugely successful career as an actress and financially supports her husband and family. But Don Black and Lloyd Webber consider her only worth to be how good she looks.

"The beauty myth is not about women at all. It is about men and power" (*The Beauty Myth* p. 4). Naomi Wolf's observation leads us to the logical conclusion of male gaze. A woman becomes so accustomed to being looked at by men, being reduced to an object, that she consequently defines herself in this way. She then changes her appearance to correspond with what the male wants to see. She surrenders her power to be an individual and allows her essential qualities to take second place to her external features, because this is what men prefer. The musical, sadly, reiterates this belief over and over again by dressing women as sexual objects, putting them in blonde wigs to indicate their stupidity, by denigrating the overweight or older woman, and by insisting on an unrealistic body shape among performers.

If women controlled the musical theatre industry instead of men, would these views remain in place? Or would the innate values upheld by *The Color Purple* or *Violet* begin to take precedence?

Notes

1. John Berger, 1972, *Ways of Seeing* (London: British Broadcasting Corp.), 47.

2. Laura Mulvey, 1999, "Visual Pleasure and Narrative Cinema, in *Feminist Film Theory: A Reader,* ed. Sue Thornham (Edinburgh: Edinburgh University Press), 46.

3. Book and lyrics by Steven Sater; music by Duncan Sheik.

4. Book by Michael Weller; Lyrics by Michael Korie and Amy Powers; music by Lucy Simon.

5. Kristin Hanggi and Kelly Devine.

6. Patricia Zipprodt.

7. New York, 1993. She returned to the show on Broadway in 1996 to play Fantine, making her the first actress to have played both roles.

8. Book by Isobel Lennart; lyrics by Bob Merrill; music by Jule Styne.

9. Book by James Kirkwood, Jr. and Nicholas Dante; lyrics by Edward Kleban; music by Marvin Hamlish.

10. Book by Mel Brooks and Thomas Meehan; lyrics and music by Mel Brooks.

11. Book by Ken Ludwig; lyrics by Ira Gershwin; music by George Gershwin.

5

It's Not Just for Gays Anymore!

The Influence of Gay Culture on Musical Theatre

Sung by Neil Patrick Harris at the opening of the 2011 Tony Awards ceremony, "It's Not Just for Gays Anymore"[1] lampooned the fact that musical theatre has traditionally appealed to gay men. The song was effectively an "in joke," the audience at the Tonys being made up of theatre professionals, and the song worked as a comic number by highlighting one thing we all recognize but rarely discuss openly: that musical theatre is dominated, onstage, backstage, and in the audience, by gay men. That is not a criticism; it is merely a fact. In musical theatre, gay men are so heavily represented that it is often safer to assume that the male you are dealing with is gay rather than straight. While this could hardly be described as a problem, the predominance of gay men on creative teams of musicals has particular ramifications for women in the industry.

It is impossible to pinpoint the reasons why so many gay men are attracted to musical theatre. Perhaps it is—and I apologize for the generalization—partly due to the fact that gay men appear to be more in touch with their emotions. Subsequently the heightened passion of musical theatre connects with a gay man in a way it does not with a straight man. It could also partly be due to gay men's adoration of camp, so often on display in musicals. Perhaps it is simply that musicals are more fun than much of what passes for entertainment in the heterosexual male world. An evening of *Hairspray* is likely to be more appealing and less alienating than spending the night in an aggressively straight bar watching football. Or is that a cliché? Whatever the reason, there is no denying that the audience for musicals is made up of women and gay men, and that fact is as true of the audience 60 years ago as it is today. While women are more likely to be found at *Wicked* and *Mamma Mia!*, gay men will congregate at a sophisticated Sondheim show, *Light in the Piazza*, or any of the diva musicals—*Hello, Dolly!, Mame, Call Me Madam*. The character of Jack in the TV series *Will and Grace* is the perfect example of how the cliché of a gay man loving show tunes has been adopted by popular culture and accepted as a given. Show me a gay man without a musical theatre CD collection, and I'll show you a Judy Garland fan.

In the days before the Stonewall uprising in Greenwich Village in 1969 gave birth to the gay rights movement, homosexual men lived in fear of being outed. Many writers of musicals pre–Stonewall were discreetly homosexual and closeted gay men in the audience sought signals in the words of these creators to reassure them they were not alone. A gay code, if you like. Musical theatre felt more inclusive to the homosexual man, because it was easy for him to project his fantasies onto the larger-than-life characters onstage, especially the leading ladies (it is not just a coincidence that many of the drag queen's favorite songs are showtunes.) Gay men identified with the romantic dilemmas of the leading lady, and her—often thwarted—search for love from the heterosexual man. They heard messages of suppressed homosexuality in songs such as "Matelot," "I'll Follow My Secret Heart," "My Heart Belongs to Daddy," "You'd Be So Easy to Love," "My Funny Valentine," "There's a Small Hotel" and substituted themselves, and their longing for male love, in place of Sally Bowles, Mamma Rose, or whoever it was singing the tortured victim song that particular evening. Gay men equated the suffering of women in musicals with their own personal trials and placed themselves in the center of the world they saw onstage, where the handsome, dismissive, straight man was the cause of all suffering. The fact that the story was a heterosexual one was neither here nor there.

This action of choosing to ignore the position of the text in favor of one's own political interpretation is described by Judith Fetterley[2] as the resisting reader. The resisting reader, as opposed to the assenting one, learns to re-read the text and the assumptions contained within it. In this instance, the text is musical theatre, and homosexual men re-read it from their personal or political stances. The world they are viewing onstage is heterosexual, but they resist this reading and transform it into a homosexual one. This is easier to do with a musical than other art forms because the creators of musicals are predominantly gay men, as are many of the performers. A gay sensibility—however subtle—is therefore already in place. Just as I read *My Fair Lady* as a lesson in misogyny and Stacy Wolf reads *Wicked* as a lesbian love story, homosexual men can read Bobby in *Company* as a man struggling with his sexuality or Auntie Mame as a man in drag. The resisting reader is conscious of the position of the text but refuses to fully accept it. The resistance involves reinterpreting the text to fit the position of the reader.

In an era less accepting of homosexuality than the current one, musical theatre was the one place where a closeted gay man could celebrate the associated culture of camp without drawing attention to himself or inviting accusations of effeminacy. Straight men were overjoyed to find someone who would willingly escort their wives to the dreaded musical, and gay men were more than happy to oblige. What could be more delightful than an evening of snappy tap routines, love ballads, and a brassy heroine? And let's not overlook the pretty chorus boy. It is not a myth that the male chorus members in musical theatre are predominantly gay—they are. That's a fact that is barely noteworthy in 2015—the hit TV series *Smash* acknowledged the predominance of gay chorus boys with barely a straight boy in sight—but 50 years ago, the very thought that a man onstage might be "like me" was enough to thrill gay men in the audience who could not dare exposing their own sexuality. How many gay men started attending musicals purely to witness what they recognized as homosexuality onstage? Closeted gay men could see homosexuality on show in the queer male chorus and silently celebrate it. A night of musical comedy was less somber or daunting than the decidedly middle class opera or ballet, and there was the added attraction of an assemblage of like-minded men in the dress circle bar.

It is highly possible that the gay men who initially attended musicals preferred interacting with like-minded men in the audience to the show itself. This was an era, remember, where the few gay bars that existed were regularly raided by police on a witch hunt. A theatre where a musical was playing was a public space where gay men could mingle with other gay men without fear of public exposure. Consciously or not, gay men turned theatre into a safe gay space and musical theatre auditoriums even more so. It could almost be claimed that attending a musical gave gay men tacit permission to be gay in public. Among the homosexual men in the audience, there was a sense of collusion. They knew why they were really there, even if the colleague's wife whom they were escorting for the evening did not.

Out of this, possibly, arose the notion that musical theatre was something you adored if you were a gay man, along with Judy Garland and Joan Crawford. It became learned behavior, partly as a result of the fact that attending the theatre was an acceptable and respectable pastime for a cultured or artistic man to have. Straight men utilize sports and unite behind a particular team as a way of expressing their masculinity within a crowd of other straight men. In the same way, homosexual men adopted musical theatre as part of a gay sensibility. Loving musicals and being knowledgeable about the genre became one way of belonging to the culture of the gay male. Over time, this has mutated into becoming an almost compulsory identifier of the homosexual male—he likes showtunes. In order to fit in with the tribe, you'd better know a few Sondheim lyrics. Or at least be aware of the contributions Ethel Merman and Angela Lansbury have made to the industry. And over time, perhaps the gay man did indeed learn how to love musical theatre. Certainly the diva musicals corresponded with the homosexual male worship of black and white screen icons such as Joan Crawford, Bette Davis, Mae West, and Gloria Swanson. Musicals such as *Gypsy, Mame, Call Me Madam, Anything Goes, Hello, Dolly!* and almost anything by Kander and Ebb had a larger-than-life leading lady at the heart of the show. Wise cracking, indomitable, and with a Broadway belt that could reach the back of the stalls without a microphone, these female characters, and the shows they inhabited, were adored by gay men. So what was—is—the attraction?

Perhaps it is the bitchy repartee on display in musicals such as *Mame, A Little Night Music, La Cage aux Folles, Company,* and *Follies* that appeals. The cutting remark and the acerbic put-down are trademarks of the diva and have been appropriated, or imitated, by gay men for years. Pre-Stonewall, bitchy repartee and the witty retort were a form of ammunition against a hostile heterosexual society, and, to a degree, they still are. What the homosexual man saw in the tough, brassy broad was a survivor who used her quick wit and a feminine assertiveness to take on the enemy—the dismissive or disrespectful straight man. Homosexual men empathized with the diva and her mistreatment at the hands of a heterosexual society, as they had experienced the same thing. The attraction of the resilient, ballsy leading lady was her victory over her oppressor. She either got her man or shot him down in flames. Either way, it reflected what many gay men wanted to see or how, in fantasy, they saw themselves. They imitated their wise-cracking, tough, and glamorous idols and wore the façade as a suit of armor to protect themselves from the hostility of straight society.

One other characteristic of the Broadway diva of musical theatre that appeals to gay men is that she is asexual. Her femininity is heightened to such a degree that she is not a realistic representation of a sexual woman. Subsequently, homosexual men in the audience do not have to see beyond the heterosexuality before they can appropriate or re-read the text.

The diva is also camp, and while camp as an aesthetic is not confined to the homosexual male world, it is particularly prevalent within it. In 1964, Susan Sontag wrote her now seminal essay "Notes on Camp" in which she asserted that the whole point of camp was to "dethrone the serious."[3] Wikipedia defines camp as "an aesthetic sensibility that regards something as appealing or humorous because of its ridiculousness to the viewer."[4] A close relation to "kitsch," the exaggerated nature of camp emphasizes style over content in a glamorized and theatrical manner, and the style is invariably flamboyant. Musical theatre, particularly the diva musicals and traditional musical comedy, is inherently camp. The glitzy costumes, the over-the-top set, the tap routines all contribute to the extravagant, overblown, and often comic version of reality that appeals to many within the gay community.

Critics are well aware of the use of, and attraction of camp within musical theatre. In his *New York Times* review of *Grey Gardens*, Ben Brantley maintained the show "tilts perilously toward cheap celebrity camp" and went on to say that "the show often coasts on the allure of loudly dropped names and the gay-bait thrills of women in extreme states of glamour and grotesqueness, preferably at the same time.... It is a musical you might expect to see performed by men in Max Factor and thrift shop drag in a downtown bar lighted by Christmas tree bulbs." Brantley was clearly aware that a large proportion of the audience at this show would be gay men, the group largely responsible for turning the original documentary into a cult movie.

Reviewing the 2003 West End revival of *Joseph and the Amazing Technicolor Dreamcoat* Lyn Gardner opened her article in the *Guardian* with the words:

> "Camper than a Christmas tree and fonder of gold lamé than Lily Savage..." Like Brantley, Gardner was well aware that the flamboyant production would appeal to a certain demographic. "Sometimes it is Cecil B. DeMille on the cheap, sometimes pure Liberace. When Stephen Gately's 'poor, poor Joseph' is imprisoned and sings, 'Do what you want with me,' it sounds more like an invitation than a lament. Maybe it is the way those beefy jailers are waving the chains around."

And Charles Isherwood, in his *New York Times* review of *Priscilla, Queen of the Desert* referred to the story as "campy sentimentality about drag life" and described the jukebox score as "the kind of mix you might find blaring from the jukebox in a Florida gay bar if patrons of varying ages and argumentative tastes were on hand."

Far from denying that the musical employs—even exploits—the camp aesthetic, these critics assume it is a given—that we all understand camp is a cornerstone of the genre. They are also acknowledging—actually, they are assuming—it is a given that men from the gay community will embrace these shows as a reflection of their own culture. Rebecca Caine notes:

> Gay men are a huge part of musicals, and they love the Mames and they love the Dollys, they love all that stuff. But I just did a Sondheim recently, an

entirely female concert with three other women.... He's a gay man and he writes brilliantly for women. And they're not drag acts. I mean, Mrs. Lovett, there's a lot to that role. It's Grand Guignol and there's a certain heightened element to that whole piece anyway.... But there's a great tragedy about Mrs. Lovett in that she's desperately in love with Sweeney Todd and I don't think you can get away with playing that role as a drag queen.

The great diva roles in musicals—Mamma Rose, Sally Adams, Dolly Levi, Reno Sweeney, Norma Desmond, both Vera and Mame, and Little Edie in *Grey Gardens*—walk a fine line between actress and drag queen. They epitomize the kind of camp that appeals to the gay male. This is partly due to the style of the show—the audience has come to expect a larger-than-life caricature—but it is also a result of the way in which the roles are defined by the script and lyrics. They are written as a flamboyant, stylized versions of a woman. They are not quite the parodies of femininity that drag queens are (although they can be played in that way), but they are not meant to be real. They are a heightened version of reality and were more in evidence 40 or 50 years ago than they are now. This could be a result of the political climate of the time. The writers of musicals then—who were predominantly gay— wanted a gay sensibility onstage, but could not blatantly represent homosexuality without fear of retribution. The diva leading lady embodied the camp aesthetic, and her close correlation to the drag queen gave the knowing wink to the gay men in the audience. It was a homosexual sensibility disguised as a heterosexual one.

But isn't there something insulting to women about turning them into a pseudo drag act for the amusement of the gay men in the audience?

The problem with the diva roles, of course, is that those female characters have no foundation in reality. They are a gay man's version of what a woman is. If I were to adopt my humorless, separatist pose, I could accuse the creators of those roles of appropriating femininity, and women, for their own needs. I, however, am not humorless, and I thrill to Dolly Levi draped in a feather boa and cavorting with adoring waiters as much as any show queen. I fully admit I find a drag rendition of Rodgers and Hammerstein's "I Enjoy Being a Girl" from *Flower Drum Song* enormously entertaining and the height of camp. But a drag queen singing showtunes in a gay bar is an entirely different thing to an actor appearing in drag in a musical. In the former, it is arguably part of the culture that has defined the gay rights movement and it is a form of entertainment designed specifically to appeal to a certain audience. The musical claims to have a broader appeal.

There are a number of musicals in which there is a male role that requires the actor to dress up as a woman, either for the whole of the show or for a part of it—*Rocky Horror, Hedwig and the Angry Inch, Hairspray, Taboo, Chicago, La Cage aux Folles, South Pacific, Kiss of the Spiderwoman, Matilda, Kinky Boots* and *Priscilla, Queen of the Desert*. The tradition of male-to-female drag onstage is more established in the U.K. than the U.S. and is an accepted part of the cultural identity of the country. Far from being confined to seedy gay bars, drag in the U.K. was—and still is—a staple of what is classed as family entertainment. From Benny Hill to *Little Britain* (David Walliams and Matt Lucas), British comedians have frequently appeared in drag in their prime-time TV shows. The main attraction of the Christmas pantomime has always been the Dame. The televised annual Royal Variety Performance regularly has a drag act, with luminaries such as Les Dawson, Hinge and Bracket (George Logan and Patrick Fyffe), Danny La Rue, Lily Savage (Paul O'Grady), and Dame Edna Everage (Barry Humphries) appearing in past years. The "burlesque cabaret" *Funny Girls* still performs nightly in the traditional variety/music hall mecca of Blackpool and is an upmarket drag show aimed at a straight audience.

But drag as family entertainment is different from a man in drag performing in a gay bar, just as the drag acts that were (and probably still are) a popular form of entertainment among the armed forces in combat zones are very different to the drag employed by the Lady Boys of Bangkok. Drag in the army is what I would refer to as "straight drag"—the men are not in any way assuming a female identity in the way some gay drag artistes (such as the Lady Boys) believe they are. Army drag was never about imitating women; it was about parodying them. And it gave the men in combat zones a form of release: they could flirt with and fawn over a man in drag, thereby colluding in the pretense that this was a "woman."

While men dressed as women can form part of a political statement—count the number of drag queens at a Gay Pride march or a rally for marriage equality—not all male actors who play pantomime dames are gay, just as not every leading man singing a love ballad to a woman onstage is straight. Far from it. But either as a political tool or as family entertainment, the underlying message of drag remains the same. A man dressing up as a woman is automatically funny, in a way that a woman dressing up as a man is not. Geraldine Turner notes:

> I do think … and I've always thought this, that a drag queen … is taking the piss out of women. I can't get away from that fact. And you know, it's kind of funny and yeah, yeah, some drag queens are good, I accept that. And I respect the art form and I respect that they're doing well and they're doing it well, but there's a part of me that sits there and thinks, "Nah. Don't like this." It's

another way of getting at women. [An] "I can do a woman better than you can," kind of thing. They're sending up women at the same time, you know?

I agree with Ms. Turner, because from whatever angle you look at it, male-to-female drag is ridiculing women. What it is essentially saying is that a woman is less than a man, so for a man to dress up as one is funny, because what real man would want to be a woman? The audience is laughing at the man who is big enough to demean himself in front of an audience by strapping on fake breasts and eyelashes and performing a monologue littered with clichéd sexual innuendo. It is a particular form of entertainment, highly popular, as already observed, within the armed forces during the war—as Luther Billis in *South Pacific* demonstrates. But it is really saying women are there to be laughed at—to be parodied in costumes that exaggerate the body to make it grotesque and with excessive makeup and wigs that transform femininity into vulgarity. There is nothing innocuous about a man in drag. Nothing about it is affectionate. It is designed to make fun of women. Ms. Turner's comment "they're sending up women at the same time" is the heart of the issue. Drag is not about being funny; it's about ridiculing women and reminding them of their place in the hierarchy. And whether the perpetrator is gay or straight, drag has, at its core, contempt for women. So what does that say about musical theatre shows that utilize a man in drag? What message are the women in the audience supposed to take away from it?

The straight drag act, where the man is not attempting to be a real woman but is lampooning essential aspects of femininity—Luther Billis in *South Pacific*, Edna Turnblad in *Hairspray*, Miss Trunchbull in *Matilda*—takes as its starting point the "ugly" woman. By making her even more unattractive she becomes yet another male joke at the expense of women. It establishes masculinity by making fun of femininity and, in doing so, raises the "manliness" of the male performer. While that is a very different thing to the drag queens on the gay circuit—their style of drag is considered an art form in itself—women are still used as the foundation of the joke. It comes from exactly the same school of thought as the "kicks like a girl," "screams like a girl" comments so prevalent among young, straight men. Girls are less than boys, and so to be called one is to be insulted. To dress up as one is hilarious, but only because women are inherently laughable.

In *The Rise and Fall of Gay Culture*,[5] Daniel Harris refutes what he labels a feminist belief that drag queens are misogynistic and claims that drag queens are not taunting women in particular. Unsurprisingly, I disagree. If drag queens are taunting heterosexuality in general, then why aren't they parodying football players or truck drivers? Why is their disdain—and yes, I do believe it is disdain—reserved only for women? If you want to show empathy with the oppressed, you don't do it by making fun of them—you dress up as the oppressor. *The Producers* showed us that brilliantly. Perhaps I am, again, making too much of this, but I have always struggled to understand why a man dressed up as a woman is automatically funny. And I keep coming back to male arrogance—the assumption that women are there to be used. Whether as a sex object or as a joke is irrelevant. It's the thinking behind it that it is the problem. Do drag queens ever stop to consider how women feel about this disrespectful parody?

The Tim Minchin/Dennis Kelly adaptation of Roald Dahl's book *Matilda* is a British musical that won seven Olivier Awards in 2011, including Best Musical. In the musical, the character of Miss Trunchbull is played by a man. This is odd, given that he is drawn as a woman in the original book. Actor Bertie Carvel won an Olivier Award for playing the role and no doubt had them rolling in the aisles cavorting in his tweed twin set, but why was the role played by a man? More to the point, why did no critic ask that question? What exactly did the production gain by having a man play a woman? It's impossible to know if it was a directorial decision or if it was written that way in the script. Either way, a man on the creative team decided that the role should not be played by a woman, and in subsequent replica productions worldwide it never will be. No doubt because it is so much "funnier" having Miss Trunchbull played by a man. Maybe the all-male creative team managed to convince themselves that it reflects the anarchy prevalent in Roald Dahl's book. "It's subversive. It's pushing boundaries." Or perhaps it was a nod to the British theatrical tradition of the pantomime Dame. Who knows? Who cares what the reason was, actually? To me, it's just another example of the male derision and condescension towards women in British musical theatre. (I can almost hear the shrieks of laughter from the creative team when Bertie Carvel first appeared onstage in costume.)

Think about it. Who is most likely to find a man dressed up as a vulgar parody of a woman funny? Straight men. But who is in the audience? Women, and lots and lots of little girls, absorbing a message that they exist to be made fun of because they are not as good as boys. Incidentally, I never fully understood why Edna in *Hairspray* was a drag role either, but probably because I am a woman and therefore incapable of understanding the multitude of ways in which a man in a dress enhances the comic effect. For me, the problem with putting a man into a woman's role and dressing him up as a woman is that the focus of the entire piece is subsequently distorted.

In 2010, Sasha Regan's all-male production of *The Pirates of Penzance in London* became a huge hit when it transferred from the tiny Union Theatre to Wilton's Music Hall and was named Best Off-West End Production at The What's On Stage Awards. The production toured to Sydney in 2012 in partnership with the Sydney Theatre Company and was promoted in the STC brochure as "this irreverently funny and entirely fresh take on *The Pirates of Penzance* is a must-see for lovers of all things musical, comedic and high-camp!" The key word in there has to be "irreverent," and I suspect it is referring to the lofty regard in which Gilbert and Sullivan and their works are held. A sophisticated "G and S" is normally deemed more suitable for state or city opera companies than fringe theatre, so Regan's scaled-down cast size, minimalist set, and one piano is the antithesis of what is normally associated with a Gilbert and Sullivan operetta.

A thesaurus search of "irreverent" brings up "disrespectful" and "mocking." So who exactly was being mocked with this production of *Pirates of Penzance?* Gilbert and Sullivan, or women in general? I saw this production and I did enjoy it, but it was not *The Pirates of Penzance* in the way the creators intended, because the focus was in the wrong place. The audience was not admiring the music of Sullivan or fully engaged in Gilbert's plot; they were marveling at how delicate those boys looked in dresses and wondering how "Mabel" could sing a top C when she is a boy, as critic Michael Church in *The Independent* confirmed. "The girls' choruses are entrancingly done, with on-the-note falsetto and a believably male idea of femininity played straight.... When Mabel makes her entrance—played by the extraordinary Alan Richardson—the whole game is raised: how on earth does a man sing such accurate coloratura, so high, and with so little apparent effort?"

I'm curious as to what exactly a "male idea of femininity played straight" is. I suppose I should be grateful he does at least acknowledge that it is a male idea of femininity, in place of an authentic female one. But "played straight"? Not the night I saw it. The audience experienced a gimmick, not *The Pirates of Penzance.*

Ian Shuttleworth in *The Financial Times* did admit to finding the production "rather disconcerting" and commented that "Samuel J. Holmes could have turned the plain, middle-aged nursemaid Ruth into a pantomime dame, but instead achieves all the effects he needs by ignoring the gender issue altogether (aside from being the sole exception to the no-make-up rule)." Shuttleworth was aware that the performers could easily have slipped into drag queen parodies—which, in their defense, they seemed at pains not to do. But how is it possible to "ignore the gender issue altogether" when it is the one thing the entire production is built on? How can boys playing girls *not* be a gender issue?

We can never know if Gilbert and Sullivan would have agreed to this interpretation or not. I suspect the fact that they were not around to argue made it a more attractive proposition than trying to persuade John Kander of the benefits of an all-male production of *Chicago*. I'm just not sure what the point of the production was. Why stage an all-male version of *Pirates of Penzance* in the first place? And, even more depressingly, follow it up with all male versions of *Iolanthe* and *Patience*? For what purpose? If it is an attempt to woo a gay audience, fine. Admit that. Or, even better, commission a new musical that does not have obviously gay men pretending to women but being themselves. And be honest about the fact that this is clearly a company that abhors the idea of seeing women onstage. If I am mistaken and it is not, then why not do an all-female production of a Gilbert and Sullivan operetta? And if men dressed as women are inherently funny, then who exactly is laughing? Sasha Regan who, it could be said, betrayed the sisterhood by giving women's roles to men but certainly did not harm her career in doing so? Gay men in the audience? I'm sure they did laugh—it was a good production that brought out the comedy well. Female performers denied roles? Women in the audience who found it all slightly insulting? It depresses me enormously that this production—and the two subsequent all-male G and S operettas—came from a company with a woman artistic director. What's next, I wonder? An all-white production of *Jelly's Last Jam* or *Porgy and Bess*? Of course not, because that would be insulting to black actors. Call me over-sensitive, but appropriating female roles for male actors strikes me as an insult to women. It's not as if there aren't enough roles written for men in musical theatre.

Men playing women's roles in musicals is not something new. Danny la Rue started the ball rolling in 1982 when he played Dolly Levi in *Hello, Dolly!* in the West End. Lily Savage (Paul O'Grady) played Miss Hannigan in *Annie* in 1999 in the West End. (What is it about the British and their love of drag?) I struggle to understand why anyone would go and see a drag queen play a leading lady in musical theatre. Not because the drag queen may not be good but because it is a *role*, a role for a woman, not a man dressed up as a woman. By removing the women from *Pirates of Penzance* the director is effectively removing the female voice and replacing it with a male one.

I don't believe that happens by accident. (I could also say the same about Matthew Bourne's *Swan Lake*. What did the story gain from having men dance roles that were originated by, and choreographed for, women? Why not do a new all-male ballet?)

In musicals, it often comes back to the fact that the diva roles are so closely related to the drag queen—the gay male caricature of a woman—that a man in a dress can play Dolly Levi and not overtly upset the balance of the show. How long before we have a man playing Madame Thenardier or Norma

Desmond? There are many producers who would see nothing wrong with that idea. Get in a celebrity drag act—RuPaul or Dame Edna—and it might even sell a few more tickets. To hell with artistic integrity.

Here's an idea. In the spirit of Edna Turnblad and Miss Trunchbull, let's cast Elder Price in *The Book of Mormon* as a young woman instead of a young man. Now that really would be subversive, given that women are not deemed worthy enough to go on the two-year sabbatical demanded by the Mormon Church. (In 2007, 80 percent of Mormon missionaries on the two-year mission were young unmarried men. Women generally serve shorter 18-month missions and are not actively encouraged to serve.) Wouldn't it make *Book of Mormon* even funnier (assuming one finds it funny in the first place) to have a female Elder Price? Why not, if Miss Trunchbull is so riotously amusing when played by a man? We don't accept blackface any more because it is acknowledged as offensive. So why is a man playing a woman's role not similarly distasteful? Again, I have to wonder if a woman had been on the creative team of *Matilda* (a show about a little *girl*) would Miss Trunchbull have been played by a man?

It seems to me that where producers once staged musicals with the fictitious straight male audience in mind, they are now blatantly aiming shows at the gay male audience known to frequent the musical. And that's fine. Productions featuring gay male characters, or gay storylines, or drag queens are well represented, and I understand the concept of claiming back territory and making a political point. But in 2011, only 3.8 percent of the American population—around 9 million adults—identified as being gay, lesbian, or transgender.[6] Fifty percent of the population is female. And more women than men—gay or straight—attend musical theatre (I'm beginning to sound like a broken record). Why, dare I ask, are women not being given the same consideration when it comes to creating shows that reflect a particular way of being, or living, that gay men are?

In bringing up the drag queens, camp, and bitchy leading ladies, the point I am making is that a gay sensibility pervades musical theatre and this sensibility does not do any favors for women in the industry. The gay mindset imposes a certain viewpoint or direction onto the genre—it may even be due to this sensibility that the musical evolved into its own unique art form. But it is a viewpoint in which there is no place for the authentic woman onstage because the gay male creators actively desire the caricature. The same point could again be made about the fashion industry, where the desire for a real woman with a realistic womanly figure is an anathema. Designers want the image, not reality.

If, as I assert, a gay sensibility is in operation in musical theatre, then how is homosexuality depicted onstage in musical theatre? If we agree that musicals reflect prevailing attitudes in society, then it comes as no surprise that the gay man could only be put onstage as a figure of fun.

Fifty years ago hostility towards homosexuality was inherent in society. In order to reinforce a belief system that labeled homosexuality as a perversion, any outward representation of the gay male had to be disrespectful. Despite the predominance of gay men in the musical theatre genre, the straight, conservative audience—the majority—had to be appeased, or at least pandered to. So the few representations of homosexual men onstage (gay women were rarely even acknowledged) had to adhere to clichéd populist thinking. Regardless of the sexuality of the creators of the show, the camp, effeminate stereotype was the only acceptable rendition of homosexuality onstage. He was a figure of fun, ripe for derision by a homophobic society. It reassured the audience that what they were seeing was a freak and was confined to the debauched world of theatre.

The overtly effeminate gay man was acceptable as a joke because no one wanted to admit the presence of any other kind of gay man. This was a society operating on compulsory heterosexuality, a viewpoint which upheld masculinity as the ultimate goal—think of the popularity of John Wayne and male action heroes—and defined women as second-class citizens. Compulsory heterosexuality was sidestepped through pseudo drag acts masquerading as leading ladies or the bitchy diva with her vicious lyrics. Sondheim was the master of this—think Joanne in *Company* and her scathing appraisal of the joys of marriage. While no one was openly gay in a Sondheim musical, gay men discovered Sondheim long before anyone else did, perhaps because he often seemed to be criticizing heterosexual relationships. Few of the straight relationships in *Follies, Company, Into the Woods, Merrily We Roll Along, Passion,* even *Sweeney Todd* are positive reflections of marriage or heterosexual couplings. Easy, then, for gay men in the audience to make assumptions about Sondheim's sexuality and re-read the subtext of the lyrics as a gay one.

In other musicals, too, it was easy for gay men in the audience to give certain characters a queer reading. Max in *The Sound of Music* is often played as the effeminate aesthete. Ali Hakim in *Oklahoma!* is easy to reinterpret as gay. The Emcee in *Cabaret* was typically asexual until the Sam Mendes revival in 1993, when he flaunted his bi-sexuality. It required little effort to impose a queer reading on *Company*—Bobby's reluctance to marry must indicate he is gay. The two Princes in *Into the Woods* are reluctant to settle down with the "right" girls. Queer readings can also be applied to women's roles— Calamity Jane, Flora the Red Menace, Ado Annie in *Oklahoma!,* Elphaba and Glinda in *Wicked.* There is even a hint at bisexuality in *Aspects of Love,* but it is only a kiss between Rose and Guilietta—hardly the free-for-all romping we see in *Witches of Eastwick*—which is defined by its heterosexuality. The women are all having sex with the same man. Whether they have sex with each other at the same time is never discussed—way too much information for the supposed family audience.

Paul in *A Chorus Line* was the first significant sympathetic portrayal of a gay man in a musical. It is likely he was allowed to exist because the show centered around Broadway dancers whom we all suspected were gay anyway. Albin in *La Cage aux Folles* got away with being a drag queen because it was easy for the audience to re-read the text as a heterosexual love story. After all, Albin's partner Jacques has a son who is as straight as straight can be—even down to his casual dismissal of the needs of his "mother." The Maid in *La Cage* however, is the freak show, the derisory figure of fun, there to reassure the audience that these people are not normal. Fun to spend an evening with, but thank God we can go home to the suburbs where people like that just don't exist.

In 1992, *Kiss of the Spiderwoman* opened in the West End, and a year later it premiered on Broadway. Adapted from the Manuel Puig novel *Él Beso de la Mujer Arana*, one of the two central characters, Molina, is in jail for his sexuality. While some elements of his "gayness" are stereotypical—the diva worship, the effeminacy, the repartee—Molina is a character we sympathize with, not just for his present plight, but because of how his sexuality causes him to be reviled by the overtly masculine South American society he lives in.

More importantly, 1992 saw the premiere on Broadway of William Finn's *Falsettos*. Not only did this show depict two "ordinary" gay men—no feather boas or sequins here—carving out a relationship, it was the first musical to honestly represent the AIDS crisis and the devastating effect it was having on the gay community. (*The Life* had touched on it, but only in terms of how the female prostitutes were at risk.) *Falsettos* also featured a lesbian couple living next door and was remarkable for its honesty, given the period and the hostility towards the gay community due to adverse publicity around the AIDS crisis. But it was also significant in its portrayal of gay relationships in a way that we had only ever seen heterosexual relationships depicted—as the norm. These were real people, in love, and dealing with the everyday problems we all face in our lives. On top of that, they spoke out loud about the disease no one wanted to mention, and that the media referred to as "the gay plague."

In 1996, Jonathan Larson's *Rent* took Broadway by storm. Using Puccini's *La Bohème* as source material, the show featured a group of young artists and musicians—gay and straight—living under the shadow of HIV/AIDS. There is a character who is a drag queen, there is a lesbian relationship, conversations occur about the importance of taking HIV medication, all portrayed in a matter-of-fact manner—"this is how it is." It is impossible to know if the worldwide success of *Rent* contributed to a greater acceptance of the portrayal of homosexuality onstage in musicals. Certainly, the show appealed to a younger generation of theatregoers who were perhaps more broad-minded to start with and coincided with less stereotypical gay characters appearing in television drama/comedy and on film. By the time the musical version of *The Full Monty*[7] premiered on Broadway in 2000, the gay relationship between Malcolm and Ethan barely drew comment from the other characters. Roger De Bree in *The Producers* was the camp stereotype, but the difference in 2001 was that the audience was laughing with him, not at him. Only six years later in 2007, the *Gay or European?* number in *Legally Blonde* completed the full circle and assumed an acceptance of homosexuality onstage from the audience.

The *Book of Mormon* and *Avenue Q* both make much of the fact that one of the characters is suspected of being in the closet, and *Kinky Boots* gives us characters who, 30 years previously, would have had no place on a Broadway stage. In 2015, homosexual characters in musicals are well and truly out and proud, written and directed by gay men who never saw the inside of the closet. It is not a big deal—except, I would argue, for women in the industry. Geraldine Turner notes:

> You know, there's been a lot of talk—not just in musical theatre—in Sydney over the last twenty years, thirty years, about gay men running theatre. From producers to directors to writers and a sort of underlying ... you know, the gay mafia. They talk about Sydney as a very gay city. We have the gay Mardi Gras, and I think it's understandable from a point of view—I'm being the devil's advocate now—but a lot of gay men would want to do shows that claim back. You know, that say ... now we're in charge we ... want to show gay stories and we want to do this and that. But I think if you're gay in musicals it's easier to get a job. And if you're a pretty gay boy you'll always be in work. And that's a little sad.

In a rehearsal room dominated by men, it is all too easy for the female actor's character interpretation to be distorted by the male director's influence or his misunderstanding of women, or for the women's roles to be ignored. Female actors are frequently isolated in the rehearsal room, due partly to belonging to a minority group, but also due to a male director being more concerned—and interested—with the male performers and performances. Women are often left to their own devices or given such superficial direction that their resulting performance can end up being based around clichéd male concepts of womanhood—especially gay male clichés. How often do the female stars of *Mame, Call Me Madam, Hello, Dolly!, Funny Girl, Sunset Boulevard, Gypsy,* or *Kiss of the Spiderwoman* give performances that veer perilously close to the drag queen grotesque, encouraged—however subconsciously— by the gay male director? All too often, what we end up seeing represented onstage is a male understanding of what women are or how men would like them to be—an interpretation heavily influenced by the Madonna/Whore theory, or the director's sexuality. The resulting performance can consequently become grounded in caricature rather than a realistic portrayal of womanhood, drawn from personal experience. To be able to rise above this requires immense strength and self-confidence from women performers.

Believe me, this is not a homophobic rant against gay men, but I have worked in musical theatre for more than 20 years and I can honestly attest, with no hostility whatsoever, that it is a gay man's world. (I worked on a show in the U.K. where the gay men in the ensemble were actively hostile in rehearsals and disparaged the creative team as "the hets" because the director and book writer were straight men.) But however unintentionally, the domination of musicals by gay men has an adverse effect on the women within musical theatre. The performers are asked to interpret roles in the way a gay man believes women behave. The women in the audience are increasingly denied stories about women and featuring realistic female characters they can relate to. And for the creative women in the industry, who are excluded from positions they are more than qualified to be in. The lack of women on creative teams often comes down to the fact that the gay men who are the majority of the creative force in the business—including producers—quite simply do not want them there, for whatever reason. It might be informative to tally up how many female directors, writers, choreographers, composers, and musical directors Sir Cameron Mackintosh, for example, has employed over the years within his worldwide empire. I'll put money on it that one hand would be sufficient. (I must, however, say here that the gay male directors I have worked with have been far more supportive and encouraging to me personally than the straight male directors.)

The fact that homosexuality is now out and accepted by modern society has elevated—however unconsciously—a brand of male chauvinism to new levels. In the days of Cole Porter and Noel Coward, gay men attending musicals were alert for signals from the stage that acknowledged their presence, and preference, and assured them they were not alone.

But the gay men involved in the creation of musicals now are no longer shunned, shut out, or despised for their sexuality. They are an accepted—for the most part—part of society. So the gay men who took women to see a musical as a cover for their homosexuality or used female characters to articulate their yearning for a forbidden love have now no need to hide behind a smokescreen. And the straight men with power within the industry now have a new male ally. Straight men keep women out because—I'm hypothesizing here—they either do not like them or do not want them. Gay men do not necessarily have the same enthusiasm for keeping women out, but they are more intent on serving the interests of their own community. It is similar to the Catholic church (again) which would sooner allow male priests to marry to counteract falling numbers, than consider admitting women to the priesthood.

The blurring of boundaries between the young straight man and the young gay man has also contributed to this edging out of women. Young straight men today are not afraid to admit they use skin products, wear designer clothes, cry at "girly" movies and even enjoy certain musicals. They populate local gyms, intent on sculpting their bodies in a way that was once considered fit only for gay men. They talk about feelings. They buy men's health magazines, which often include fashion spreads, and take the time and care with their appearances that a generation before would have earned them the "queer" insult. The result of this is that young gay men no longer consider straight men the enemy. They have achieved the unthinkable and made friends with the dark side. In short, gay men no longer need women on the side.

What this means for women in musical theatre is that the ranks of men putting a personal agendas onstage have swelled with the welcoming of openly gay men into the mainstream. And the personal agendas, for many of those men, do not include women. In joining the ranks of their previous oppressor, gay men have abandoned the group that stuck by them in the dark times. For decades women gave emotional support, empathy, and tacit approval to gay men in a way that straight men never did. But now that the job is done, women are dismissed by the younger gay men who appear to have the musical theatre industry on their own terms. It feels similar to attitudes within the workforce that now divide parents and non-parents. When childless women join the rank of childless men to complain about maternity leave and flex time for working mothers, the sisterhood feels betrayed. When gay men exclude women from music theatre, it too feels like betrayal of everything we fought for together. I could take this argument one step further and say the new generation of gay men are actually aping the behavior of straight men by denigrating women onstage and erecting barriers to keep them out of the workforce. In order to be part of the straight establishment, they are behaving in the same disrespectful manner towards women as their straight male counterparts, which was not at all how gay men behaved in the Golden Age of musicals.

We have already seen how, 60-odd years ago, many women made their names as lyricists, composers, choreographers, and stars within musical theatre. Gay writers put women center stage in shows that appeared to worship femininity. In this time of so-called liberality and acceptance, young gay composers/writers/directors have no need to disguise their sexuality onstage with a procession of sequin-clad women descending a staircase while belting the end of the Act One number. They can go to their local gay bar and do it themselves. Now that the stigma attached to being gay has been removed, gay men can be out and truly proud and feel no shame in placing their view of the world center stage. This is indeed a good thing. But like any point of view, it can be abused to the point where one particular viewpoint appears to be taking precedence.

The revival of *On a Clear Day* was a perfect example of this. The character of Daisy was never intended to be a gay man called David. That is not how it was written. The result of this revision was that the whole dynamic and original intention of the show was discarded in favor of the director/book writer's personal or political position. Why was that allowed? Why were the intentions and wishes of the original creative team so arrogantly dismissed? Why not just do *Village People: The Musical* and be honest about what you want to see onstage? Did no one at any point question the ethics behind appropriating a female role and turning it in to a male one? If a female creative team did exactly the same thing—transforming J. Pierrepont Finch in *How to Succeed* into a lesbian woman, for example, completely upsetting the original intentions and the balance of the show, they would be labeled separatists and humorless feminists, at best. It feels as if gay men have the permission of the wider musical theatre community to make up for the years in the wilderness by placing a political agenda onstage. I understand why this is the case. It's just a shame the same opportunity—or permission—for women to place their personal or political (the personal *is* political, remember?) position onstage is not being so readily presented.

This could be as much a generational issue as anything else. The younger gay creators have no desire to see a diva musical because it is, to them, old-fashioned—a reminder of the days of suppression when closeted men were forced to reinterpret the leading lady or the chorus boy as a way of fulfilling personal romantic fantasies. Perhaps it even stems from a sneering disdain for the old show queen who goes to every revival of *My Fair Lady* and reverently discusses the night he saw Bernadette Peters play Dot in *Sunday in the Park with George.* Young musical theatre queens sing songs from *Smash.* They tweet about *Spring Awakening.* They consider Sondheim passé. With the arrogance of youth they appear to consider the great musicals, and the gay men who created them, as dinosaurs and of touch with a modern gay culture. In the same way that some young women consider sexual promiscuity proof of their new-found equality, some young gay men believe the battle for gay rights has been won. *Priscilla, Queen of the Desert* is the proof they cite. But just as young women in the audience credit the girls in *Lysistrata Jones* with girl power without stopping to think about the image they are really being sold, young gay men are so busy singing along to "Someone Left My Cake Out in the Rain" that they do not question if the image of gay men onstage is a truly respectful one.

As gay culture has changed, so in turn has the musical and the gay sensibility within it. If the writers are writing for a specifically gay audience, or at least acknowledging that a large proportion of the audience will be gay, then what kind of gay audience do they have in mind? I suspect it is a young one—certainly not the audience that would rush out and buy tickets for a revival of *Passion.* Which in turn leads me to ask if the older gay audience— the traditional one—is dying out. Not in a physical sense, but as the type of shows they loved disappears—the diva musicals, the wise-cracking comedies—are older gay men deserting a genre that once spoke to them, because it no longer does? It's hard to know what would appeal to the cultured gay man about *Rock of Ages* or *King Kong the Musical.* The mature Sondheim aficionado may still go to shows, but I suspect the shows no longer resonate with them in the way that they used to. On this point, at least, they can join hands with women, who are just as starved of musicals that speak to them.

The gay men who have taken control of the musical now couldn't care less about women because they don't need them in order to appear respectable. Just like the gay men dominating the fashion industry whose interest in women is purely aesthetic, the consideration given by the gay men creating new musicals towards women barely extends beyond what they look like onstage and rarely takes into account the fact that the majority of the audience members will be female. The fact that straight men are allowing this to happen is hardly surprising. It is another strand of Faludi's asserted backlash—heterosexual men claiming back territory won by the Women's Rights Movement by standing back and watching women be pushed out of the industry. Anneke Harrison notes:

> Recently, I was in the auditorium during the production period of a show. I looked around at the dozens of people working hard and making it all happen. There were plenty of women there. And then I looked at the levels … and the

further up in importance, the fewer women there were. And further up again, the fewer straight men there were. I thought, in a way, that makes sense because if you are in a position of power, you'll employ people who support you and who are like-minded. You need a cohesive support team. You're not going to employ someone who might rock the boat.

What we now define as musical theatre owes much to the contribution of gay men. Where would the musical be today without Noel Coward, Cole Porter, Lorenz Hart, Jerome Robbins, Michael Bennett, Jerry Herman, Stephen Sondheim ... the list is endless. The development of the genre into an art form has gay men to thank, and I do thank them. Anyone who loves musical theatre fully understands the gay sensibility at the heart of it—it is what makes the genre what it is. Gay men have always claimed ownership of musicals, mainly due to the high proportion of homosexual men appearing in them, creating them, and buying the tickets. But it is time that claim was challenged. Not necessarily onstage, where the gay sensibility has utilized camp to effectively define much of the genre—to remove that would be an affront to the musical itself, but certainly offstage, on creative teams.

When I was involved in the premiere of *Dr. Zhivago: The Musical* in Australia and an internship became available, I suggested a particular young woman who had all the right credentials and would have benefitted enormously from involvement with a new musical. I was told that this was not possible, as the (gay) male producer felt there were too many women on the production team already. There were five, and three of those were in resident or associate positions, which are never considered as truly part of the creative team as they are there to maintain, as opposed to create. Why is "too many women" looked upon as a problem when the number of men is never an issue? It is because women are viewed with suspicion, or hostility. They will "cause problems." Roughly translated, that means they might have the temerity to question what the male creators are putting in place, particularly with regards to the way in which the female characters are written, or in terms of how the female actors are treated in the rehearsal room. The idea that a similar remark concerning the numbers of gay men on the creative team would ever be made is laughable, mainly because there would be no one left.

The above incident illustrates a point I made earlier—that it is almost impossible for young women in the industry to even get a foot in the door, regardless of how talented or experienced they are. Nine and a half times out of ten, the job will go to a young man, particularly if he is pretty, unless a woman is doing the hiring. But even then, as proved by the *Viva Forever!* debacle, sisterhood may not be high on the agenda.

(I must state here that the issue of women being spurned by gay men appears to be a much bigger problem in the U.K. and Australia than in the U.S. Few of the women I spoke to in the U.S. even mentioned it. All of the women in the U.K. and Australia brought it up at some point.) Susan H. Schulman notes:

> But there's all sorts of clubs—you know, boys' clubs, the gay mafia. You drift to people who you feel comfortable with. I think that has more to do with it. And maybe there was a gay mafia because people drifted towards people they felt comfortable with. A sensibility, a working sensibility, or creative sensibility. People who'd been educated at Yale worked together because they felt comfortable; they had a common language. I mean, that happens everywhere, in everything.

Yes, there have always been clubs. And clubs become mafias when people who feel they should be given opportunities are not. Someone has to be blamed: the gay mafia, the white mafia, the Jewish mafia, Oxbridge. In some instances the accusations are correct; in others they become excuses. It's a fine line. Women are under-represented on musical theatre creative teams, and women's stories are under-represented. No one can argue with that. What I'm saying is that the people who have it in their power to change the imbalance show no inclination to do so. Perhaps that is deliberate; perhaps it just hasn't occurred to them.

What would the cultural landscapes of the U.S., the U.K., and Australia look like today without the past input from gay male writers, directors, dancers, actors, choreographers, designers, artists, gallery directors, musicians, opera singers, composers, architects, or film makers. A barren wasteland, I suspect. But if the fight for acceptance and respectability has now been won by the gay community—and thank God it has—then perhaps the club doors could open a little further and allow other people in such as the group who offered support when times were tough: women.

Notes

1. Lyrics by David Javerbaum, music by Adam Schlesinger.
2. Judith Fetterley, 1977, *The Resisting Reader: A Feminist Approach to American Fiction* (Bloomington: Indiana University Press).
3. Susan Sontag, 1966, "Notes on Camp," in *Against Interpretation and Other Essays* (New York: Farrar, Straus and Giroux).
4. http://en.wikipedia.org/wiki/Camp_style.
5. Daniel Harris, 1997, *The Rise and Fall of Gay Culture* (New York: Ballantine Books).
6. Review conducted by the Williams Institute, April 2011.
7. Book by Terrence McNally, lyrics and music by David Yazbeck.

6

Why Can't a Woman Be More Like a Man?

Difference and the Musical

In *My Fair Lady,* Henry Higgins poses the question "Why can't a woman be more like a man?" He sings of all the wonderful qualities men possess and asks why women—who are lacking these attributes—can't be more like men. The answer is glaringly obvious. A woman can't be more like a man because she is not one. She is different. And while many women claim their difference as their strength, Sheila Jeffreys in *Beauty and Misogyny* succinctly outlines why the notion and theory of difference is problematic for women. "If women are different, there must be something that they are different from. That something turns out to be men, who are not themselves different from anything else, they just are." (p. 21).

In other words, men—white, heterosexual men—are the yardstick against which everything else is measured. To be a woman is not to be a man. To be black is not to be white. To be gay is not to be straight. And instead of celebrating this diversity, difference is taken to mean inferiority. Anything that is not what society considers the norm—white, heterosexual, and male— is deemed lacking.

Despite often placing women at the center of a musical, the scripts often subscribe to the theory of women as different. *Next to Normal* uses women's biological difference on which to hang an entire show—women have babies, women get depressed, men deal with the fallout. The song "How to Handle a Woman" From *Camelot* has its foundation in an attitude that designates women as different. This, of course, is perfectly true, but the song treats the difference as negative. A man has to learn how to "handle" a woman, the implication being he knows how to interact with a man.

As with *Next to Normal,* women are presented as impossible to understand because they are not men. The theme of difference is also prevalent in musicals such as *Jelly's Last Jam, The Wiz, Porgy and Bess, The Color Purple, Memphis*—shows still categorized as black musicals, i.e., not white. Musical theatre, as we have seen, is created and produced by white men, resulting in women and characters of race being defined as other.

Highlighting difference is the cornerstone of bullying, and we only have to look at the schoolyard to see it displayed. A child who looks different—skin color, weight, red hair, freckles—or who sounds different is an easy target. The persecuted child is derided for what he does not have—white skin, acceptable accent, the right clothes, etc. Despite moves by communities and governments to embrace diversity, difference is still regarded as lacking, because it is not the norm.

Higgins's lament for women's lack of male qualities is designed to make us laugh and reveal aspects of his character. I'm sure there are many people in the audience who find it hilarious, but it illustrates perfectly the dangers of defining a group by its difference. By highlighting the good qualities in men, Higgins shows us what he considers to be lacking in women because his assumption is that male qualities are the standard to which everyone else should aspire. This takes us back to the arguments around biological determinism, where the qualities of compassion, empathy, and nurturing—considered innate in women—are used against them: too compassionate to be a leader; not strong enough for management. Instead of celebrating the qualities women do possess, a society that places a man on a pedestal just for existing, has, in effect, permission to dismiss women as inadequate—but only because men are defining the norm.

If women are used as the blueprint to define difference, then it is men who are lacking, because their testosterone levels deprive them of an ability to be as compassionate as women. Men and male behavior, however, continue to be the reference point to which women are compared. If one day out of the entire year is deemed International Woman's Day, are we to draw the conclusion that every other day of the year, by default, is International Men's Day?

The musical not only characterizes women as different, but assumes that the men in the audience are in accord with this viewpoint. Just as male gaze takes for granted that the viewer is heterosexual and male, so *My Fair Lady* assumes the audience will agree with Higgins misogyny, or at least find it amusing. That the women in the audience may not appreciate this depiction is irrelevant. Men may nod sagely at Arthur's conclusion in *Camelot,* that the way to handle a woman is to "simply love her," but women, already bristling at being described as something that has to be handled, may not appreciate being reduced to a passive imbecile who requires control.

Feminism and feminist theory have long argued the equality vs. difference debate. Should woman aspire to be equal with men, or should they regard their difference as their strength? If their difference makes them stronger, then seeking equality with men is selling themselves short. Many women are of the opinion that their ability to give birth and to withstand the pain involved makes them both physically and emotionally stronger than men. Some men will argue that it is exactly that difference that makes women unsuitable for the workforce, as their hormones render them over-emotional. We can go on for decades discussing this single point without ever reaching a conclusion that is satisfactory for both parties.

The difference vs. equality debate is increasingly pertinent to women and sexuality, as a younger generation embraces a sexual freedom that not so long ago was available only to men. For many young women of Generation Y, being sexually available equates with personal power—the right to do as she pleases—and equality. Certainly, it is progress from an oppressive patri-archal ideal based around women's purity and innocence, but I'm not convinced that replacing male controls around women's bodies with a sexualized culture where girls as young as ten wear boob tubes and lip gloss and pout for the cameras is either power or equality. Is this really what the suffragettes starved themselves for? The younger generation of women appear to have abandoned the innate qualities in being female that set them apart from men and embraced a belief that sexuality alone embodies womanhood. But far from empowering women, this notion merely deludes women into regarding their bodies as their only weapon against misogyny. When women deny their innate differences, they all too often end up aping the worst traits of male behavior. Anneke Harrison notes:

> The women that I enjoy working with the most lead in a consultative way. There tends to be more consultation and more involvement. I'm never in any doubt that they're the boss, but I feel like a collaborator, not a subordinate. I think women are better at that. Maybe in men that's seen as a kind of weakness. Maybe that's the problem. That women have to behave like men to be taken seriously and given any kind of currency in a male world.

Margaret Thatcher was the prime example of a woman behaving like a man in order to be accepted by the men in her political party and later her cabinet. No doubt she felt the need to do this to combat the conviction of those around her that her femaleness alone rendered her unsuitable for the position of prime minister. Yet she was criticized for essentially denying her womanhood by embracing power with such enthusiasm. It's another Catch–

22 situation, in which women are damned if they do, and damned if they don't.

On one hand, society uses women's difference as the excuse to exclude and control them—difference being equated with lacking. On the other hand, when a woman does display any of the qualities so admired in men—ambition, sexual freedom, indifference to romance—she is derided as unfeminine. Susan Stroman, Wendy Cavett, and Susan H. Schulman have all emphasized earlier in this book that women lead differently from men, and that is not necessarily a bad thing. Wendy Cavett says a woman is "nurturing, as well as a leader." It is an addition, not a loss. When women take on male characteristics in order to be accepted, they deny what is unique about the female experience and they become mere imitators of a male paradigm of power. Wendy Cavett notes:

> Sometimes female musical directors have perhaps felt a need to make sure that they are seen to be strong. And they lose a dimension of their humanity in order that someone doesn't perceive them as weak. And maybe the places I've worked, the shows I've done, I've been very lucky. There's a much greater latitude, a much greater appreciation of individualism. Including sexuality.

The gay rights movement faces a similar equality dilemma—denying that any difference exists in order to be accepted by a heterosexual society could ultimately destroy the unique qualities that form the foundation of gay culture. The crux of the matter resides in the notion that equality means we are all expected to fit a straight, male definition of society. True equality would recognize difference and individuality and acknowledge that one size does not fit all. Instead of fighting for inclusion through legalized gay marriage, the homosexual community could come up with an alternative legal ceremony that is tailored to suit their specific requirements. A truly egalitarian society would operate from a "separate but equal" standpoint. It would rethink how it defines itself, instead of demanding that women, homosexuals, and ethnic minorities conform to a white, heterosexual, patriarchal definition.

While the musical operates from a position that regards women as different, it fails to acknowledge that not all women are the same or have the same concerns. The second-wave feminists quickly realized that in order to unite all women, the movement had to recognize differences within various groups of women. Ethnic women have different priorities from white women, and work/lifestyle balance is more likely to be an issue for educated, professional women than women employed on casual or part-time contracts. Childless women are raising concerns about benefits awarded to female employees with children, and lesbian women are likely to focus on issues that do not apply to straight women. Yet the musical insists that there is only one kind of woman, the kind who is seeking, and will be fulfilled by, the love of a good man.

Difference, in musical theatre, has particular implications for women on and offstage due to the fact that the industry is controlled by men who translate difference as "not one of us." Offstage this informs the choice of members of the creative team, the "too many women" excuse. Onstage, the male voice affects the characterization of female roles that are written from a point of view that regards a woman as something that has to be "handled," or by comparing them to men. In *Next to Normal,* Dan is depicted as the stronger sex because he does not, and will never, suffer from postpartum depression. Women are weaker because they do. So if women are different, and the thing they are different from is men, then how are men defining these differences? What is it about women that makes them different from men? First and foremost, it appears to be their femininity.

Billy Bigelow in *Carousel* imagines his daughter as dressed frilly pink with ribbons. This is the embodiment of passive femininity, i.e., everything that men are not. His son may rule the country, but his daughter will grow up to be compliant—no doubt still wearing pink ribbons as she gives birth to another generation of submissive, frilly girls. Thirteen years later, when Rodgers and Hammerstein wrote *Flower Drum Song,* their image of woman-hood as sweet and frilly and girlish had not evolved into anything deeper. The character of Linda enjoys being a girl because of the trappings—the make-up, the hair-do, the lace dresses, and the cold cream—that men attribute to femininity. Linda is "sugar and spice and all things nice"—the antithesis of the strong, masculine hero. Kim in *Bye Bye Birdie*[1] (1960) also associates being female with an abundance of accessories. Her reasons for considering it "lovely" do not include the innate qualities—compassion, empathy, nurturing ability—but center around mascara, lipstick and high heels. By emphasizing the paraphernalia associated with femininity and the look of femininity, the male writers reduce the women to little more than shop mannequins, something to hang clothes on and arrange in suggestive poses to please the male eye. Linda and Kim and countless other female characters in musicals are depicted as superficial beings whose main preoccupation is personal grooming. Men have much worthier issues on their minds. Women are not expected to possess brains, strength, or integrity, because those are male characteristics.

Daniel in *Once on This Island* professes to admire the fact that Ti Moune is not like the other girls who obsess over their looks, paint nails, and powder their faces. He claims to be attracted by her individuality and by the fact that she sidesteps convention and marches to the beat of her own drum. Yet Daniel abandons Ti Moune in order to marry a woman who does paint her nails and obsess over her hair. In other words, he marries the woman who conforms to the male ideal of passive femininity, as opposed to a woman with character. Billy Bigelow's image of a woman dressed in pink and lacy frills could never be mistaken for anything other than obedient, unthreatening, and childlike.

Female characters in musicals who do not fall in line with the male vision of femininity, either physically/visually or emotionally, are classed as deviant. And deviant is a more extreme view of difference. In musical theatre, deviant women are the only group within their entire sex who are acknowledged as having concerns or living a life apart from the prescribed norm. Unsurprisingly, this subgroup is depicted in negative terms, because the people doing the depicting are the very same people defining the unconventional woman as deviant. Instead of applauding the strength and courage these women display through their refusal to adhere to a restricting set of rules governing their behavior, the musical condemns them.

Rose in *Gypsy* is deviant because she has ambitions beyond her station and refuses to live a conventional life with a husband, a home, and her children in school. She is repeatedly told by her father and later by Herbie to "settle down," to give up the only lifestyle she has ever known because it does not conform to the rules defining the family and the role of mother. Her ambition—her difference—is not presented as something to be admired, and Rose is to be scorned, or pitied for her hopes of a better life. So much for the American Dream. But Rose is a woman, and first and foremost a mother, and that makes her ambition a problem. Mothers are not supposed to require anything more than their children to feel fulfilled and good about themselves. Naturally, her punishment for having the guts to go after what she wants is to be abandoned both by her daughter and her disappointed lover.

Desiree in *A Little Night Music* is also an actress and also a mother. Desiree's daughter Fredrika, boarded out with her grandmother while Desiree earns a living to support her child, defines her mother by what she isn't. And what she isn't is society's definition of a good mother. Desiree doesn't do housework, or cook, or lead an "ordinary life." She is different. The fact that the image Fredrika paints of "ordinary mothers" presents their lives as excruciatingly dull compared to Desiree's lifestyle is neither here nor there. In *Grey Gardens,* Little Edie is condemned in Act One for her spirited and willful character and repeatedly told how she should behave. In Act Two, both Little Edie and Big Edie are presented as deviant because they live apart from society in their own chosen world, shunning a normal life. Eva Peron in *Evita* is so aware that she has overstepped the prescribed boundaries that classify women as passive (and pink) that she feels the need to justify her actions in a song. Because she has succeeded in a man's world and displayed qualities considered innately masculine—ambition, strength, emotional detachment—she has to explain herself to her public in order to keep them on her side. Juan Peron never gives a balcony speech/song explaining his motives, because no one ever questions them. Eva, as we know, dies of cancer. That's what's happens to women who dare to be different.

A pattern emerges with these and other deviant female characters in the musical. They are feisty. They are at odds with a society that defines pink, decorative femininity as the ideal to aspire to. These women want more challenging lives and regard their needs as of equal importance to men's. Because they do not marry, live in the suburbs, have children, and bake cakes with the neighbors for the church sale, they are classed as unconventional, at best, dangerous rebels at worst. Which returns us again to the question of who is making the rules that dictate how women should live their lives. If musical theatre is a reflection of society, then the few deviant women it presents us with are a mirror image of countless women across the world rebelling against a constricting set of rules and being forced to face the consequences of not doing as they are told. Obedience has always been a bigger issue for women than for men, because men make and, more often than not, enforce the rules that women are obliged to obey. When I say rules, I am referring to the often unwritten laws surrounding female behavior—how women should dress, how they should behave, where they should and should not be after dark, what is an appropriate career, where they should live and with whom, etc.

Women who question these rules, or deliberately flout them, are classed as deviant in a way that men are not. Men, it seems, can do as they please. Musical theatre—that hotbed of escapism—is not immune to this way of thinking. The real problem with Maria in *The Sound of Music*, for example, is that she has a personality, and her rebellion, tame as it is, is seen as a deliberate flouting of the rules designed to stamp out individuality. The bigger issue is that her independent streak is regarded as unfeminine. She behaves like a boy, climbing trees and scraping knees. Fortunately she does conform, marries Captain Von Trapp, and is spared the ignominy of being thrown out of the Abbey onto the streets of Salzburg, where she would no doubt fall into prostitution and die in a gutter with a needle in her arm.

The musical tells us over and over again that women who do not fall in line will come to a sorry end, and the only way of avoiding the inevitable judgment from on high is to marry the man today. In the land of musical theatre, nothing sorts out a troublesome woman like the love of a good man.

Look at *Calamity Jane* and *Annie Get Your Gun*. God knows where those two women would have ended up without Frank Butler and Wild Bill Hickok to take them in hand. If the women in *Chicago* had made more of an effort at being good wives and uncomplaining partners, they wouldn't be in jail now.

If Sally Bowles didn't sleep around and associate with dubious characters in seedy nightclubs, she could have snared the scintillating Cliff, instead of ending up alone and childless. Norma Desmond is dragged off to the asylum because she refuses to conform. Admittedly she shoots her younger lover, but let's be honest, by the end of that musical, who didn't want to shoot the selfish, dishonest, grasping Joe Gillis?

The crime that these, and other female characters, are really guilty of is behaving as men do. They do not live up to men's expectations of women as pretty, ineffectual ornaments. These women ignore the differences that are used by men to define them in a constricting way. The audience at a musical is not asked to empathize with a female character who displays the same resolve/courage men are endowed with, because women are *different* from men and having the nerve to imitate men and their behavior, is reprehensible. The way these female characters are written and the punishment they subsequently receive indicates that the writers expect the audience to condemn the deviant female. She is not supposed to be worthy of respect because she is not living up to the ideal of womanhood. No one pauses to consider that it could be the ideal itself that is the problem, not the deviant women.

The easiest way to tame a troublesome woman and to bring her into line is to marry her off: the "a baby will sort her out" attitude. You may laugh, but yes, that way of thinking does still exist. A woman with three children under five will hardly have time to sleep, let alone agitate for change. Musical theatre reflects this patriarchal standpoint by insisting that being married is the natural state for all women, and women who show no inclination towards it are dangerous and must be controlled. Lizzie in *110 in the Shade* is an oddity because she is not married. Adelaide in *Guys and Dolls* is acutely aware that her unmarried status is a problem. Big Edie in *Grey Gardens* intimates that if Little Edie had married, they would not currently be living in squalor with only flea-ridden cats for company. In Act One of the same show, Major Bouvier sings a song entitled "Marry Well" to his young granddaughters (the future Jackie Kennedy and her sister Lee Radziwill). The alternative, that they may remain single, is never considered, because that would make them stand out; they would be different. In Meredith Wilson's *The Music Man*, Marian is judged as deviant because she is more interested in music and literature and refuses to dumb down to please a prospective husband. Her mother considers Marian's single state a disgrace and spends most of the show urging her to find herself a man, even going so far as to inform Marian that without a husband she has no place in society, so no one will listen or even be interested in hearing her opinions. Marian's entire worth is defined by the status of the man she marries.

The *Music Man* is undeniably a wonderful example of a classic musical comedy, and the fact that it is regularly revived by regional theatres almost 60 years after its incarnation proves the quality of show. But I wonder what women in the audience today make of being told they have no status in society without a husband: slight impatience, or just boredom?

The message around non-conformity is patently clear. If women do not conform to male expectations of passivity, marriage, and motherhood, they will be labeled deviant and will be punished in some way. But what the majority of these supposed abnormal women are doing is merely being themselves: individuals. They are living their lives as the women they know themselves to be, not the women men are telling them to be.

Women who do not conform to marriage and motherhood are derided as "not real women" because they are ignoring the difference that is utilized to define women as the weaker sex. If a woman's ability to carry a child and give birth renders her weaker than men—as opposed to merely different—then women who make a deliberate choice not to have children are immediately suspect. They are denying the difference that can be construed as weakness and used against them. They are, in effect, declaring their equality with men by leveling the playing field, which could partly explain why childless women are disparaged as unnatural, emotionless, cold and immature, or assumed to be either gay or a "career bitch." Their denial that difference equates with weakness renders them a threat to patriarchy.

By treating women as other, i.e., not men, and regarding female-ness as a lack of male-ness, the musical reinforces an attitude of women as weak, simply because men are deemed strong. If women are not men, then a real woman has to be the antithesis of the ideal man. And if the ideal man is summed up by his manliness and strength, then the opposite would have to be weak and feminine. When women do not behave according to the male vision of female difference, they are derided as manly. How many star female athletes have their sexuality questioned because they display muscles and aggression on the sports field?

Musical theatre has very clear ideas—embedded in this vision of men as strong and women as weak—on how women should behave and approach life. It is hard not to make the connection between this patriarchal vision of women onstage and the fact that men control the genre. Even the nuns in *The Sound of Music* are aware that Maria's problem stems from her difference. As the Mother Abbess points out, "she's a girl." That is, she is not a boy and cannot continue to behave like one. Conforming, in the case of young women, invariably means suppressing their true natures, and Maria's defiance is an indication that she is not ready to do so. Girls may well be girls, but women will do as they are told.

If white and male is taken to be the normative, the yardstick against which everything is measured, then ethnicity proves as problematic as gender for an art form grounded in that normative.

Ethnic minorities have been even less well served by the musical than women—at least women were once leading ladies—with ethnic characters defined within a context of otherness. Martin Gottfried, author of *Broadway Musicals*,[2] takes until page 329 to recognize any notion of difference within the entire genre. The final chapter of the book (which extends a full ten pages, five of those being pictorial) is given the heading "Black Musicals," immediately placing the subject within the context of otherness. The black musical is so designated because it is not white. All other musicals are just musicals.

> I don't mind them calling it a black musical. The problem comes when that comes with consequences: where it being a black musical means that nobody … buys tickets … and it being a black musical means that some producers won't touch it. Or means they have to sanitize it in a particular way. If the theatre-going audience heard all these words—black musical, women's play— they go, oh well, that's what it is. But it's just a descriptive term. Like opera. It's only because the labels have costs that it is problematic. And there's an implied judgment that it's not going to be as good.—Melanie La Barrie

In *Parade* it is Leo's Jewishness that sets him apart as "other." He may be white, male, and heterosexual, but his religion prevents him from being accepted by a community already divided by racism and the Civil War. No matter how Leo and his wife Lucille assimilate to Southern ways, they will always remain outsiders because they are Jews and therefore different. In *Caroline, or Change*[3] (2004) both Caroline, the maid, and Noah, the eight-year-old son of the house, are different: Caroline because she is African American, and Noah because he is a Jewish boy in a Southern town. There are also hints in the lyrics that Noah might be gay, in which case he is likely to be more ostracized by the community than Caroline will ever be, even with the hostility surrounding the growing civil rights movement. In both of these shows it is not the race of the character that is the issue, but the prejudice towards their race from other people. The shows tackle the touchy subject of racism with real respect, and both Leo in *Parade* and Caroline in *Caroline, or Change* are complex characters who inspire empathy. We witness how they suffer through being classed as other.

West Side Story and *Fiddler on the Roof*—both conceived, directed, and choreographed by Jerome Robbins—take the issue of racial prejudice as their starting point. The gang warfare between the Puerto Ricans and the white Americans in *West Side Story* and the persecution of Eastern European Jews in *Fiddler* provide the backdrop and the plot for the shows. Both groups are persecuted for their otherness—be it religion or skin color. *Rags*[4] (1986) picks up where *Fiddler* left off, with the arrival of Eastern European Jews in America, and *Ragtime* (1998) also imagines the immigrant and African American experience.

The number of Jewish men represented on the creative teams for the above shows allowed an authentic Jewish story and characters truthfully to come to life. They were writing about what they knew, or at least could relate to, unlike men writing shows about women, or white men writing black stories. Susan Stroman notes:

> There are not many African-American composers or lyricists in musical theatre. I don't know if that's the result of some larger exclusionary action, or because that specific style of music and performance isn't a big part of popular culture, and therefore new talent isn't being generated in quite the same way. During The Scottsboro Boys, there was the issue that a white creative team couldn't tell a story based in a black experience. The Scottsboro Boys has an all-black cast, and what they brought to their characters is something I could never teach them. I could only give them a path, a plan, and they made it their own. I have never done a show like that in which the actors were so invested in telling the story—they invested body and soul to tell that story, and I've never experienced that in such a powerful way. We need more African-American writers who want to be in musical theatre so those stories and those experiences can be heard.

In the 1920s and 1930s, the all-black revue was a familiar form of entertainment on Broadway, but the shows were rarely written or produced by African Americans. Just as the minstrel shows before featured white actors in blackface performing their idea of the black experience, the all-black revue was a white man's caricature of black culture.

The depiction of black stories or characters was wholly imagined by white men and had no basis in reality. In the same way as women in musicals speak with a male voice, or a male idea of a female voice, black performers spoke with a white voice—a frequently patronizing voice, that had no foundation in authenticity. Outside the revue, roles for ethnic musical theatre performers were rare, although in the late 1930s black versions of white musicals started appearing. Gilbert and Sullivan's *The Mikado* became *The Hot Mikado* in 1939 starring Bill "Bojangles" Robinson, and in 1943 Oscar Hammerstein wrote a new book and lyrics for *Carmen Jones,* essentially Bizet's opera with a World War II/African American setting.

In 1967, four years into the run of *Hello, Dolly!,* legendary impresario David Merrick, in an attempt to boost flagging box office receipts, replaced the Broadway company with a black cast headed by Pearl Bailey. While the move did entice a black audience into the theatre, they were still watching a white story, played out by black actors. And black actors were only being employed on musicals when their difference, their ethnicity, became the selling point of the production. In other words, they were a marketing tool. Unless the rules were bent to accommodate black performers and their difference, there was no room for them on the Great *White* Way. The only way for a black performer to be employed on Broadway was to dismiss any personal belief in their difference as their strength. Difference, in terms of race, was unlikely to be looked upon favorably by a Broadway producer. In 2015 we understand the vital importance of diversity within the arts, readily accepting (for the most part) that the ethnic experience is as relevant to the cultural makeup and history of a nation as the white story. Seventy years ago, however, ethnic actors really only had two choices—appear in a black version of a white story, or play the Maid. It was not until the 1970s that the black musical made its particular mark on the genre, most notably with *The Wiz*[5] in 1975. A retelling of Frank Baum's *The Wonderful Wizard of Oz* within the context of African-American culture, *The Wiz* won seven Tony awards, including Best Musical, and was made into a film starring Diana Ross and Michael Jackson in 1978.

Broadway had seen musicals with a predominantly black cast, or a black story, before *The Wiz—Purlie*[6] in 1971 and *Raisin*[7] in 1973 (which also won the Tony for Best Musical)—but the all-black cast and the large-scale/big-budget production made *The Wiz* a breakthrough for Broadway. *The Wiz* can justifiably claim much of the credit for laying the foundation stone on which later musicals that told black stories with black performers were built. Some of the more memorable of these shows were *Dreamgirls* (1981), *Jelly's Last Jam*[8] (1992), *The Color Purple*[9] (2005) and *Memphis*[10] (2009).

But the defining characteristic of these musicals, regardless of their success or otherwise, is their ethnicity. They are Different from other musicals because they are not white—yes, even today.

Nina Lannan offers:

> It is still a very white industry and this was never more evident to me than when we worked on *The Color Purple* and … had a hard time finding company managers and stage managers … anyone of any ethnicity to work on the show. And another show we worked on was *Flower Drum Song*, which was an entirely Asian cast.… When you look at those actors … those brilliant, won-

derful actors, and then at their bios in *Playbill*, you see credits for roles in regional theatre—not Broadway. The actors in both shows just hadn't had the opportunity to be on Broadway. And it hit me right there looking at the *Playbill*, these actors had to be itinerant performers going round the country to get work.... But if you look at the bios of ensemble actors from the other predominantly Caucasian casts, you see bio after bio filled with Broadway show credits.

Issues around race and musical theatre bear striking similarities to the issues around gender and the musical. There is a distinct lack of ethnic representation on creative teams and characters are often written within a narrow set of stereotypes, with few leading roles written for non-white actors. And there is still a lack of African American, Asian American, or Hispanic stories that could be classed as empowering making it to the musical theatre stage— the oppressed victim making a regular appearance. There has been some improvement in the appropriation of the ethnic voice by white writers as a growing cultural sensitivity rightly decries the suggestion of an inauthentic voice telling an ethnic story. Unlike *Miss Saigon* in 1989, when the white, male creative team gave us their version of the Vietnamese experience complete with two white actors—Keith Burns as Thuy and Jonathan Pryce as the Engineer—donning eye prostheses to play an Asian and a Eurasian. Today, one hopes, this would be decried as offensive, both to the audience members and to Asian actors who are denied the opportunity of major roles for which they are more suitable than white actors.

In 1990, Broadway actor B.D. Wong filed a complaint with Actors Equity about the casting of Jonathan Pryce as the Engineer in the Broadway production of *Miss Saigon,* arguing that it was "racially false" to allow an Asian role to be played by a Caucasian. (A similar argument could be made for the casting of wheelchair-bound Nessarose in *Wicked* with an able-bodied actor.) After protracted negotiations, Pryce was allowed to reprise his London success as the Engineer on Broadway in 1990, but subsequent productions have employed an actor of Asian extraction in the role. In 2015 it is quite simply unacceptable to have a white actor play a role of any ethnicity; we are mostly in agreement on that (although Opera Australia recently mounted a production of *The King and I* with a Caucasian in the title role and not one critic or arts commentator appeared to notice). Why, then, is a similar demonstration of awareness and sensitivity not in evidence when it comes to gender within musical theatre? Why is it irrelevant that the female voice is appropriated by men when it is unacceptable to have a black story told by a white writer? Why does the concern with offending a group with an outdated or inappropriate portrayal not extend towards women in the same way it does to ethnic minorities?

As the quote from Tim Rice at the beginning of this book clearly indicated, the British sensibility around gender and musical theatre appears to affirm that women have no place in the debate.

Which brings me back to the visibility and empowerment issue. Put quite simply, this argument attests that visibility in itself is empowering—that the more ethnic actors in the cast, the more empowering it is for the performers and for audience members of that particular racial group, who see themselves and their stories represented onstage.

But I would argue that visibility in itself is not enough, not when the depiction of the racial group is bound within a narrow and demeaning set of stereotypes. All too often the issue of race—and, I would argue, gender—in musical theatre comes down to quantity over quality. Do we quibble about authenticity in *The Lion King*—the Disneyfication of Africa—when the show employs so many black actors? Is the portrayal of the Asian girls in *Miss Saigon* a positive image or an offensive stereotype rooted in a colonial vision of Asian sexual prowess? Why raise the issue at all when so many Asian women finally have a role on Broadway? Similar questions arise with *The Book of Mormon.* Is the fact that black actors have a presence on Broadway and the West End in the hit show of the season more important than the roles they are asked to play? Does the actor who repeatedly announces "I have maggots in my scrotum" empower other black actors and audience members with this line? Or is he, and the entire show, fulfilling a white view of ignorant Africans as something to be laughed at? On the other hand, a hit Broadway musical with a predominantly black cast can send a message to the white audience that there are black actors out there who are perfectly capable of playing leading roles and who are just as talented as white performers.

Female politicians are acutely aware that their numbers alone are irrelevant. Unless women are represented at senior levels of government—the cabinet, the Senate—they are powerless to effect change. When Tony Blair's New Labour Party swept to power in the 1997 U.K. General Election with an unprecedented 101 female MPs, the photograph of Blair on the steps of Westminster surrounded by 96 of those elected women was captioned "Blair's Babes"—hardly respectful or empowering. In the same way, boosting the number of ethnic performers in musicals does not necessarily mean that they will be empowered or that their difference will become their strength.

When the visibility vs. empowerment debate is applied to gender and musicals, the similarities to race are striking. More women onstage do not guarantee a positive portrayal—think back to the discussion around *The Life,* or *Nine*—because men are still creating the shows. No woman in the audience is empowered listening to Queen assert that he's no good, but she's no good without him, or by watching intelligent women put their lives on hold to appease their self-obsessed lover Guido. Can we really assert it is important to do *Sister Act* or *Legally Blonde* purely to have a show dominated by women, when the roles are clichéd and one-dimensional? If I had bought a ticket to *Lysistrata Jones,* certainly I would have seen more females onstage than males, but it doesn't necessarily follow that I would have witnessed a show that treated women as equal to men. Some will argue that the power resides in the fact that women are at least seen onstage, and in leading roles. They therefore have a voice. But what *kind* of voice is it? Is the adoring/simpering/victim voice so prevalent in *Nine* better than no voice at all? Christine Toy Johnson notes:

> I think it has become more diverse compared to what it was, say, twenty years ago. But it's still only in the ensemble and supporting roles. And people say, oh, you've got Audra [McDonald] or Norm Lewis and they're fabulous. But that's it. I mean, can you imagine someone saying, oh, there's one white actress on Broadway and for the last ten years she's played the same three roles?

Melanie La Barrie agrees that "there will always be little roles that they will give to Indian or black people." But not many leading roles. Diversity is all very well in the ensemble, it would seem, but not center stage. The trouble with visibility is that it often calls for the sacrifice of integrity. Black performers appearing in a black version of a white musical, or playing domestic servants in a drawing-room comedy, are hardly a unified call to arms for Black Power in the arts.

And nor is agreeing to play Sandy in *Grease* striking a blow for feminism. But what is the alternative? Women and actors of ethnicity who want a career in musicals have to accept that their difference is unlikely to be treated with respect. They can either get over it or leave the business. Maybe visibility— sheer numbers alone—is indeed the best solution for now and the only hope for an authentic voice for women and ethnic actors. There is always the outside chance that someone in the rehearsal room will be listened to.

In the last couple of decades, significant moves have been made by producers, directors, choreographers, and unions to boost ethnic representation onstage. I say two decades, but it is probably only the last decade in the U.K. and the idea has yet to take root in Australia. The notion of color-blind, or mixed-race casting, in musical theatre is well established in the U.S., where an all-white cast would now raise eyebrows. The cast of a musical should reflect the country or society in which the show is produced, and therefore an all-white cast is at odds with the multicultural societies of the U.S., U.K. and Australia. Musical theatre reflects a nation's culture, and therefore has to reflect the range of people who contribute to that culture. Simple enough, one would think. But color-blind casting can still be a major issue for musical theatre purists who argue that it is not a true representation of the story and characters—particularly with a historical piece—or a true interpretation of the writer's original intention.

While liberals ask why the Baker's Wife in *Into the Woods* cannot be played by a black or Asian or Hispanic actress, conservatives argue that the role was written for a white actor and to tamper with this unbalances the story. But this is assuming that the role was indeed intended for a white actress. Nowhere in the script does it specify the race of the actor playing the role. In fact, most musical theatre scripts only denote the race of the character when they are not white, proving that white is normative and anything else is considered other. But if the script of *Guys and Dolls* does not specifically say "white caucasian female" in the character breakdown, then why can Sarah Brown not be played by an actor of ethnicity? Arguing that it makes no sense historically is a redundant point—gangsters weren't dancing down the streets singing "Sit Down, You're Rockin' the Boat" either. Musicals are make-believe—anything can, and should, happen. If we can accept that Edna Turnblad in *Hairspray* is played by a man, what is to stop an audience accepting Audra McDonald playing Lizzie in *110 in the Shade* as she did in 2007 in the Roundabout Theatre Company production. A production which had black and white actors in equal numbers onstage, a truly wonderful production to experience as an audience member because the notion of equality, in terms of race at least, was clearly on display. Christine Toy Johnson notes:

> So, *Mamma Mia!* … really those friends could be anything…. There's the mother Donna, there's Tanya, and there's Rosie. So Tanya and Rosie are the friends. However, somewhere along the line and I don't think they would say it was even a conscious decision—I would bet that—somewhere along the line they decided that the character of Rosie could be cast with a woman of color. So you've seen … an African American woman has played it on Broadway, I know an Asian American was cast in one of the tours but she couldn't do it. But that's the part. So they won't really think about the other two because they have it in their head that that's the woman of color slot. And I find that this happens a lot. That they get it in their heads that that is the only role. And this one is a good supporting role. Leading roles— no, they don't do that much.

Audiences have seen an Asian actress play Eponine in *Les Misérables*, an African American actor—Clarke Peters—as Darryl van Horne in *The Witches of Eastwick*, and Audra McDonald take the leading role in *Carousel*. If we are now beginning to recognize that there is no real reason why Sky Masterson cannot be played by a black actor, is it too much to ask musical theatre creators to make a similar leap of imagination where gender is concerned? That they think outside of the box when creating female roles and move beyond the passive, dependant stereotype? If the chains that restrict actors of ethnicity to playing caricatures can be broken, can't the attitudes towards female roles in musicals—on and offstage—be similarly torn apart? Christine Toy Johnson notes:

> [*Miss Saigon*] employed a lot of Asian people, for sure. And here's the thing about the stereotypes. The prostitute Asian stereotype is painful to watch. But what happened on Broadway in the last year of the show: they cast the part of Ellen, which is, you know, his white wife—with an Asian American woman. And it started, I think, because this woman was an understudy and over the years they were looking internally for who could be the cover, and this one woman was great. I mean, she would never have been cast originally because she wasn't a white American, but she was in the cast already. And then she took over the role and it seemed like wow, that's so deep. Because that means Chris went home and found someone who looked like Kim. The substitute. So in that case it was a really interesting example of how ... when people start thinking outside of the box it can really deepen the story. And I wish that more people would understand that.

Unfortunately, few producers appear to think outside of the box when it comes to the representation of women in musical theatre. They are prepared to acknowledge that an all-white cast in this day and age is inappropriate and not a true reflection of a multi-cultural society and audience. Yet they do not see that the way women are depicted onstage is just as offensive to a contemporary audience who may not so readily regard their perceived difference as a weakness. Perhaps, in terms of gender inequality on creative teams, the problem stems from familiarity. People are more familiar with a male director or musical director. They are familiar with the body language, the tone of voice, the gestures. The female version of the same is confronting because it is unfamiliar. But again, that is assuming that the male way of doing things is the correct way and that the female way is not just different, it is wrong. Some producers/directors and audience members subconsciously want to see white actors in leading roles because it is what they are used to seeing. It is what they are familiar with. Yet when they are presented with a black actor playing Enjrolas (Kyle Scatliffe, in the current Broadway production of *Les Misérables*) or Audra McDonald as Lizzie, they accept it. They follow the emotional journey of the show and still engage with the character in exactly the same way as they would if it was a white actor onstage.

If audience members can rethink their expectations of characters in terms of race, why do we assume they cannot do the same with female roles? Do we know for a fact that no one in the audience wants to see a strong, independent, free-spirited leading lady? If the first step toward shifts in gender perception were implemented, then over time, as has been proved with so-called blind casting, difference becomes just that. Different. But not wrong. Melanie La Barrie notes:

> The role that I play right now in Matilda is the librarian. And in the drawings in the Roald Dhal books she wasn't portrayed as a black Caribbean woman, but they wanted that flavor … and I was in. But I think that's what I bring. I don't think it's my blackness that makes the role, or the fact that they're being color-blind, I think it's a way of being.… I think that when it comes to fantasy there is color blind casting, but I am not sure—and I might be wrong—I am not sure that there is color-blind casting in things that aren't based in fantasy. So therefore I don't know if it happens. I don't know if it happens for real, you know? Maybe it does and I'm just not aware of it, or part of it.

While positive steps are being taken to address the lack of actors of race being cast in musicals, nothing is being done to address the lack of assertive women's roles onstage or the lack of women on creative teams. *Matilda the Musical*—a show blatantly aimed at little girls, and starring a number of them, was created entirely by men. *Charlie and the Chocolate Factory* premiered last year in London, also with an all-male creative team. The West End show *Made in Dagenham*,[11] about women in a factory striking for equal pay, has a female choreographer in an otherwise all-male creative team (which I find so astounding as to be almost laughable—men know so much about fighting for equality). The Richard Eyre revival of *The Pajama Game* currently in the West End did not have one single woman on the production team. Ditto *Dirty Rotten Scoundrels*, *Billy Elliot*, and the revival of *Miss Saigon*. At least *The Commitments* had a female choreographer. Let me just remind you that this is the West End in 2015, not 1954. (Actually, women were better represented in the choreography department in 1954 than they are now.)

Broadway fares slightly better with directors Susan Stroman and Leigh Silverman for *Bullets Over Broadway* and *Violet* respectively. Lynn Ahrens wrote the book for *Rocky* (which also had a female choreographer), but Marsha Norman was the only woman on the creative team on *The Bridges of Madison County*. The Idina Menzel vehicle *If/Then* has an all-male creative team,[12] as does *Cabaret*, *Newsies*, and the forthcoming Sting venture *The Last Ship*. The last two shows tell male stories, so a heavy male presence is understandable. (I didn't say forgivable; I said understandable.) The creative department on the Carol King musical *Beautiful* is male heavy and the only female creative representative on *Kinky Boots* is Cyndi Lauper, a woman whose success in the rock world gives her sufficient credentials to be taken seriously as a composer. So while there is an energized debate and action happening around the lack of actors of race onstage and we acknowledge that a show about an ethnic community needs representatives from that culture on the creative team, a show about women can still be conceived, written, and directed by men and no one questions it. Susan H. Schulman notes:

> I have—probably—a bit more insight into … what would motivate a woman to do certain things. Just like I think a man would have a bit more insight into what would motivate a man to do certain things.

I'm still reeling at the idea of a show about the instigation of the Equal Pay Act in the U.K. being written and directed by men. Am I really the only person who queries the integrity behind that?

Again, I pose the question, why does political correctness not cross over into gender? Why are stereotypical images of women still populating musicals when similar race stereotypes would not be allowed? The same men who are patting themselves on their backs for casting ethnic actors in roles usually played by white actors, continue to excuse themselves from the room when the gender issue is raised. If it ever is. Anneke Harrison notes:

> "I think if a bunch of creative women were putting together a show they would—well, I hope they would—have some real female characters, I hope they would do that. But I don't think they'd sit around agonizing, "Have we got a genuine male voice? Have we been fair to men? Are we stereotyping the male role?" They wouldn't give it a second thought. And should they? Or should they just portray men as women see them, or as they want them to be?

In 1990 actors took to the streets on Broadway to protest about Jonathan Pryce playing a Eurasian in *Miss Saigon* and the portrayal of the Asian girls onstage. Twenty years later and no one is protesting about men playing women's roles in drag, or the way the women are portrayed, or shows about women and aimed at women being created by men. I find that sad, because it means we either do not see it, or we do not care. Christine Toy Johnson notes:

> We're ostensibly on the same page about reflecting the world in a realistic way, but everyone passes the buck. It's "Oh, it's the playwrights, they don't want to see it. It's the directors. It's the casting directors. It's the producers. It's the actors—they're just not showing up." It's this conversation that we have over and over and over. And I can almost predict the outcome. It's always back on us. "Actors are not showing up to auditions." And I say, really? I don't believe you. Because you cannot put the onus on us. We might not be showing up to open calls for the ensemble when we have built a career playing leading roles in regional theatre, or even off Broadway. But on Broadway there's that feeling of … well, you should just take what we give you. And there are people who say, well I've built a career—a good career—and I think that I deserve to … be seen or considered. And then there's the issue of access. You know, you do get seen but you're not really being taken seriously. And you can tell. Then there's

the default position as well, "Oh, we cast the best people for the role." And I always argue—well that's [subjective]. What goes into the definition of "the best person for the role"? Does that mean the best race or ethnicity that fits your vision? And that's something we need to address. Perception and how we shift perception.… I don't think anybody will say that they are racist or that they intend to cast with that in mind. But I do think that there are a lot of people who have certain perceptions in mind … if I cast a person of color in that particular role, that then says something that I'm not intending to say. I think there is definitely that perception.

And exactly the same attitude exists towards women. "I'm not a misogynist. I just don't want a female director." Because she is not a man. She is different. And that difference is still perceived as less.

To return to the loathsome Higgins and his arrogant question, "Why can't a woman be more like a man?" Let's imagine for one second he was posing the question with regards to race. "Why can't a black man be more like a white?" Would we laugh? More to the point, would it ever even be allowed onstage? Of course not. Because it is, quite simply, offensive.

Why can't a woman be more like a man? Because she isn't one. She is different. And trust me, that's not a bad thing.

Notes

1. Book by Michael Stewart; lyrics by Lee Adams; music by Charles Strouse.
2. Gottfried, Martin, and Lory Frankel. 1979. *Broadway Musicals*. New York: H.N. Abrams.
3. Book and lyrics by Tony Kushner; music by Jeanine Tesori.
4. Book by Joseph Stein; lyrics by Stephen Schwartz; music by Charles Strouse.
5. Book by William F. Brown; lyrics and music by Charlie Smalls.
6. Book by Ossie Davis, Phillip Rose and Peter Udell; lyrics by Peter Udell; music by Gary Geld.
7. Book by Robert Nemiroff and Charlotte Zaltzberg; songs by Judd Woldin and Robert Brittan; based on the play *A Raisin in the Sun* by Lorraine Hansberry.
8. Book George C Wolfe; lyrics by Susan Birkenhead; music by Jelly Roll Morton and Luther Henderson.
9. Book by Marsha Norman; lyrics and music by Brenda Russell, Allee Willis and Stephen Bray.
10. Book by Joe Di Pietro; Lyrics by Joe Di Pietro and David Bryan; music by David Bryan.
11. Book by Richard Bean; lyrics by Richard Thomas; music by David Arnold, directed by Rupert Gould.
12. Book and lyrics by Brian Yorkey; directed by Michael Grief.

7

A Secretary Is Not a Toy

Revivals and the Contemporary Audience

I had never seen a production of *South Pacific*, I had just been in it. And of course, because it was my first show I was really excited, and I didn't even think about what it was about, I was just in it.… So this past revival—a couple of years ago—and I sat downstairs and I thought, wow, I've never actually seen this show before. Huh, let me see. Oh. It's all about people hating Asian people.

—Christine Toy Johnson

Revivals of older musicals, particularly those written by "the greats," are a staple of the diet offered to audiences on Broadway and the West End. Producers continue to demonstrate their nervousness of new musicals by returning to the tried and tested hits time after time. Musical theatre is a business, remember, and producers are in it to make money. A new production of *The Sound of Music* is a much safer bet than risking a hefty investment on an unknown entity. For the inexperienced theatre-goer, a familiar show and recognizable songs are a more enticing product than a new musical, especially when the price of the ticket is taken into account. The majority of the audience wants to know what they are going to get before spending hundreds of dollars for a night out. Some producers will argue that it is necessary to revive older shows because there are simply not enough good, new shows being written. No doubt John Kander, Steven Flaherty, Lynn Ahrens, Adam Guettel, Michael John LaChiusa, Jason Robert Brown, Jeanine Tesori, and William Finn—among others—would take issue with that, arguing that the shows are being written but they are not being produced. It's an argument that goes around in circles. Writers create new works, but producers are too fearful of losing money to put those shows on. Consequently, the writers are denied the experience deemed necessary to write the "great" works favored by producers, because the only way they can learn from their previous shows is by having them produced. In the end, it comes down to what will make producers money, and both Cameron Mackintosh and Andrew Lloyd Webber have staged revivals when they were in need of a hit.

While I am in complete agreement that Rodgers and Hammerstein, Lerner and Loewe, Frank Loesser, Cole Porter, and Irving Berlin wrote some truly wonderful musicals, I am not so convinced that all of their shows can withstand scrutiny from a contemporary audience. As discussed in previous chapters, musicals reflect the prevailing attitudes in society at the time in which they were written. The passing of years has introduced more enlightened attitudes towards race and gender, and some of the views expressed in the classic shows are now considered, at best, outdated, at worst, offensive.

Oklahoma!, for example, premiered in 1943 and was adapted from a play, *Green Grow the Lilacs*, that was written over a decade earlier. The musical is set in 1906, and the scene where the ranch hands bid for a girl to take to the dance may well be a true depiction of dating methods in 1906. The subtext of the scene—that of ownership, and women belonging to men—was not so far removed from attitudes towards women in 1943, so it was unlikely that audiences seeing the show for the first time would find the scene offensive. Seventy years later, however, the entire auction scene and the message it conveys cannot be viewed as anything other than distasteful to a contemporary audience.

Unfortunately, the same can be said of a number of the older shows that were adapted from a book or a play that already contained entrenched attitudes towards men's and women's behavior and their place in world, or towards ethnic minorities. Since these musicals premiered, society has moved on to such a degree that an outward display of what we now class as chauvinism, racism, homophobia, or anything that contravenes our new obsession with political correctness will come under scrutiny in a way it never used to, and rightly so. In 1934, the characters of Ching and Ling, the Chinese gamblers in *Anything Goes,* may well have elicited laughs from the audience. Today, the characters are more likely to be condemned as one-dimensional and insulting stereotypes.

So how then do we stage the classic musicals in 2015, when we know certain lyrics or characterizations have the potential to offend? Do we attack the script with a pair of scissors and simply cut the auction scene in *Oklahoma!* and all derogatory references to Pacific Islanders in *South Pacific?* But then the rest of the show makes no sense. Where would we even start with *The King and I* and its patronizing, colonialist view of the inhabitants of Southeast Asia? Should directors stage these shows as "period pieces" and assume that an audience realizes that the attitudes expressed onstage belong to a distant past? Or should producers eschew them in an acknowledgement that attitudes have moved on to such an extent that it is no longer acceptable to have these misogynistic or racist views expressed within modern popular culture? I agree wholeheartedly with Christine Toy Johnson when she says, *"I think there are some shows that really don't need to be done any more."* I, personally, would cite *The King and I, Flower Drum Song, Carousel, South Pacific,* and *My Fair Lady* as obvious examples of those. Not because I lack respect for the achievements of the great composer/lyricists, but because I harbor unease that some of their shows serve now only to reinforce a racial and/or gender stereotype, a stereotype that we, as a society, are endeavoring to move away from.

But if we have moved on from outdated attitudes towards gender and race, why do revivals continue to be so popular? Why do audiences still laugh at the chauvinistic Higgins or applaud the clownish King of Siam? Perhaps the answer to that lies within the audience demographic. I know if I was taking my mother to the theatre, *The King and I, Flower Drum Song,* or *My Fair Lady* would be exactly the kind of show she would want to see—something she regards as "safe," its familiarity reassuring. The majority of the audience for revivals is an older generation, and they flock to those shows for nostalgic reasons. They know the songs, they know there will be no offensive language, nudity, or sexual preferences displayed onstage that they prefer not to think about. Possibly, they are not even aware that the views expressed by some of the characters onstage are now considered offensive, because they are of a generation that grew up with those attitudes. Fair enough. Should they really be denied the opportunity to see their favorite shows because feminist sensibilities or political correctness has gone into overdrive? They may not notice that the depiction of the King of Siam is less than respectful; they are there to see him sing "Shall We Dance" with Mrs. Anna. Despite their age, the audience for revivals shows no sign of flagging. But where does that leave the new, younger audience who yearn for more progressive shows, or the middle generation who have grown up with musical theatre, and love it, but really don't want to hear Julie Jordan make excuses for Billy Bigelow's violence one more time? Beth Williams notes:

> There was an Encores production—a three-day concert version—of Promises, Promises, probably in 1995[1] ... and the critics at the time talked about how in this day and age you just can't represent women like that on stage. It's too

offensive. I read that and we talked about it, because here we were 15 years later producing that very show. Yet it somehow didn't resonate the same way for any of us. Why was that?

The revival of *Promises, Promises*[2] that Ms. Williams is referring to opened on Broadway in April 2010. Yet 15 years after initially raising concerns about the portrayal of women in the show, none of the critics—including the few female ones—appeared to have a problem with the way women were represented. That could possibly be due to the distance of time and a belief that society has moved so far away from those attitudes that to raise an issue about them now is redundant, even passé. Elisabeth Vincentelli in the *New York Post* described the show as "fun" (there's that word again), and compared it to a "dessert cart." *USA Today*'s Elysa Gardner seemed more concerned with frocks and hair, than feminism. Elysa Gardner notes:

> Those who come for the kitsch won't be disappointed. Like last year's revival of *Bye Bye Birdie*, this *Promises* revels in pre-cultural revolution fashion follies. Bruce Pask's brightly colored dress suits and Tom Watson's gravity-defying hair and wig design winkingly evoke working women of a more, um, innocent era.

Innocent?? 1962?

In 1997, when reviewing the Encores production of *Promises, Promises,* Ben Brantley commented in the *New York Times* on the "groaning, antiquated quality to many of the sex jokes." He also noted, "There's no attempt to disguise the sexism here. The women are unequivocally girls, expensive pleasure toys in silver Courrèges-style mini-dresses." Yet in 2010 none of the critics picked up on the misogyny rife in the show, a show which unashamedly depicts women as playthings for men. The revival added two Bacharach songs that had not been a part of the original 1968 production: "I Say a Little Prayer" and "A House Is Not a Home." Both songs are instantly recognizable and including them in the revival was no doubt an attempt to cash in on the familiarity of the Bacharach catalog. But in 2010, surely the women in the audience are aware that their lives mean more than slapping on lipstick and mascara and dreaming of a man? Remember the discussion about the victim song in Chapter 3? Fran in *Promises, Promises* wails a number about how she is not meant to live alone and that without a man, her house is merely that—a house, not a home. The audience is also treated to "Where Can You Take a Girl?," a song in which the male executives discuss places they can take their secretaries—the type of girl they could never take home—for a "little fun" on a Tuesday night. No, really, it's incredibly respectful. But when placed within the contemporary cultural context, the real reasons behind the 2010 revival of *Promises, Promises* become glaringly apparent.

It seems we have "Mad Men" to thank for the buoyant new production of *Promises, Promises*, receiving its first Broadway revival since its premiere more than 40 years ago. This musical adaptation of Billy Wilder's classic film *The Apartment* has clearly tapped into the '60s era nostalgia so vividly rendered by the AMC television series [Frank Scheck, *The Hollywood Reporter*, April 25, 2010].

This revival appears timed to cash in on the current "Mad Men"–fuelled fascination with the naughty 1960s workplace. But one of the paradoxes of "Mad Men" mania is that while it has revived interest in corporate cocktails and office affairs, the TV show is so profoundly well-written that it casts a harsh shadow over the failings of some of the era's contemporaneous literature" [Chris Jones, *Chicago Tribune*, April 25, 2010].

And this, from the ever-insightful Ben Brantley—one of the few critics who actually does write a review with an eye on the context.

When *Promises, Promises* was revived by the Encores! series of concerts in 1997, its leering view of secretaries as disposable playthings seemed uncomfortably quaint.... So the announcement last year that *Promises, Promises* was to be remounted on Broadway would have provoked a blanket "What are they thinking?" response, except for one thing: a seductive, styled-to-the-teeth little television show called "Mad Men." Set in a Manhattan advertising agency around the time of the Kennedy presidency, this AMC series made it safe for early 1960s sexism to come out of the closet, provided it was treated with anthropological distance and mouth-watering period glamour."

Brantley hit the nail on the head. The overt, leering sexism of "Mad Men" was overlooked in the heady enthusiasm for retro kitsch. More conversations took place around water coolers concerning the costuming and set design of the TV show than about the gender inequalities still rife in the workplace. *Promises, Promises* was merely cashing in on the prevailing passion for all things 1960s. As the reviews for the musical unanimously proved, the outdated depiction of women barely raised an eyebrow amidst the fervor for a pretty secretary shaking cocktails and trysts in the stationery cupboard. And we were far enough away from the era in which it was set and written to understand that it was a joke.

"Mad Men" aside, if we agree that we have moved on from the archaic values represented in *Promises, Promises* or *How to Succeed in Business* and acknowledge that these show have the potential to offend, why revive them? Because, it appears that as far as producers are concerned, "When in doubt, stage a revival."

The Royal National Theatre in London has presented *Carousel* (1992), *Lady in the Dark* (1997), *Oklahoma!* (1998), *My Fair Lady* (2001), and *South Pacific* (2001)—*Oklahoma!*, *South Pacific* and *My Fair Lady* all directed by Trevor Nunn. *The Sound of Music* was on Broadway in 1998 (directed by

Susan H. Schulman), and Andrew Lloyd Webber produced a hugely successful West End production in 2006, in which the star of the show was chosen by a television talent quest. In 1999, Michael Blakemore directed the Broadway production of *Kiss Me, Kate* which appeared in London two years later. *Seven Brides for Seven Brothers* was staged at the Goodspeed Opera House in 2005 directed by Greg Ganakas in a production so far removed from the original, with a rewritten book, new numbers and new choreography, that one wonders why they didn't just do a different show.

Daniel Radcliffe was recruited to star in *How to Succeed in Business Without Really Trying...*" on Broadway in 2011. *South Pacific* was revived at the Lincoln Center New York in 2008, directed by Bartlett Sher, and transferred to London in 2011. *Porgy and Bess* was renamed *The Gershwins' Porgy and Bess* for a West End production in 2006 (again directed by Trevor Nunn—clearly the expert in revivals), and another—more controversial—production using the same title came out of the American Repertory Theatre in 2011, directed by Diana Paulus.

The King and I is currently touring Australia and was in the West End in 2000. On Broadway, Lou Diamond Phillips played the King of Siam in 1996, and a national tour of the U.S. went on the road in 2004. Director Hal Prince revived *Showboat* on Broadway in 1994 and London in 1998. Francesca Zambello directed a large-scale production at London's Royal Albert Hall in 2006. *Camelot* was last seen on Broadway in 1993, but a U.S. touring production was on the road in 2007. Bernadette Peters played Annie Oakley on Broadway in *Annie Get Your Gun* in 1999 (interestingly, the song "I'm an Indian Too" was dropped from this production). In 2009 there was a U.K. tour of the show starring Jane Horrocks. *Guys and Dolls* had an "uninspired"[3] Broadway production directed by Des McAnuff in 2009. London had previously seen Ewan McGregor as Skye Masterson in director Michael Grandage's fairly humorless production in London in 2005. *West Side Story* was restaged by Arthur Laurents on Broadway in 2007 and the international touring company continues to blaze a trail across Europe. Other perennial favorites—*Fiddler on the Roof, Damn Yankees, The Music Man, Hello, Dolly!* and *The Pajama Game* regularly pop up on both sides of the Atlantic.

Clearly, there is an eager audience for these old favorites, or producers would not be constantly rehashing them. But if musical theatre is a reflection of contemporary society, then are these revivals actually saying that we prefer to look to the past rather than to the future? That there is, in fact, no future for the genre because the audience is of a generation that will only go to a Rodgers and Hammerstein revival? Yes, that audience certainly exists, but it is not the only audience. Casting Ewan McGregor in *Guys and Dolls* in London and Daniel Radcliffe in *How to Succeed* on Broadway was a blatant attempt to entice a younger audience in to see an old show. Why not give them a new show instead, one that reflects the society they live in and the values they subscribe to? It would have been interesting to survey the younger audience members who attended both of those shows to find out if they had come for the show or the star. I suspect they were there for the star and couldn't care less about the show. So why not put Daniel Radcliffe in a new musical and give emerging writers a fighting chance?

My issue with the producers who favor revivals over a new show (apart from their spectacular lack of imagination) comes from a personal suspicion that the producers or directors do not understand why the shows may cause offense. They see nothing wrong with the depiction of women in *How to Succeed in Business* or in the portrayal of the of the Pacific Islanders in *South Pacific*. What I consider even worse is when they admit the show *might* now offend *some* people, but they go ahead and present it anyway, assuming that the older audience will still come.

There is another reason why producers may favor revivals over new shows. They no longer have the experience, the knowledge of the genre, or the expertise to guide a new musical from conception to Broadway. The number of people calling themselves musical theatre producers these days is really quite astounding. Many of them appear to be confusing the word producer with investor. Putting up money for a show does not necessarily mean you have the skills to be a guiding and creative influence in that show. All too often, the "producers" no longer have any real experience in musical theatre. Their knowledge of the repertoire is often limited to the older shows and probably stems from their memory of the film versions. And I'm afraid I require a lot of convincing that many of the people now calling themselves "producers" have an abiding interest in the development and survival of the genre. Their passion is not for the genre itself, it is for the money they believe is there to be made from the industry. Nina Lannan notes:

> One of the things that gives Broadway its incredible vitality, and it's something that should be treasured … is that anyone can be a Broadway producer. As long as you have the money to put on your show, and as long as you can get a theatre to put it in … anyone can produce on Broadway. And you can hire us as the general manager, and we will bring industry expertise to the project.… We work for producers who have never produced on Broadway and we work for producing veterans … so while it does give Broadway its vitality … it also means you have people entering this world who don't know anything about producing theatre. And sometimes it works and sometimes it doesn't.

The great producers of musicals—Hal Prince, Cy Feuer, George Abbott and David Merrick—knew the industry inside out. They knew when a show wasn't working and they knew why. If they couldn't fix it themselves, they knew the person to bring in who could. They understood the value of an out-of-town tryout—sometimes up to three months—when the script was rewritten, songs added or removed, choreography changed, cast members replaced—anything it took to get the show working before it hit Broadway. But by and large, the producers with a passion for and an innate understanding of musical theatre as an art form have disappeared, replaced by money people who have no earthly conception of what it takes to create a successful musical because they have never truly immersed themselves in the genre. They have never heard of the "I want" number or the "eleven o'clock" number and completely disregard the blueprint established by the greats, because they have the misconception that creating a musical is easy. Throw together a few songs—not necessarily of a uniform style—hire someone with no experience of the art form to fill in a few lines of dialogue, bring in a director who regards musical theatre as slightly beneath him but a good way to pay off the mortgage, and off we go. See you at the Tonys.

Two recent high-profile examples of inexperienced producers collaborating with non-musical theatre creatives were Broadway's *Spider-Man: Turn Off the Dark* and Australia's *King Kong: The Musical*. The problems identified by many of the critics who reviewed both of these shows were mainly issues around a weak script and songs, and the fusion of the two. Writing for theguardian.com (June 17, 2013), Vicky Frost described *King Kong* as having "little cohesion" and "confused both musically and narratively—packed full of ambition and innovation, but unable to pull its constituent parts into one satisfying whole." Kate Herbert in *The Herald Sun* (June 15, 2013) echoed Frost's remarks, noting that the show suffered from "lackluster dialogue" and a lack of a "consistent voice and unified vision."

Two further reviewers drew attention to the confused nature of the production.

> Unsurprisingly, the amalgamation of these disparate resources caused the show's musical content to feel disjointed. The subsequent absence in stylistic cohesion made it difficult to ascertain the show's musical voice [Peter Burch, *The Australian*, June 16, 2013].

> Two main problems stand out: the disjointed transitions from stage action to song, and the fact that some numbers sound pretty without doing hard yards dramatically.... A somewhat flimsy book is the show's weakest link.... [Cameron Woodhead, *The Age, Sydney Morning Herald*, June 15, 2013].

Production company Global Creatures clearly learned little from the *King Kong* experience (nor, one assumes, read the reviews) as almost identical complaints of inconsistency and confusion rained down upon *Strictly Ballroom: The Musical,* directed by film director Baz Luhrmann.

Alex Needham in *The Guardian* (April 13, 2014) referred to *Strictly Ballroom: The Musical* as "a collection of gaudy set pieces," pointing out that the involvement of a number of different composers gave the show "an identity crisis." In the *Sunday Telegraph,* Jo Litson echoed Needham's concerns, describing the score as a "mish mash," stating "the songs rarely deepen character, heighten emotion or advance the plot as they do in a good musical, while the lyrics are at best, ordinary."

Clive Paget displayed a deeper understanding of musical theatre form than either Luhrmann or Global Creatures combined, with his observation:

> So what should Luhrmann have done? He might have handed it over lock, stock and barrel to an experienced musical theatre team—as was done with the surprisingly successful *Hairspray,* another much-loved film given a new incarnation in musical theatre form. That might have ensured greater cohesion. Or he could have gone properly down the jukebox musical path and shaped the show around a series of "Baz's greatest hits." Again, cohesion would most likely have ensued. As it is, what we have is at best an entertaining hotpotch, at worst, frankly a mess.—Clive Paget, *Limelight,* April 14, 2014

It all sounded eerily similar to the comments that greeted the premiere of *Spider-Man: Turn Off the Dark* in 2011, which Hadley Freeman in *The Guardian* (February 15, 2011) referred to as "a mess," and "baffling in its ineptitude."

In the *Hollywood Reporter* (June 14, 2011) David Rooney was even more scathing:

> *Spider-Man* is the ultimate apotheosis of theme-park product. It's Orlando in New York. And like an experiment of Spidey's nemesis, Dr. Norman Osborn, aka the Green Goblin, it completes the genetic mutation of both musical theatre and of audiences that demand spectacle at any cost. If that cost comes at the expense of nuanced storytelling, emotional involvement and character-enhancing, plot-advancing songs, so be it.... There's nothing that comes close to the complexity or suspense of either the original comics or the popular Sam Raimi movies. So there's no compelling reason for *Spider-Man* to be a musical.

Proof, although no one (particularly at Global Creatures) appears to be listening, that inexperienced producers combining with a creative team that knows little about musical theatre (and cares less) is a recipe for disaster.

What the critics highlighted about these three shows was that they struggled with the very basics of the form they claimed they were redefining. An experienced producer with a passion for musical theatre and a knowledge of the structure of the genre would have been able to identify these issues at an early stage, way before the lack of a unifying style and a poor script ultimately defined the show. The producers of *Spider-Man, King Kong,* and *Strictly Ballroom* were running a marathon before they had learned how to walk. Perhaps if they had started off with a couple of revivals of tried and tested classics, they might have learned something about musical theatre.

With the growing use of technology in musicals—*Spider-Man* and *King Kong* being two obvious examples—production budgets have escalated to a point where the time frame in which to ready a new show for the premiere has shrunk. Time is money, and money—not quality—is the driving factor. (Money on *King Kong,* however, seemed not to be a problem. Three workshops and a six-month rehearsal period, and still the script was described as "confused.")

For productions without a bottomless money pit, the cost of an out-of-town tryout is now almost prohibitive, but a two-week workshop does not produce the same results. And out-of-town tryouts no longer protect the show from the critics who are now prepared to travel hundreds of miles in order to be the first person to savage a new show. The arrival of the internet allows even the most inexperienced audience member to publicly share his views, whether they are qualified to do so or not. Consequently, the preparation of a new show is no longer private. The creative team trying to fix a new show is under constant scrutiny from a blogging and tweeting preview audience who believe they know what the show really needs, because they have seen *Smash.*

Three weeks of previews are now no longer the answer either, when the time and costs involved in reprogramming all the technical equipment to absorb any changes to the show will push the production over budget. *Spider-Man* had 182 previews and the opening night was postponed six times—but the show was held for ransom by technology and by inexperienced producers who refused to appreciate that the scale of the production and the time available to the creatives to stage and fix it, were not commensurate. As demonstrated above, new producers are seldom able to understand when the script is not working and, more importantly, how to fix it. Which is exactly what made the aforementioned great producers, great. They understood that where musical theatre is concerned, the book and the music are more important than the special effects. Granted, Prince, Feuer, Merrick and Abbott did not have the technology available to them that producers have today, but they still had a deeper understanding—gained from years of experience—of what intrinsically makes a show work, or not. And they, not the director, had the final say. The great producers also worked alone or with one, maybe two partners at most. Today, the sheer number of people who take to the stage as producers to accept a Tony award for best musical is staggering.

Nina Lannan outlines why this can be problematic for new shows.

> Now, because of costs and because the environment is so competitive, we have had groups of producers emerge. When you have four, or five, or six producers, it's hard for them to organize to be a strong creative force in the development of the show, thus some of that territory seems to have been ceded to the director.... Sometimes there's one producer on the team who is stronger than the others and will deal with the show creatively.... Sometimes he or she becomes the person all the other producers have to funnel their concerns through.... But still, you're having opinions from ten or twelve people, which sometimes aren't necessarily helpful—they perhaps don't know enough about theatre, or they're at cross purposes among themselves ... since that system is a bit broken, the director becomes the de facto person that is totally in charge of the show creatively. Also, at times producers don't have the knowledge or structure to challenge a director and argue effectively to reduce costs. You can see shows that are hugely expensive and wonder if the director or choreographer had been a little bit challenged, in a good way, might the outcome have been different.

With the combination of inexperienced colleagues, too many cooks, and a megalomaniac director in place, it is little wonder producers favor a revival of a show that has had proven success over a premiere of a new one. A show with songs and a script that already works requires less expertise than one that is facing a premiere. And an older show that does not rely on special effects is cheaper to mount than a new one which does.

To return to the question I asked earlier, how do we overcome the fact that many of the older shows that are regularly revived contain attitudes that are now, to a number of people, offensive? I acknowledge that Frank Loesser was a genius, but can we honestly say that the depiction of women *How to Succeed in Business* and *Guys and Dolls* is a respectful one? Or his portrait of a mail-order bride in *The Most Happy Fella* (1958)? And if it isn't, then why are those shows being revived? On the other hand, can we really abandon *Oklahoma!* when it is credited with changing the entire direction of the musical as an art form? Or *South Pacific*, which, on its 1949 premiere was considered way ahead of its time because of its exploration of racial prejudice? Where would we draw the line if we were to start censoring theatre? Forbid theatre companies to do Shakespeare because Ophelia's neediness is now mildly pathetic, Lady Macbeth is clearly mad and bad, Juliet a victim of statutory rape, and Kate submissive and sacrificial? Do we ban all plays that represent ethnic minorities as oppressed, even if, historically, they were? Do producers have the right to deny audiences the chance to see a show that, in its day, was considered groundbreaking but is now considered questionable because a vocal minority object? At the end of the day, one fact remains. No matter how sexist or racist the show now seems to *some* of us, there is still a large audience out there who wants to see it.

If attitudes towards women in some older shows could now be considered dubious, those towards non-white characters are even more so. Musical theatre has traditionally been the domain of the white male (no changes there, then) and attitudes towards characters of a non-white background were written from a specific viewpoint—that of the dominant, white male. In the same way as the woman's true voice in musicals is displaced by the voice of the male writer, the depiction of black, Asian, or South Pacific peoples is a white person's idea of those particular races. The voice those characters speak with has been imposed on them by someone who has no authentic experience of the culture he is representing. What we get onstage, then, is a caricature drawn from a narrow set of stereotypes—accents and costumes tend to be the defining characteristics, not depth of emotion. We get Annie Oakley, dressed in a white man's version of Native American dress, poking fun at the traditions and culture of an ethnic minority group by singing "I'm an Indian Too." We get the King of Siam behaving like a "barbarian."

As anyone who has seen a revival of *The King and I* (or the highly successful 1956 film) can attest, the King is indeed portrayed as a buffoon. Not just the King, but the entire culture of Siam is mocked and seen through white, colonialist eyes. The King and his wives are portrayed as childlike and simple, and the superiority of the white race is repeatedly reinforced. At least, that is the reading we bestow upon the show from our lofty, enlightened viewing position in 2015. In 1951, audiences were so enraptured with the show that it ran for three years on Broadway and another year on tour. At the time, this was a remarkable achievement—a show that lasted 100 performances was considered to have had a respectable run.

The King and I was based on the 1944 novel *Anna and the King of Siam* by Margaret Landon, and the novel was derived from the memoirs of Anna Leonowens, an Englishwoman who was tutor to the Royal Siamese children in the 1860s. Rodgers and Hammerstein had a duty to remain true to the text, and Leonowens's original memoir is an accurate reflection of how the English (not a race known for their empathy toward other cultures) regarded the inhabitants of the Far East at the time. The fact that Rodgers and Hammerstein made no attempt to broaden that viewpoint is a reflection of society in 1951, which held similar views towards ethnicity and white superiority to that Anna Leonowens displays in her 1860 memoir.

Audiences for *The King and I* were perfectly happy to have an inferior racial stereotype confirmed—it corroborated their belief in themselves as superior. And who could blame Rodgers and Hammerstein for appropriating a culture and a historical figure for our entertainment? They weren't exactly howled down by dissenting voices. If we now long for the other side of the story—a musical based on the King the nation revered—it is only because we are looking at *The King and I* from a contemporary perspective. And that is precisely what makes the show problematic to stage in 2015. We are acutely aware today that the story is being told from a blinkered viewpoint—that of the white colonialist—and the knowledge we now have of the native oppression inherent in English colonialism allows us to see beyond the one-sided viewpoint we are given in the musical. Agreed, the musical is reproducing an attitude that originated in the memoir and subsequent novel, but even knowing that, it does not make the depiction of the King any more acceptable. Perhaps producers are so seduced by the score—who can't hum a few bars from "Shall We Dance," or "Getting to Know You"?—and the potential profits that two star names could bring in that a respectful or authentic portrayal of the Thai race is the least of their concerns. And let's be honest, anyone looking for a respectful or authentic portrayal of Thai culture is hardly likely to buy a ticket to *The King and I*.

In 2011, the American Repertory Theatre in Massachusetts mounted a revival of *The Gershwins' Porgy and Bess*,[4] directed by Diana Paulus (the original folk opera *Porgy and Bess* had been significantly rewritten five years previously for a London production directed by Trevor Nunn). In an acknowledgment that the original script contained language that is now highly offensive and that some of the characters appear one-dimensional, Ms. Paulus brought in Suzan-Lori Parks to revise the script. Changes to the plot, dialogue, score, and characters were explored as the creative team strived to find a means of giving the production more appeal to a contemporary audience. Controversy erupted when Stephen Sondheim wrote a letter to the *New York Times* (August 10, 2011) disputing that the original work was flawed and arguing that "there is a difference between re-interpretation and wholesale rewriting." Sondheim was outraged that anyone would dare tamper with this classic piece (he had raised no objection when Trevor Nunn did the same thing five years earlier) and disagreed that the characters were not fully rounded in the original writing. The controversy continued online, with both sides of the argument winning support, but neither side being victorious outright.

What Ms. Paulus had been astute enough to recognize, however, was that a younger audience would simply dismiss the piece in its original incarnation as racist, due to the language and depiction of African Americans. By revising the work, she was acknowledging that it was a great piece of musical theatre/folk opera that deserved to be seen by a new audience, but she was mindful of the fact that times have changed. Without updating the script and lyrics and absorbing contemporary sensitivities, the original show would now so offend potential audience members that they simply wouldn't buy a ticket. Interestingly, Sondheim raised no objection at the "wholesale rewriting" of *On a Clear Day*, and his letter to the *New York Times* seems to be more of a personal attack on Ms. Paulus than her directorial skills. Perhaps he simply could not get his head around the idea of a woman directing a classic musical:

> Then there is Ms. Paulus's condescension toward the audience. She says, "I'm sorry, but to ask an audience these days to invest three hours in a show requires your heroine be an understandable and fully rounded character." I don't know what she's sorry about, but I'm glad she can speak for all of us restless theatre goers. If she doesn't understand Bess and feels she has to "excavate" the show, she clearly thinks it's a ruin, so why is she doing it? I'm sorry, but could the problem be her lack of understanding, not Heyward's?

It would take a genius to rewrite *Finian's Rainbow*[5] (1947) in a way that would make it palatable to audiences in 2015. Despite a score that contains the hits "How Are Things in Glocca Morra?," and "Look to the Rainbow," this show is rarely revived due to the way the script handles racism—a white, bigoted senator is "demoted" to being black. In the original production, the actor in question donned blackface for his scenes as a black man. This is absolutely unthinkable now, and the 2009 Encores production had the character played by two different actors, one black, one white. If the creators were still around to argue, I'm sure they would protest that the show is actually making a point about the ignorance of racists and that turning a character from a white man into a black man is not saying that one race is inferior to the other, or that being black is a punishment. It happens in order that the character—who is a racist bigot—has no option but to experience the oppression himself that he is guilty of serving up to the black characters he encounters in the show. But it is a telling statement on how sensibilities, yes, even in musical theatre, have changed, to the point where it is widely acknowledged that this show is problematic today.

Susan Stroman notes:

> Sometimes shining a light on what makes people uncomfortable is how you get an audience to examine those attitudes. Take *Show Boat*—the miscegenation scene was ahead of its time. It's still relevant. Watching now, you see how the ugliness comes out of ignorance and fear. And the choreography was another way to look at the color line. The Charleston is a dance created by African Americans and appropriated by white people—Kim's Charleston

shows that. Same with a step like the Cakewalk, which comes from slaves making fun of the plantation dances thrown by the white owners. The chore-ography gave us the chance to show how the African American contribution to music and dance has been dismissed or ignored. I could illustrate those moments using just dance—whoever got it, got it—and it was empowering.

What intrigues me about *Finian's Rainbow, Annie Get Your Gun, The Gershwins' Porgy and Bess, Show Boat, South Pacific,* and *The King and I* is this: If producers and directors are able to recognize that an outdated stance towards race in older musicals is likely to offend members of the audi-ence, why can they not make a similar mental leap where gender is con-cerned?

If we are all in agreement that staging a revival of *Finian's Rainbow* is unlikely to increase a black audience and dispel the notion of theatre as the plaything of white people, then why can we not similarly agree that shows such as *Seven Brides for Seven Brothers*[6] with its assertion that a woman's place is "behind her man" is unlikely to entice teenage girls or the thinking contemporary woman into the theatre? But maybe I have slipped back into the all-too-familiar humorless, separatist mode. It's just a musical, remember? Lighten up. Well, I'm sorry, but faced with another revival of *My Fair Lady* (1956) and an evening of the chauvinistic bullying Higgins, I can't.

"It's a joke," traditionalists cry. It's funny. Really? Who laughs at the description of women as "vacillating, calculating, agitating, maddening and infuriating hags!"? Men who agree. So what the show is really doing is rein-forcing outdated views to the unenlightened audience members who still cling to them. *The King and I* does exactly the same thing. Who laughs when Mrs. Anna refers to the King as "a barbarian"? People who think the white race is superior. So, am I at fault for not being able to relax enough to find Higgins's lyrics amusing, or should producers be more aware that this kind of misogyny is now more likely to alienate a female audience than enrapture it?

Oklahoma!, Carousel, My Fair Lady, Seven Brides for Seven Brothers, and *How to Succeed in Business* are only a handful of the shows written before the rise of the women's movement that present a view of women that is now repugnant. Since the sixties and the rise of feminism, the role of women in society has changed so dramatically as to be virtually unrecognizable from the society into which these shows premiered. While it was perfectly accept-able in the 1950s—funny even—to see women represented onstage as man-mad bimbos, subservient victims and less important than the male characters, contemporary women in the audience might not find Higgins as funny as their grandmothers did, nor offer the same easy forgiveness to the violent

Billy Bigelow as Julie Jordan does in *Carousel*. Am I really the only woman in the audience who bristles at the description of women in *Guys and Dolls* as "broads"?

I know it's a comedy. I am aware it is not reality. But something in me just wishes that we could see fewer shows where the image of women as manipulative, conniving "little broads" is presented as humorous. Or excused as "affectionate." We understand that certain words that refer to a person of another race—words also justified with the "term of affection" explanation— are no longer acceptable. Why do those same rules not apply to women? There is nothing affectionate about being referred to as "some little broad." It's dismissive, contemptuous, and a clear indication that the person singing considers himself superior to the person he is singing about. Substitute any racial slur if it makes my point clearer. Maybe overexposure to musical theatre has diluted my sense humor—it's *Guys and Dolls* for heaven's sake, it's not meant to be taken seriously. But I can't help wondering whether if it was a gay man who was the object of such ridicule—read "fag" instead of "broad"— would the show be quite so enthusiastically revived? Beth Williams notes:

> I've just produced *Promises, Promises* and *How to Succeed in Business*—you know—"A Secretary Is Not a Toy," "Happy to Keep His Dinner Warm"—and neither of those shows have a lot that is good to say about the way women were treated in the workplace. Other than to say it's funny. OK, it might be a little different if it was a serious musical but those two are musical comedies. I really think that today's audience views it so differently. The world has so changed around us, we don't take this behavior seriously any longer. It's just like watching *Mad Men*. You think it's … funny … and you know that the world isn't like that today. "Look how far we've come!"

What Beth Williams is saying is that songs such as "Happy to Keep His Dinner Warm" work for a contemporary audience purely because we understand that times have changed and that we have moved on. The situation and/or lyrics come from another era, and the era itself is now amusing. Part of the attraction of "Mad Men," part of what made it funny, was imagining what would happen if a man behaved in that way toward a woman in the workplace today. And *How to Succeed* and *Promises, Promises* are comedies, not reality. If the scene/song is played sincerely, then hackles (certainly mine) may rise. If the actor and the audience *share* the joke, then it is possible to make this work. We all acknowledge that things have progressed since the lyrics were written, and that's what makes it amusing for a contemporary audience to watch. They laugh at what is now considered as the ridiculousness of the era. That's the theory, anyway. I'm sure the same argument is put forward as justification for "Everybody Ought to Have a Maid" from *A*

Funny Thing Happened on the Way to the Forum. It still doesn't make me laugh.

When the musical is not a comedy—a revival of *Carousel*, for example—there are few opportunities to exploit humor to offset outmoded notions of gender. The second of the Rodgers and Hammerstein canon, *Carousel* premiered in 1945 and was adapted from the 1909 play *Liliom* by Ferenc Molnár. The show was widely anticipated after the resounding success of *Oklahoma!* and audiences and critics were not disappointed. Writing in the *New York Times*, reviewer Brooks Atkinson referred to the show as "a masterpiece" and the show was an immediate, and lasting, hit. The iconic bench scene in which Julie and Billy sing "If I Loved You" is described by Stephen Sondheim as "probably the single most important moment in the revolution of contemporary musicals."[7] The song "You'll Never Walk Alone"—the finale of the show—has taken its place in popular culture in the U.K. as the anthem for Liverpool Football Club, and in 1999, *Time* magazine named *Carousel* as the best musical of the twentieth century. When the show was first revived in New York in 1954, Brooks Atkinson had lost none of his original enthusiasm for the piece.

> *Carousel* has no comment to make on anything of topical importance. The theme is timeless and universal: the devotion of two people who love each other through thick and thin, complicated in this case by the wayward personality of the man, who cannot fulfill the responsibilities he has assumed.... Billy is a bum, but *Carousel* recognizes the decency of his motives and admires his independence.

I find it odd that Atkinson claims the show has nothing to say that is of "topical importance." He rightly acknowledges the theme as "timeless and universal," but he and I obviously perceive different themes in the show. As I see it, *Carousel* is about male violence toward women, and the show makes a comment on how women suffer as a consequence of this male propensity toward physical aggression.

Surely that was as topical in 1954 as it is today? I, personally, don't see the "decency" that Atkinson cites in any of Billy Bigelow's motives. Was Atkinson so impressed with Julie's unswerving devotion to Billy that the fact that he hit her was irrelevant? Atkinson claims *Carousel* admires Billy's "independence," but viewed today, the show also appears to admire—or at least excuse—Billy's violent behavior towards his wife and daughter. In his book *Enchanted Evenings: The Broadway Musical from* Show Boat *to Sondheim*,[8] Geoffrey Block identifies this as the main problem inherent in a revival of *Carousel* today: "In an age increasingly and justifiably less tolerant of wife-beating in any form and for any reason, Billy might be considered a much less wonderful guy than he was in 1945" (p. 174). Indeed he might. And audience members, myself included, may not want our daughters and nieces exposed to the distorted ideals of forgiveness contained in the subtext in this dialogue between Mother and daughter.

> LOUISE: But is it possible, Mother, for someone to hit you hard like that—real loud and hard—and not hurt you at all?
>
> JULIE: It is possible, dear, for someone to hit you—hit you hard—and it not hurt at all.

I know I cannot be the only person who visibly flinches at Julie's response. So, is it simply a case of cutting the line in productions today, or does that remove the whole point of the show, leaving it unbalanced? Retaining the line in contemporary productions gives the impression that domestic abuse is a topic not worthy of our attention—there are other more deserving issues in the show. Undoubtedly it was easier to sideline the subject in 1945, but to dismiss it as irrelevant today—to gloss over it in a show—is disrespectful to women and a complete rejection of any notion of equality in a modern society.

The greatest challenge for any actress playing Julie Jordan is to find a way of revealing to us the strength of the character, when her dialogue and lyrics make us view her in the opposite way—as a victim. Only by playing against what is written can the actress persuade us that this is a woman we should admire and not pity. Susan H. Schulman notes:

> But *Carousel* ... I think you need to understand three different historical perspectives: the period in which the musical is set, the period in which it was written, and the period in which it is being performed. In the period *Carousel* is set, women had to find a way to deal with being treated the way Julie is.... A negotiated equal partnership was not common in marriage. It would not be accurate to time or place. Actually, not even to the time it was written. If you are doing a revival today, you have a modern perspective and see the evolution, so ... there are ways that you can show Julie awakening too: the fact that she doesn't really have to deal with that; that's not something she has to accept any more. She is not a wimp. She's a factory girl. But ... you can't take these shows and pretend they weren't written at a certain time or that they're not set in a certain period, for a reason. I think that needs be the jumping-off point. You must find the resonance for today's audience, completely. Look at *Sweeney Todd*. People would ask me all the time ... how does that resonate to today? And I'd say, excuse me, you've never done something terrible because you've been in love? Maybe you don't chop up pussycats for meat pies, but I bet you've caused great emotional damage.

Interesting that Ms. Schulman talks about finding the resonance to today in the older shows. Does that mean that as a society, we have actually not moved on from the attitudes of the 1950s? If the shows still resonate, is it because we have not evolved as much as we claim? Or is it the old adage of "the more things change, the more they stay the same"?

Composer Richard Rodgers (1902–1979) and lyricist Oscar Hammerstein (1895–1960) were one of the most influential and important musicals theatre writing teams in the history of the genre. Their first show together was *Oklahoma!* in 1943, and their partnership lasted almost 20 years, until Hammerstein's untimely death in 1960. Rodgers and Hammerstein musicals have endured in a way that other shows from the period have not, possibly due to the fact that their six major hits were all made into films. *Oklahoma!* in 1955, and *Carousel* in 1956 both starred Gordon MacRae and Shirley Jones as the romantic leads. Yul Brynner won an Oscar for his role as the King in *The King and I* in the 1956 film, and Deborah Kerr was nominated for best actress. *South Pacific* appeared on screen in 1958, and three years later the now much-criticized, *Flower Drum Song* was released. But it was the phenomenal success of *The Sound of Music* in 1965 that really cemented Rodgers and Hammerstein as household names. The film won five Oscars, including Best Picture and Best Director for Robert Wise, and remains the most financially successful screen adaptation of a musical ever made. The popularity of the film continues today, with cinemas worldwide screening sing-a-long *Sound of Music* nights, when audience members dress up as their favorite characters and are encouraged to shout out lines of dialogue and sing along with the songs. Whatever it was that made Rodgers and Hammerstein shows so appealing has not waned over time.

When the Royal National Theatre in London staged the aforementioned *Carousel* in 1992, director Nick Hytner and independent producer Cameron Mackintosh frequently referred to the production as a "re-examination" rather than a revival. Like Diana Paulus and *The Gershwins' Porgy and Bess*, Hytner and Mackintosh were publicly acknowledging that the show would benefit from some updating if it was to be embraced by a contemporary audience.

Consequently, the score was re-orchestrated, the Agnes de Mille choreography was replaced with a new ballet from Sir Kenneth MacMillan, and the darker themes of the original Molnar script were brought out by Bob Crowley's stark set design. Yet in among all that "re-examination," no one thought to remove the one line of dialogue that now undermines the entire piece—well, undermines it if you are an enlightened human being who understands that there is no excuse for domestic abuse, ever, and that ignoring the problem doesn't make it go away. Maybe, as gay men, Mackintosh and Hytner were so unaware of the enormity of the issue of domestic violence that the line did not jump out at them in quite the same way it does with women. I like to think that if a woman had been on the creative team, the line would have been cut.

> To me, the only way I can look at a revival is to think it's never been done before. Of course, it's been done before, that's why it is what it is, I totally understand that. But me as the director, I have to say this is the first time this show is ever going to be done. What in it appeals to me? If someone had plunked this script down and said, "Susan, we want you to direct *The Music Man*." … Why would I want to direct *The Music Man*? What can I personally find in this story that makes me want to tell it?—Susan H. Schulman

I have to lay my cards on the table here and admit that *My Fair Lady* is one of my least favorite shows in the entire history of musical theatre. To me, it is not only sexist, but racist and classist. I can watch an English premier league football match on TV if I want to see those three qualities on display. I do, however, acknowledge that *My Fair Lady* is a classic and I am certainly not deaf to the brilliance of the score. I also take my hat off to Lerner and Loewe for discovering the musical within Shaw's *Pygmalion* that had previously eluded Rodgers and Hammerstein. My problem, I suppose, is that I get so fixated on Higgins's controlling behavior and misogyny that I miss Eliza's blossoming as a woman of spirit. To me, it is a show about men—Higgins, Doolittle, and Freddie have all the best numbers—and about a feisty woman being tamed. But I am humble enough to acknowledge that I am in the minority. Audiences love it. And who am I to argue with box office returns?

Prior to the 2001 opening of the Royal National Theatre production, directed by Trevor Nunn, critic Kate Kellaway discussed the character of Eliza Doolittle in an article in *The Observer*.[9]

> Eliza has been hailed as a feminist heroine, a first cousin to Nora in Ibsen's *The Doll's House*. Diana Rigg played her this way in the 1974 production directed by John Dexter. And Liz Robertson, who played the role in *My Fair Lady* opposite Tony Britton in the late seventies, still champions Eliza for her "courage, her fierce ambition to better herself. The suffragettes would have admired her."

The suffragettes may well have admired Eliza, but would the Eliza of *My Fair Lady* have gone on a hunger strike for votes for women? I doubt it. All her actions are entirely selfish and based around self-improvement. Eliza wants a better life for herself, not for women in general. Actually, that outlook fits in perfectly with the current "me" generation of young women who are Eliza's age—the generation wooed by advertisers with reassurances that "you're worth it." Perhaps that explains the apparent resonance of the show with audiences today. And if she is a first cousin to Nora, then *My Fair Lady* is a sister to *Kiss Me, Kate*. Both shows are adapted from a classic play and feature "troublesome" women mending their ways and submitting to arrogant, bullying men.

Both shows manage to dodge the "sexist" accusation by exhorting us to laugh at the antics of the chauvinistic men, rather than be outraged, and ask us to be thankful when both women—Kate and Eliza—do finally learn how to do as they are told. Their submission, we are asked to believe, comes out of their love for their men. And at the end of the day, it's their choice.

In the same article on Eliza Doolittle in *The Observer*, Kate Kellaway goes on to say:

> Nowadays, I find myself as much discomforted as amused by Higgins's merry misogyny.... Worst of all, I suspect Shaw of being on Higgins's side to a disagreeable degree. I fear he enjoys the shaming aspect of the experiment (how to turn cabbage leaf into cabbage rose), but at least he had the grace to give Eliza the temperament (as opposed to a fully realized character) with which to win her audience's heart.

Lerner and Loewe manage to get away with the blustering and thoroughly disagreeable Higgins by bestowing upon Eliza enough pluck and determination that she can never be mistaken for a victim. Higgins, therefore, cannot be a bully, and we are seduced into believing it is a fair fight. It is not Eliza I have the problem with—if she is happy to fetch his slippers, that's entirely up to her. It's not even the show itself, which, I admit, has moments of genius—the Ascot Gavotte, "I'm Getting Married in the Morning." It is Higgins and the fact that Eliza returns to him. I loathe the fact that Lerner and Loewe appear to be exhorting us to actively desire a match between Higgins and Eliza—I could think of no worse fate for her. And neither could Shaw himself, who, during the original run of *Pygmalion* in 1914, professed to be furious at the romanticism introduced by the actors into the ambiguous final scene. Shaw repeatedly avowed that marriage to Higgins was the antithesis of a happy ending for Eliza. But musical theatre is steeped in romance—or distorted male perspectives of heterosexual love—and *My Fair Lady* gives us the ending we are all, apparently, hoping for. Why would we be glad that a spirited, intelligent, and determined young woman would return to a self-obsessed, mother-fixated, controlling, ill-mannered man, 40 years her senior, who has not exhibited one moment of kindness, empathy, or concern for her throughout the previous three hours? The fact that it is Eliza who comes back, not Higgins who goes looking for her, indicates that he has learned nothing from the entire experience. It's a good thing she is a woman and therefore so easy to forget, because he is not exactly rushing out to find her.

I admit I am missing something—the show ran for six years on Broadway and was undoubtedly the most popular musical of its era. I just don't understand the appeal of it today. There is only one thing that would make me go and see a new production of *My Fair Lady:* a female creative team. I believe a female director would be less amused by Higgins and have more empathy with Eliza. Maybe we would even see a return to Shaw's more credible ending and do away with the dewy-eyed romanticism that serves only to benefit Higgins.

The sibling of *My Fair Lady,* Cole Porter's *Kiss Me, Kate* is another favorite for revivals. This show has the advantage of being a show within a show—*The Taming of the Shrew* within *Kiss Me, Kate.* "A group of strolling players" perform Shakespeare's play, but it is the players themselves—in particular Lilli and Fred—around whom the action of *Kiss Me, Kate* revolves. As actors in the touring company, they play the roles of Kate and Petruchio in *Taming of the Shrew,* while offstage they engage in an on/off romantic liaison. As with any contemporary production of Shakespeare's "The Taming of the Shrew," Kate's final speech—rendered in the musical in a song—creates a serious challenge for feminists.

In the show, Kate/Lilli comes freely to Petruchio/Fred, but she sings lyrics which are hard to interpret as anything other than degrading to women. Is *Kiss Me, Kate* therefore a sexist musical that has no place in contemporary theatre? Surprisingly, no, I don't believe it is. I believe it comes down to the direction and a contemporary approach to the piece. If we are sufficiently engaged by the stormy romance of Lilli and Fred, then what they say as the characters of Kate and Petruchio becomes almost irrelevant. The lyrics saying how "simple" women are may indeed make us wince, but seeing the song played out, with the foreknowledge of Lilli's and Fred's tempestuous relationship, we understand what Lilli is really saying to Fred with this song. She is not submitting; she is apologizing and professing her love for him. If the director has done a good job, the audience understands that the chances of Lilli cradling Fred's foot offstage are so remote as to be laughable. Kate does it for Petruchio as part of the show they are performing to their own audience, not the audience witnessing *Kiss Me, Kate.* That is the joke that the audience is being asked to collude in.

In *My Fair Lady,* however, we are left in no doubt that Eliza will continue to fetch Higgins's slippers and allow herself to be dominated by him once the curtain falls. Her meek return indicates that her earlier outburst was an aberration and will not happen again. Unlike Lilli and Fred, Eliza loses her backbone when Higgins is around and allows her temperament to be suppressed. There is no way of updating *My Fair Lady* for a contemporary audience, mainly because so few people acknowledge that there is anything wrong with it in the first place.

And my absolute final word on *My Fair Lady*: well, it's not mine. Jonathan Pryce played Higgins in the 2001 National Theatre production and gave an interview to *The Telegraph* journalist Jasper Rees,[10] in which he shared his enlightened thoughts on Rex Harrison playing Higgins.

> [Pryce] mentions reading Patrick Garland's hilarious book, *The Incomparable Rex*, about directing Rex Harrison in the Broadway revival of *My Fair Lady*. Harrison was uniformly unpleasant to his various Elizas. "You think what a shit Rex Harrison was, and as you do it you think, 'I think he had something; maybe he was right.'"

Need I say more?

Roundabout Theatre Company's 2007 production of *110 in the Shade* achieved a contemporary feel without rewriting any of the script or updating lyrics. The show dates from 1963 and is steeped in the patriarchal values of society in the early 1960s, but the production—almost effortlessly—transcended these viewpoints and felt modern, purely because of the mixed-race cast. From the moment the first characters appeared onstage, the audience knew it was a contemporary production of an older show, because current sensibilities, in terms of cultural awareness, were visible onstage. It was then relatively easy to overlook the outdated attitudes towards women in the script, because it was so obviously a modern production of an older work. We forgave the song *Old Maid* because a giant leap forward had been made in another area. Beth Williams notes:

> But … I don't think you can change the writing and have shows still work the way they worked originally. If you try and … update it, you ruin the show. See, if you didn't have Rosemary singing "Happy to Keep His Dinner Warm," then you wouldn't really have the right character playing across from the young climber … the guy who, if taken seriously, is really being nothing but manipulative. But he charms you because it's all fun. Musical comedy. You have to have Rosemary to make that work…. And I think if you start tampering with that … no.

One of the most pressing issues facing the creative team of a revival is the question of whether or not to update the script and lyrics. As discussed earlier, *The Gershwins' Porgy and Bess* was updated in an attempt to attract a new audience and to tackle the racism implicit in a script from an era less culturally sensitive than our own. But there is always the danger that in updating the musical, the essence of the show—what it was originally built upon—will get lost. If a director was, for example, to remove every racial slur in *West Side Story* as a nod to political correctness, the audience would not understand the anger and frustration emanating from the Puerto Rican Sharks. In some instances, updating or reviving a musical to accommodate contemporary sensibilities, only succeeds in dissipating the overall impact of the show.

Melanie La Barrie notes:

> I did *The Sunshine Boys* in Leeds and ... we had all these old vaudevillian characters, one of them being a character in blackface. Now it was just a moment ... in terms of the story.... However, somebody came to see it and said, "you can't have a blackface character in there, because it will offend black people." Well, I was in the show and I wasn't offended by it, because it was telling the story in the time, in the language of that time ... in the way that it is supposed to be told.... So then it is not our place to change it. We are story-tellers. We are also story makers, so if we were to make one today then no, that language is not acceptable. However, this is a story that was told then. And I don't think it is right for us to try to sanitize history, because you know what? Black history, black people need to be proud of their struggle. We need to be proud of how hard it was. If we're going to tell that story then we have to make people feel uncomfortable hearing it.

When playwright David Henry Hwang first proposed a rewrite of Rodgers and Hammerstein's *Flower Drum Song,* many wondered where on earth he would start to address the political incorrectness rife throughout this story of the immigrant Chinese community in San Francisco. Although Hwang was given permission to rewrite dialogue, he was not allowed to change lyrics—which more or less defeated the purpose of the entire exercise. Regardless of how cutting-edge Hwang's dialogue was, the show still had to contend with songs such as "Chop Suey," "Grant Street" and the all-time favorite of the drag queen circuit, "I Enjoy Being a Girl." Hwang and his collaborator, Robert Longbottom, subsequently found themselves in the unenviable position of trying to fashion an updated version of the show that remained faithful to the spirit of the original C.Y. Lee novel, dealt with contemporary themes such as assimilation and loss of traditional values, portrayed the Chinese American community—and women—in a realistic and complex way while retaining outdated lyrics. It's difficult to see how anyone thought this was a production that could work. The revival lasted only five months on Broadway, and the critics were not kind. While applauding the creative team's "honorable intentions," Ben Brantley in the *New York Times* referred to *Flower Drum Song* as "terminally out-of-date." As Christine Toy Johnson articulates, "I think there are some shows that really don't need to be done any more." This would appear to be the case in point.

An easier, although more superficial, way of "updating" a show is to simply remove it from the era in which it is set and place it in contemporary society. This approach is one favored by less able or less intelligent directors and/or producers and very often makes the entire premise of the show ridiculous.

Giving Charity a mobile phone in *Sweet Charity* (as I saw happen in a recent production) makes the rest of the show implausible. She would have rung for help when Charlie mugged her in Central Park, and instead of singing "If My Friends Could See Me Now," she would ring and tell them exactly where she was and with whom. She'd probably post a selfie on Facebook.

Even a show as supposedly "contemporary" as Sondheim's *Company* (1970) does not convincingly make the shift to a present-day setting, as the entire foundation of the show—why is Bobby not married?—is irrelevant today. This is a society of soaring divorce rates, single parents, "friends with benefits," long-term gay relationships, and declining church attendance. Who cares if someone is not married? He won't be the only one. And the scene where there is a hint that Bobby might be gay is now so passé as to border on insulting. If it's 1970, we understand why Bobby might be reluctant to be open about his sexuality. If it's 2015, we are more likely to be slightly impatient with him.

That is not to say that some aspects of an older show can't be revised without taking away from the original intentions of the show. When Susan Stroman was approached by director Trevor Nunn to choreograph the Cameron Mackintosh/Royal National Theatre 1998 revival of *Oklahoma!*, she knew she had to move away from the original Agnes de Mille choreography. Susan Stroman notes:

> [Trevor] wanted me to choreograph a new production he was directing and explained his plan to approach *Oklahoma!* as a new piece, to go back to the original essence of the stage play. I told him I would do it, but only if the Rodgers and Hammerstein Estate would allow me to develop the music for the choreography, which they did. Basing the show in its historical period, a time when Americans were fighting for territory, informed me how the piece should be choreographed. I brought in a dance arranger, the wonderful David Krane, and restructured the music to match my choreography. The movement is very fight-oriented, combative, and the women are pioneer women, tough and strong—which is very different from the original. So it truly was approaching it like a new piece.... I'm very lucky because the three revivals I've done in my career—*The Music Man, Oklahoma!* and *Show Boat*—are the big ones. They're great slices of America, and they're great shows you can learn from as a creator. Immerse yourself in that music and you understand why it all works.

So it is possible to revisit certain aspects of an older show and highlight things that would not have been highlighted then, to pull the focus away from what we now regard as politically incorrect. Susan Stroman notes:

> The way *Oklahoma!* was done—Hugh Jackman was Curly—and I think it was the first time that *Oklahoma!* had been really seen through the eyes of Curly.

And it was directed through the eyes of Curly. So it took the onus of the bidding of the picnic baskets away. It was about love. And Curly's love for Laurey. So it was directed and staged in a whole new way.

Even little tweaks here and there can make a difference. The 1998 Broadway revival of *The Sound of Music*—directed by Susan H. Schulman—made a telling change to the lyrics in "Sixteen Going on Seventeen Reprise" when Maria sings to Leisl, "Lo and behold you're someone's wife/and you belong to him." In 1998 this was changed to "Lo and behold you're someone's wife/and you belong **with** him." Not a major change, but belonging "with" someone indicates a choice that belonging "to" him does not. Men's ownership of women was accepted as an archaic concept in 1998. If Maria had told Leisl that she belonged "to him" and not "with him," there is the chance that some audience members would lose their emotional connection with Maria. This was an unlikely reaction when the show premiered in 1959, a time when women could not open a bank account without their husbands' permission, and wives often regarded themselves as belonging to their husbands. Melanie la Barrie notes:

> When we put these historical, these museum pieces—that's what they are—they're ancient pieces of theatre.... There is a serious failing in all the theatre we have created since then … if we still need to be flogging these old dead horses every so often. If we still need to be dragging out *My Fair Lady* … come on now, you mean we haven't made a musical since then that has any worth? That we have to keep dragging out the *Olivers*, the others. The failing is not the museum pieces. The failing is the work that has been done since then that has absolutely—apparently—no value. We just keep making all these disposable musicals. Life has become so disposable and they keep making all these throwaway shows.

Melanie la Barrie makes an interesting point. Are we creating disposable shows? Do any contemporary musicals have the staying power of *West Side Story*, *The Music Man* or *The Sound of Music?* So many recent shows have been built around a concept or story that belongs specifically to contemporary popular culture—*The Addams Family, Shrek, Ghost, Legally Blonde, Spider-Man, The Lion King, Wicked, Jersey Boys*—that prior knowledge becomes a necessity. How many people who had never heard a song by The Spice Girls (yes, those people *do* exist, I am one of them) bought a ticket to *Viva Forever!?* I suspect most people who go to *The Addams Family* are fans of the TV show. Would anyone buy a ticket for *We Will Rock You* if they loathed the music of Queen? In 50 years' time, those shows will be obsolete because their reference points will have disappeared from living memory.

The current audience for revivals—the Rodgers and Hammerstein devotees—are, with the greatest of respect, not getting any younger. There will come a point where that generation disappears. Will tickets to *The Sound of Music* and *My Fair Lady* be bought by that generation's surviving children? Or will we have a new batch of revivals making the rounds, spearheaded by Sondheim? I wonder if the Rodgers and Hammerstein/Lerner and Loewe canon will become part of the repertoire of opera companies—the new Gilbert and Sullivan operetta slot. With their full orchestras and large casts these shows have to guarantee a long run in order to be financially viable. Opera companies are already producing *South Pacific, Sweeney Todd, The King and I, Pacific Overtures, Fiddler on the Roof,* and *The Most Happy Fella.*

Viewing those shows as part of an opera company season actually makes it easier to overlook the gender/race political incorrectness. We expect opera to be melodramatic, to have grand passions and unrealistic characterizations. In 2013, The Royal Opera in London staged Verdi's *Othello* with the white singer Aleksandrs Antonenko singing the central role. Critics were unanimous in their praise for the production and Antonenko—"breathtaking," "outstanding," and "glorious"—but not one of them commented on the fact that a black role was being sung by a white man in dark makeup. Something about the world of opera seems to make this acceptable.

Rebecca Luker notes:

> But in many of the classic musicals, the heroine had to deal with very real issues. Anna in *The King and I* and Nellie in *South Pacific*—which I would love to have played—those are great characters. And that's what I love about the R and H women. Those women face such challenges. Especially Nellie, who has to overcome her ingrained prejudices. And Julie in *Carousel* is so powerful in the end. She too faces the real challenge of spousal abuse, one that many women face. But in Julie's time it was even more rampant and very misunderstood. Rodgers and Hammerstein managed to put these very real issues into a musical and make them poignant and meaningful.

The older shows have passed the test of time because they were brilliantly constructed by people who understood the business and had a lifelong passion for it. And competition was more intense in the Golden Age, simply because so many good shows were being produced. Now we get the occasional one, every second or third season, that seems destined to last. Producers appear more concerned with a franchise show than with the quality of the product, and that is exactly why shows such as *Ghost, Shrek,* and *Legally Blonde* will not be revived in 50 years' time. They are instantly forgettable. So maybe there is indeed value in producing revivals that remind an audience of how far we have come, and how truly great the art form of musical can be when in masterful hands.

Susan H. Schulman says that some of the themes in the older shows still resonate with contemporary audiences. I'm not sure if that's a good thing or a bad. On the one hand it shows how truly great those shows were, that they still hold relevance after 60 years. On the other hand, it saddens me that as a society we have not moved sufficiently far away from certain viewpoints to find them instantly offensive. We still smile and say, "Oh, it's all good fun, really." Christine Toy Johnson notes:

> Sometimes I think that there is a point to seeing controversial things onstage if it teaches us that we shouldn't think that way any more. If it can be successful in saying ... here is a show where the women are portrayed in this horrible way and somehow the director—if it's a revival—can put a frame around it and can make it clear to an audience member that ... oh, that's not the case any more. I'm seeing a snapshot ... a museum piece. But that doesn't happen very often.

I admit, I don't know what the answer is. I would be distraught if I thought there was a good chance I would never again see a production of *Oklahoma!* or *The Sound of Music.* But I am convinced that there are great new shows out there that are simply not being produced. And I do not believe that it is purely down to the fact that producers are reluctant to risk money on an unknown entity. I believe there are too many producers who neither understand nor care about musical theatre as a genre now. *Shrek the Musical, Addams Family, Rock of Ages, Spider-Man, Kinky Boots, The Bodyguard, The Commitments, 9 to 5, Rocky, High Fidelity,* and *Thriller Live* are not born out of a heartfelt desire to push the boundaries of musical theatre. They are about enticing an audience into the theatre with a familiar product—much the same as revivals.

The one thing I do know is that I never again need to see a production of *My Fair Lady, Annie Get Your Gun, Guys and Dolls,* or *The King and I.* I believe those shows now do more harm than good to the genre as a whole.

If musical theatre is to be taken seriously within a cultural debate, then producers need to turn away from revivals of shows that in their day may have been innovative—cutting edge, even—but that have now long passed their sell-by date. We need fresh, original material if the genre is to progress and keep up with the move forward in drama and television—and if musical theatre audiences in 50 years are to have anything worth seeing. Rebecca Caine notes:

> I know that I always came up against a brick wall with My Fair Lady because it was changed. In the Shaw, she walks out. In the musical, she stays. And even though I was very young when I was doing it, when he says, "Fetch me my slippers, Eliza" and I was supposed to, I think, hold the slippers to me and

look at him adoringly, every night I would think, "Ouch, ouch. I don't know how to play this. What on earth am I doing here? What am I thinking?" And that was every single night. Because … it was against all of my instincts. I mean, I'd just played the girl all night, what on earth was she sticking around for? And in the Shaw she doesn't. It's interesting, isn't it? I mean, that's a very interesting moment. And *Carousel*—I nearly did it, and I wonder how I would have dealt with that famous line. I mean, there are abused women who do end up thinking like that … so somehow you'd have to present it through those eyes. You know, it's the Stockholm syndrome. You start to identify with the person holding you prisoner…. But I don't see how we cannot present those shows. They are fine works of art. We can't get to the point where we don't put them on. Like *Othello*, you can't have people blacking up any more; you've got to have a black actor. We've moved on in that regard. How do you do *Taming of the Shrew*? What do you do? And *Kiss Me, Kate*. How do you do, "I am ashamed that women are so simple?" Do you do it with a twinkle in your eye? Maybe you somehow let the audience know that you think this is a pile of crap, what she's saying? It's tricky. But then do you not do *Merchant of Venice* because of the depiction of Shylock? I don't know.

NOTES

1. The production took place in March 1997 at New York City Center. Directed by Rob Marshall, the show starred Martin Short, Terrence Mann and Kerry O'Malley.

2. Book by Neil Simon; lyrics by Hal David, music by Burt Bacharach; based on the 1960 film *The Apartment*.

3. Ben Brantley. *It's a Cinch That the Bum is Under the Thumb of Some Little Broad The New York Times* March 2, 2009.

4. The show was first retitled as *The Gershwins' Porgy and Bess* for Nunn's 2006 production. Among other revisions, Nunn replaced recitatives with dialogue in an attempt to move the show away from opera and more into the musical theatre realm.

5. Book by E Y Harburg and Fred Saidy; lyrics by E Y Harburg; music by Burton Lane.

6. 1954 film directed by Stanley Dolan; script by Albert Hackell, Frances Goodrich and Dorothy Kingsley; lyrics by Saul Chaplin and Gene de Paul; music by Johnny Mercer.

7. Frederick Nolan, 2002, *The Sound of Their Music* (New York: Applause Theatre & Cinema Books),159.

8. Block, Geoffrey Holden,1997, *Enchanted Evenings: The Broadway Musical from Show Boat to Sondheim* (New York: Oxford University Press).

9. "Oh, Wouldn't it be Luvverly…" *The Observer*, March 4, 2001.

10. "Work with Martine again? I think not," *The Telegraph*, March 18, 2003.

8

New Ways to Dream

> I don't know if there is a woman's voice. If there is, it's not a strong one. It's only a tiny one. It's in the wilderness, really. But I do think it's becoming stronger.
>
> —Melanie La Barrie

Just like Norma Desmond in *Sunset Boulevard* we need new ways to dream. Everyone, she asserts, needs "new ways to dream." Indeed we do. We need new ways to approach musical theatre. Ways that include women. This means not just accommodating a contemporary female viewpoint onstage with leading roles of complexity and substance, but also finding ways to embrace a woman's voice within the genre. That involves actively encouraging female book writers, composers, choreographers, and directors and building a new foundation for the genre that incorporates women, and women's viewpoints, as well as men. Because the musical is languishing far behind other art forms in terms of contemporary gender practices, and if the industry is to hold onto the predominately female audience, it has to acknowledge that women have progressed, both in terms of their thinking and expectations and in workplace equality.

All the women I interviewed were keen to stress that the industry had changed or was in the process of changing. And perhaps my impatience stems from the fact that it is not changing quickly enough. That is purely personal, I admit that, because I will not be around to take advantage of a more enlightened attitude. Certainly the culture of sexual harassment so endemic in the eighties and nineties (and not just in theatre) is no longer tolerated, either by management nor by young female performers who are more aware of their rights within the workplace. The horror stories I heard (and witnessed) of directors, composers, producers and leading men behaving with a sense of droit du seigneur towards much younger girls in the cast are history. Removing some of the power bestowed upon the star has actually been a good thing in one respect: at least young female principals are no longer expected, as Rebecca Caine was, to take notes on their performance from a bullying or predatory leading man. I cannot categorically say that a male star would not be able now to have a female co-star fired, but I do believe it would be met with much more resistance from management, and the woman in question, than it was 20 years ago. I believe that is a direct result of more women in management in the theatre or in positions of authority within production companies and a more supportive attitude from men in similar positions around them. Individual producers, composers, and directors have learned the hard way that firing a contracted leading lady because "we don't like her any more" or because the producer/composer/director prefers a younger model will end up in a lawsuit, which the performer will win. That is indeed progress.

The issue that has emerged regularly throughout this book is the lack of an authentic woman's voice in musical theatre. There are many shows that claim to have a woman's voice—*Next to Normal, Legally Blonde, The Life, Sunset Boulevard, Passion, Miss Saigon*—but that are, in fact, an imitation given to us by male creators. Unfortunately, the men who are writing about women appear to be stuck in a narrow set of stereotypes that no longer truthfully represent contemporary women. It has to be indisputable that a woman understands the female experience better than a man, so why are female writers not being sought out and utilized?

The BMI workshops and regional theatre prove that they exist, despite claims that they do not. So are they simply not being given the same encouragement as men? Surely the patronizing belief from the sixties and seventies that "women can't write as well as men" is not still in place 50 years later? The fact is, woman book writers and librettists do exist. They have won Tony awards—and would win more if they were given the chance.

This is a debate we have heard before, albeit in the field of science. Throughout the 1990s, questions were raised about the lack of women in scientific fields. An attitude had prevailed for decades that deemed women as too emotional to attain the level of detachment that was believed necessary to engage with "good" science. The female brain, it was claimed, was not designed to comprehend engineering, physics, architecture, or even medicine. This viewpoint was traced back to high school, where intelligent girls were steered away from science subjects towards the arts, and continued in colleges and universities, where the numbers of young women admitted to science degrees was, and still is, woefully low. The belief that girls are artistic and boys scientific continues to dominate educational institutes. The irony, of course, is that the arts is the last place a woman is likely to get a job in management. How many major art galleries are controlled by women? How many women do we see holding the conductor's baton in the pit of the great opera houses? How many artistic directors of major theatre companies (particularly state-subsidized ones) are women? How many women conduct major symphony orchestras, direct Hollywood movies, run television companies, produce musicals? Yet girls in high school are still told they are more artistic than boys. What they are not told is that they are unlikely to get the positions they are qualified for if men are in the running for the same job.

Musical theatre, like science, is not a level playing field. The difference, however, is that scientists and educational institutions now recognize the unique qualities women bring to the fields of science and are actively trying to encourage women to participate. Who is encouraging women into creative roles in musical theatre? How will we ever have a woman's voice if there are no women writers and directors being given opportunities? Susan Stroman notes:

> Theresa Rebeck, Marsha Norman, and Julia Jordan just started the Lilly Award, which has only been around for a few years, but if there's a woman playwright or composer out there taking a chance, they want to recognize her. The more you celebrate women who have accomplished something, or women who are on their way, the more present and visible it makes women—even to other women in the same field. It can embolden a woman who dreams of working in the theatre to get out there and try.

Young women need more encouragement to pursue a career in musical theatre, and the women already in the profession need encouragement to stay, because far too many talented and creative women on the fringes of the industry are bailing out and seeking careers elsewhere due to the lack of opportunities. Awards such as the Lillys, which recognize the achievements of women in theatre, are vitally important in keeping women not just visible, but optimistic and forward-looking, instead of feeling depressed or helpless in the face of the blatant inequality surrounding them in the industry. Beth Williams notes:

> I believe so strongly that giving credence to any issue is going to help it get in your own way. Just because I'm told there is something I can't do doesn't mean it's true. I know that. I believe that the best thing we can do for the twenty-year-old women in college is to teach them to work hard and make a strong commitment to themselves—to understand that only they can stop themselves from achieving their dreams. I'm trying to let my niece know, she's seventeen, that my journey has been what it is because I stayed true to what I knew and believed in.

After the U.K. launch of the Spice Girls musical *Viva Forever,* David Lister, writing in *The* Independent,[1] came up with the perfect scheme to encourage female composers and writers into musical theatre.

Original musicals from fresh, young British writers are a rarity, in fact they're an endangered species; musicals from young, female writers are particularly rare. Now there's a thought. What could be a better illustration of true "Girl Power" than to empower female composers and lyricists for British musical theatre? It would just need someone to fund a scheme to find and encourage them, an Orange Prize for the musical-theatre world. David Lister notes:

I can think of seven people immediately who could fund such bursaries: the Spice Girls, Miss Craymer and Miss Saunders. By diverting the tiniest fraction of the profits from the upcoming show to a scheme to find new female creators of musical theatre, they would be empowering women artists and, at the same time, greatly enhancing the future health of the stage. It would be wonderfully philanthropic. Now, that would be "Girl Power."

Funnily enough, Susan Stroman articulated a similar plan in her interview with me the previous year. She notes:

It would be great if a producer took the initiative to start a program offering aspiring female artists the opportunity to do a workshop or a lab, and gives her the means and the space to do it. A sustainable program that supports women trying new work, helps them develop their ideas and exposes them to other women as potential collaborators.

Yes, it would be great. But how likely is it that such a scheme would ever come to fruition? Call me cynical, but I find myself chuckling at the mere idea that Cameron Mackintosh or Andrew Lloyd Webber might fund a scheme to encourage women to create musicals. How many female directors has Mackintosh ever employed, or librettists or book writers? Ditto Lloyd Webber. Has the Royal Shakespeare Company redirected any of the profits from *Les Misérables* or *Matilda the Musical* into workshops for new musicals written or directed by women? What have Mark Platt and David Stone, producers of the feminist musical *Wicked*—the same show attended by thousands of little girls every week—ever done to encourage women to create a musical?

Again, it comes back to the fact that the producers and production houses such as the Royal National Theatre are oblivious to the lack of women on creative teams because they are so accustomed to seeing a group of men with creative control that they take it as the norm. It never occurs to anyone to question this exclusivity, let alone make moves to change it. So what hope does the authentic woman's voice have of ever being heard in mainstream musical theatre, especially when the majority of men producing musicals today wouldn't know the difference between a true female voice and an imitation? Their view of women *is* the imitation, not the reality.

And that view is not limited solely to producers. Theatre critics are just as incapable of recognizing the gap between how women are represented onstage and how women behave in the real world. By not noticing or ignoring this anomaly, they too become complicit—however inadvertently—in maintaining the imbalance inherent in the industry. Women such as Theresa Rebeck, Marsha Norman, and Julia Jordan, with their Lilly Awards, are holding up the gender inequalities for all to see.

Theresa Rebeck is billed as the creator of the hit TV series *Smash*, which premiered in 2012. (She is also listed as one of the nine executive producers of the series—not surprisingly, the only woman.) *Smash* was set around the creation of a new Broadway musical based on the life of Marilyn Monroe. The characters, scenarios, and dramas that go hand-in-hand with the creation of a new musical were delightfully familiar to anyone who has ever worked in the genre—as Rebeck has.[2] The success of the series possibly owed much to its authenticity, which dripped with insider knowledge of Broadway musicals. For the star-struck *Glee* or *Wicked* fan, this was the backstage world they longed to see. But one area of *Smash* was not a truthful reflection of the contemporary musical theatre industry. The writer of the fictional show *Bombshell* was a woman—Julia Houston—played by Debra Messing, and the producer of the show was another woman—Eileen Rand, played by Angelica Huston. Perhaps this was wishful thinking on Rebeck's part—a view of the industry as she would like it to be. Or was she making a point about the lack of women in an industry patronized by other women?

The characters of both Julia Huston and Eileen Rand are strong, independent women who are extremely good at their respective jobs. Was Rebeck showing us that there is really no excuse for keeping women out of the industry when they can perform just as well as men? Unlike the real world, no one in the series ever questioned Julia Huston or Eileen Rand's credentials or their right to be in the industry. I suspect the producers of the TV series were well aware that a truly authentic depiction of the creation of a new Broadway musical would result in "too many men" onscreen—something their female viewers would not forgive. *Smash* was more likely to appeal to women and the Glee generation, and the producers of the series would not want to risk alienating that audience by giving them no one to identify with. Hence two women in leading roles and a major plot line centering around another two female characters competing for the leading role in the new musical. What a pity musical theatre producers do not give their female audience the same consideration.

Smash was also interesting because the show within the show—*Bombshell*—had a clear woman's voice. The musical being created was about a woman and was written and produced by women, and discussions took place within the series about not turning Marilyn Monroe into a victim. Yes, it was

TV and fiction, but what a sweet fantasy to watch play out. *Bombshell* is exactly the kind of musical we should being seeing on Broadway in 2015 (and probably will when some savvy producer realizes the hit he could have.) It is a musical where, both on and offstage, women are regarded as equals and individuals. How sad that we have to turn to the small screen and a make-believe production to see a glimpse of a musical with a woman's voice. How sad that the reality—particularly the West End in London—is so far removed from the tantalizing fantasy of *Smash*.

The TV producers of *Smash* may not have been as sensitive to their audience as I am giving them credit for. Perhaps the roles of Eileen Rand and Julia Huston were created with the sole intention of luring two female stars into the series, thereby pushing up viewing figures. But I do believe that a television (and film) audience and critics are more likely to recognize gender discrimination and protest about it than a musical theatre audience, and critics. This is what I do not understand.

Why is musical theatre allowed to get away with such blatant stereotyping and prejudices, when other art forms are scrutinized in terms of gender and culture studies? *Mad Men* ignited debate around women and the workplace. The lack of a woman's voice in contemporary theatre drama is widely discussed. The fashion industry is criticized for an unhealthy and unrealistic view of women. Books are written about the consequences to society of the sexist depiction of women in music videos, rap songs, TV commercials, comic books, even animated films. I recently read an academic thesis devoted entirely to Lara Croft, the main protagonist of a video game. Why is musical theatre never included in discussions of gender and the media, or gender and culture? Do we return again to the "escapist" justification? I may be displaying my own prejudice here, but are video games and the fashion industry really more culturally significant than musical theatre? It's not about one art form having more depth than another; it is about a debate that encompasses all art forms and does not dismiss one as irrelevant.

I have never agreed with the detractors who dismiss musical theatre as mindless. Personally, I find reality television shows mindless, but I still appreciate what *Wife Swap* contributes to a debate about gender roles in contemporary society. Yet I would be more likely to be awarded a research grant for a study on the cultural impact of *Jersey Shore* or *Dance Moms* than I would be for a similar project on musical theatre. And this is the crux of the problem in igniting a debate about gender and musicals. Musical theatre is not awarded a place of significance within a cultural context because it is not regarded as a serious contributor.

But, as I brought up in the introduction to this book, musicals have historically tackled a wide variety of serious social concerns and continue to do so. And the sheer number of people who have engaged with musical theatre in the last decade, even on film, make it hugely relevant to any debate concerning culture. Yet studies rarely consider it. Books debating the women's voice in theatre ignore musicals, and books about musicals ignore women. Until musical theatre can be accorded the same academic and cultural respect that is given to video games and MTV, the industry will not change. Because it is not subject to any form of scrutiny. And that, I'm afraid, returns us again to the critics and arts commentators, who persist in closing their eyes to gender issues within the musical theatre industry. If we are to have any hope at all of changing attitudes towards women within musical theatre, then the way in which the genre is viewed within a wider context is the first thing that has to change.

Nina Lannan notes:

> I was in the TKTS [half-price] ticket line the other day and I got into a random conversation with two women and asked, "What are you going to see?" They told me their three choices for shows, then pointed to the man with them, who must have been the husband of one of the women. They were probably in their thirties, early forties and said, "But we have to find something that he'll like." It was interesting. It was clearly his choice. They were looking at *Bonnie and Clyde, How to Succeed in Business, Anything Goes* … the three they were really hoping for. But what was fascinating was that he clearly was the decision trigger. The decision maker was the man.

Nina Lannan's anecdote brings up the touchy subject of women's collusion in their own oppression. Women constantly sacrifice their own desires for the men in their lives—no one could disagree with that. It could be a result of upbringing, societal pressure, religious beliefs, low self-esteem, fear of being single or a combination of these and dozens of other factors. And let's be clear about one thing: they very often do it willingly, to please their men.

That sacrifice may not be as monumental as giving up a satisfying career to placate an insecure husband; it can be as seemingly insignificant as seeing the show he wants, rather than the show she wants.

Not all women comply with the various societal pressures to put their men first, but they often end up single, and possibly happier—who knows? But by giving the male in the group the power to make the decision, the women Nina Lannan met in the ticket line are doing far more than simply appeasing him. They are reassuring him of his innate superiority over them. Why do they acquiesce? Why can't they—there are two women to one man— insist on seeing the show they want to see. Perhaps he is paying for the tickets?

Doubtful, given that more women today have financial independence, which translates into buying power, than women 30 years ago. At the end of the day, it comes down to keeping the male in the group happy, despite the fact that he is the minority. It's a startlingly accurate reflection of the genre itself. More women than men attend musicals, but producers put on shows designed to appeal to men, and the women watching them understand that it is pointless to argue. I will admit here that I find women's collusion in maintaining a patriarchal society bizarre. Why do women take on more than their fair share of housework and child-rearing? Why do they do what their husbands want instead of what they want? Why do young women believe the advertising that tells them they are nothing more than their bodies and subsequently dress like sex objects? Why do smart, sensible women tolerate behavior from their boyfriends/spouses that they would never tolerate from their sisters? It's because they are told by the media, by society, by the church, the judiciary—every area of life—that their needs are less important than men's, and keeping men happy is why women are here. Can we really blame men when women pander to them. When women simper and gush, "Whatever you want, honey," instead of voicing their own desires? But if women sit through *Rock of Ages* and say nothing about how uncomfortable they are at the way women are portrayed for fear of upsetting their boyfriends who thought the show was "awesome," how will the shows ever change?

I find it hard to believe that the resounding silence from women concerning the sexist attitudes currently on display in musicals is due to the fact that they do not notice. I believe they are well aware of the male perspective dominating the stage, but because it is what they have come to expect from a musical, it seems futile to question it. Women I spoke to about *Rock of Ages* found it demeaning toward women. Women I know who saw *Next to Normal* found it patronizing. No woman with whom I discussed the issue embraced the idea of men playing women's roles. So I find it impossible to accept that the female consumer is blind to the sexist clichés of womanhood onstage. But perhaps she too has been influenced by attitudes that dismiss the musical as irrelevant to cultural debate, or by husbands who denigrate the musical as "girl stuff" and therefore not something to be taken seriously, (unless, of course, it's by the creators of *South Park* and therefore a "must see"). Maybe women feel slightly silly at voicing disquiet over a musical, something they are told is irrelevant, unlike sports. A major part of the "pleasing your man" creed is that women agree with his opinion. If he thinks *Book of Mormon* is the best musical he's ever seen, is there any point in bringing up how offensive she found the portrayal of women? It will only lead to a fight.

Women's collusion in maintaining the status quo in musical theatre is a genuine problem, because if the women who buy the tickets don't complain about the lack of a woman's viewpoint, then how will producers and creators absorb the message that this is not what they want? The box-office figures for *Mamma Mia!* indicate without a doubt what women really want to see. If what they are being offered is not quite that, well, they'll take it anyway, because it's better than nothing. They'll order a hot dog if steak is not on the menu, because at least that way they won't go hungry. And perhaps I am wrong in assuming that other women are as impatient as I am with the depiction of their sex onstage. Perhaps a societal view of women as passive and compliant, decorative and sexy, is so embedded in women that what they see up onstage is exactly what they see in life. They love *Mamma Mia!* because it is an authentic representation of their own experience. They continue to attend *Phantom of the Opera* because it offers romantic escapism.

Anneke Harrison notes:

> If you were knee deep in nappies and washing up and housework, with a boring part-time job ... and that was the reality that had set in after the roses from the first days of romance had faded ... if that was your reality, then the notion of romance would be very appealing. You know, to be sought after purely for yourself and your own beauty, and to be wooed and treated like a princess, it must be quite alluring. Because they're not getting that in real life anymore.

I firmly believe it is the women in the audience who could change the industry, or at least raise questions about why women and women's desires are being overlooked. There are just too few women represented at the top level of the industry to change it without mass support, which they are unlikely to find among the men dominating the genre. Ticket buyers may be unaware of how much power they actually wield in an industry that is dependent upon them for survival. If no one goes to the show, the show closes. But the female audience has to demonstrate an impatience with a product that demeans them, and so far, they have shown no inclination to do that. If that is due to their limited expectations—no one goes to an Andrew Lloyd Webber show to see enlightened men and free-thinking women—then how do we raise their expectations? How do we persuade women to demand a more respectful and truthful product?

We could start by making the women in the audience aware of the gender discrimination that I maintain still exists in the industry: the cliquey boys' club, the lack of women in creative or senior management roles, the bullying, the dismissive attitude towards female performers, the sexist jokes in the rehearsal room, the lack of consideration for working mothers, the sexualization of women onstage, the patronizing attitude toward female associates/

assistants, the "too many women" viewpoint. Bear in mind I have worked in musicals for more than 20 years and have witnessed and/or experienced all of the above. I believe if the female consumer was conscious of how the industry actually operates in terms of gender, she might be less eager to financially support it. Women are not passive by nature and will join forces and respond to a cry for action—witness the campaign to end female violence against women in India, or Girl Rising[3] promoting world-wide universal education for girls. Recall the female peace protesters at Greenham Common in the U.K. in the eighties or the women rallying for an end to civil wars in Northern Ireland, Liberia, Bosnia, Nigeria. All testament to the incredibly powerful force a group of women can be or become.

For example, the U.S.–based organization *Miss*Representation.org is a "call-to-action campaign that seeks to empower women and girls to challenge limiting labels in order to realize their potential and to encourage men and boys to stand up to sexism."[4]

Formed on the success of the 2011 award-winning documentary film *Miss Representation* by Jennifer Siebel Newsom, which traced a direct link from the misrepresentation of women by the media to the lack of women in positions of power and influence in the U.S., *Miss*Representation.org is proving to be a powerful tool against sexism. Visitors to the website are encouraged to take a pledge in which they agree to challenge the media's limiting portrayal of women and girls, and the "I'm Not Buying It" campaign encourages website viewers to utilize social media sites Twitter and Facebook to protest against sexist advertising. Supporters can use the hashtag #NotBuyingIt to register their disapproval when a product is advertised in a way that demeans women or reinforces a gender stereotype. A recent success story was a campaign against Disney provoked by Avengers and Iron Man T-shirts for children sold in the online store. The Avengers T-shirts for boys carried the slogan *Be a Hero,* while the girls' T-shirts declared *I Need a Hero.* The Iron Man T-shirts for boys announced them as *The Invincible Iron Man* while the girls'—in pink of course—claimed *I Only Kiss Heroes.* After over 1,000 #NotBuyingIt tweets and nearly 8,000 signatures on a petition, the Disney Store removed the offending "I Need a Hero" T-shirt from its website. Whether they will follow suit with the "I Only Kiss Heroes" pink monstrosity remains to be seen.

Another good example is Mumsnet,[5] a British website formed in 2000 by Justine Roberts and Carrie Longton to provide parents with the opportunity to swap information and exchange views in discussion forums. Since its formation, the site has become a powerful political tool and a resource for journalists who cite discussions on the message boards in the daily press. In

2009, the print media referred to the forthcoming U.K. general election as "the Mumsnet election," and in February 2013, the BBC Radio 4 program *Women's Hour* assessed Roberts and Longton as the seventh most powerful women in the U.K. In 2010, Mumsnet launched the Let Girls Be Girls campaign against the premature sexualization of young girls and challenged retailers to withdraw items that emphasized or exploited young girls' sexuality. The campaign was extended in 2013 with a call to news agents and supermarkets not to display "lads' mags" within the sight of children.

The success of campaigns instigated by *Miss*Representation and Mumsnet proves that there is a willingness among women and men to voice their disapproval at sexism in society. The women who chat on these sites are not all fully fledged political activists—they are ordinary women expressing their displeasure at being patronized or defined by a narrow stereotype. I guarantee that some of those women attend musical theatre. They may even be the same women who tweet "I'm not buying it" or write to U.K. retail giant Marks and Spencer to complain about lacy bras marketed at seven-year-olds. If the gender discrimination rife in musical theatre was brought to their attention, who is to say those women wouldn't sit up and rethink their view of what they are being sold? If they care about the early sexualization of their daughters, surely they care as much that those same daughters are being told by *Grease* to sleep with their boyfriends in order to keep them. Or by Julie Jordan in *Carousel* that it doesn't hurt if a man hits you. The problem is that gender discrimination is the best-kept secret in musical theatre. Only those who work in it are aware of it. And if they protest, they will lose any chance at a career. Nina Lannan adds:

> Ironically, for a business all about collaboration, you have to be driven and single-minded and really, really want to direct on Broadway to the exclusion of many other life choices. And … is that at a time in a woman's life where she is trying to start a family and isn't able to be in the competitive race so much?

It is not simply a lack of encouragement and too few opportunities that keep women out of musical theatre. As I explored in the previous chapter, women are different from men. And their biological difference has always provided men with the perfect excuse for keeping women out of professions in which they are not welcome. But it is more than that. Women give birth to babies, and more often than not, they assume more of the child-care responsibilities than their male partners. No matter how many government directives—maternity leave, flexi time, subsidized childcare—are put in place to assist mothers to maintain a career, women's biological difference from men affects both their security in the workforce and their ability to progress within it.

Working mothers juggle children and a career in a way working fathers—
for the most part—do not. Biological determinism encourages society to designate the mother as primary carer with spurious claims about maternal
instinct, women as innate nurturers, and men as unemotional. Men can, and
do, bring up children just as well as women, and couples often now negotiate
full-time child care around the partner with the greater income. But the gender inequality pay gap often ensures that the primary income source within
a relationship is the male, and so the female stays at home with the children.
This, in turn, keeps women out of management positions because a working
mother is often available only for part-time work. By the time the children
are in high school and the mother returns to full-time work, it is often to a
position she would have progressed beyond had she not had children. Nina
Lannan adds:

> It would be interesting to look at countries with good child care support to see
> if more women are able to work in theatre. For example, France, or Sweden. I
> had a relative who worked in Las Vegas who had membership in a 24-hr. child
> care center. She could drop her child off at any time of the day or night, and
> the child would be familiar with the surroundings and know the people
> there.... Sometimes we have single mothers working in and on shows and they
> have to absent themselves from the show to deal with child care issues. People
> would ask, "Why isn't so-and-so showing up?" And it's because a child was
> sick and there was nobody else in the house to take care of him. It would be
> great for our industry if someone would open a child care center for men and
> women working in Broadway shows. There is no provision to support women
> working in the theatre who have families, which is particularly important
> given the work hours that theatre demands. This one act would increase the
> ability of young women to work on Broadway.

Theatre, in particular, is not at all conducive to a healthy work/lifestyle
balance for working mothers because of the awkward hours and uncertainty
of the length of employment. The intense period of technical rehearsal, for
example, is conducted in eleven-hour shifts, six days a week. In the U.K. it
is possible to claim tax credits for money spent on government registered
childcare by working parents, but taking advantage of this scheme is almost
impossible for self-employed theatre professionals, given their irregular
employment and unsocial hours. There is the old argument that women
choose to have children and they are well aware of the consequences when
they do so. But so do men. The choice to become a father does not have the
same impact on a man's career as it does on a woman's when she chooses to
become a mother, especially if that career is musical theatre, which involves
unsocial hours, uncertain employment, and, often, the necessity to tour—to
go on the road—for months at a time.

Women are not incapable of dealing with any of those issues, but when children are involved, it becomes a question of practicality. Women shouldn't be expected to choose between children and careers when men can have both. But it is undeniable that being a mother limits a woman's ability to commit 100 percent to the workplace—theatre included.

It is also a fact that women who actively choose not to have children in order to concentrate on a creative career may not be terribly supportive to women who request special treatment—days off, reduced hours—because they have children. As I've said before, theatre is not a level playing field. Just as an aside, it is interesting to note that almost none of the successful women I have worked with in musical theatre are mothers. I wonder how many of those women made an active choice not to have children in order to stay in the industry or how many women who are mothers accept that they will never get beyond a certain level and choose to prioritize their families. Beth Williams notes:

> I actually regularly find myself looking around a conference table and there's no question I'm in the minority. Always. But I don't think it's because of anything anyone in that room is doing to stop women from being there. I don't. I think that women are still choosing—for all good reasons—to not always put themselves out there while they're raising a family. I think it's fairly common in this day and age for men to share child care responsibilities. But I have often worked with women in theatre—from designers to stage managers to producing partners—who opt to limit the number of shows they take on, or choose to remain a "second" in command, as opposed to being promoted, or who have their children at the theatre with them. All of those women seem to be very happy in making these choices for themselves and for their family. I love and respect that. I guess my point is that I don't believe being a mother keeps a woman from having opportunities come her way. But I do think it may change her perspective on what's important.

Of course it does. And I'm not suggesting for one minute that women should abandon their children to launch an all-out assault on the musical theatre industry with the intent of female domination. All I am saying is that there must be more ways in which women can be given the same consideration that men are within the industry. And within that, an acknowledgment must be made that women have additional responsibilities in terms of family demands, not just through children but also caring for elderly relatives. Neither of these commitments should exclude them from a career in musical theatre.

My fear is that the discrimination against women in musical theatre will result in dissatisfied creative women leaving the industry or young, talented women not even attempting to enter it because they know the glass ceiling and broken ladder ensure that they will progress only to a certain level—particularly in the U.K. and Australia. But is leaving the industry, or not going into it in the first place, really the only answer? Surely change has to come from within? If all the women who felt any dissatisfaction with, say, the Catholic church were to leave, would it make any real difference? Or would the church inadvertently achieve what it really wants? Because it cannot truthfully be said that the Catholic church embraces women. If women left the institution en masse in protest and started their own church around the corner, I'm not convinced that many priests and bishops would care—except that they would have to look elsewhere for their flower arrangers, housekeepers, and cake bakers. At least they would no longer have to answer awkward questions about women priests.

Is that so different from musical theatre? If women stay, can they possibly effect change from within when they are up against decades of male tradition? If creative women leave musical theatre for other professions, would anyone care? In the long term, it would probably kill the industry stone dead, so abandoning the profession to the men who believe they own it would gain nothing. But how can the few women in the industry bring about change from within? Susan Stroman adds:

> My union has a fantastic program that pairs an established director currently in production with a young observer. The observer gets to experience the process from start to finish. I always choose a female observer, and, even though they're called "observers," I always get them up and dancing, participating. They are very much a part of the process, and they experience what it takes to put up a show. We need more women helping other women get the chance to watch a piece come to life so they can go out and create something of their own.

An observership program is, as Ms. Stroman says, a great thing, but only if the women who observe have the opportunity to move beyond that. All too often the women who do progress from being an observer to an assistant find out that that is as far as the profession will allow them to go. Yes, there have been improvements in the number of women working backstage or in technical areas, but in the two and half decades that I have worked in musical theatre (in Australia and the U.K.), it has become harder for creative women to break into the industry, not easier. Even when there is a female producer driving the project—Judy Craymer on *Viva Forever!* or Carmen Pavlovic on *King Kong: The Musical* and *Strictly Ballroom*—the creative team will be predominantly male. Why is this still the case? If women can hold the top jobs in government, the judiciary, science, and medicine, if they can win Nobel prizes, the top literary awards, and distinctions in other fields of the arts, why are they still not considered capable of creating a new musical? With the greatest of respect, musical theatre is not exactly brain surgery. And women know what other women, want to see.

In the U.K. and Australia, I distinctly get the feeling from women within the industry that they feel more powerless than ever—that they believe they cannot change the way women are viewed or treated within the profession, especially when there are so few females in positions of power to back them up. (This was not echoed by their U.S. counterparts, who had a far more positive sense of shifting gender roles within the industry.) It increasingly feels as if women in the industry are resigning themselves to accepting that this is the way the profession operates, and it is a waste of time to challenge it. It shouldn't have to be the constant and frustrating fight for respect and recognition that it often is. But nothing will ever change if there are so few women left in the industry that their voices are effectively silenced. But until it is heard, it cannot possibly be effective.

If there is still an inbuilt prejudice toward women writers (and directors) in favor of men, what can be done to tackle that? How do we change decades of tradition and belief in the male talent being superior to the female? And where is the proof for this? If women had had the same opportunities as men have had in musicals, and failed dismally, then the attitude would be understandable. But a prejudice exists against an idea that has never even been fully tested.

In the U.K. and Australia, subsidized and state theatre companies are at the mercy of Arts Council funding. If the people in charge of distributing the grants from the Arts Council were genuinely concerned about the lack of women in creative positions, they could simply threaten to withhold funding until the company in question demonstrated a willingness to employ more women. Subsidized theatre companies have a board of directors—any board member could raise the issue and question the management structure of the company. Why did no board member at Sydney Theatre Company, for example, question the appropriateness of an all-male production of *Pirates of Penzance* being included in the program?

Well, perhaps because out of a current board of eleven members, only one of those is a woman. But if the corporate world can acknowledge that there are too few women elected to various boards of directors, surely theatre can too? Musical theatre is, by and large, a commercial organization and therefore not at the mercy of state funding. The producers control the product, so there is no governing body with whom a complaint could be lodged. Commercial musical theatre, therefore, is a law unto itself. Denying funding to a subsidized state or regional theatre may result in a woman being engaged to direct the annual musical (assuming there is one), but it would have little impact on Broadway or the West End, where the majority of musicals premiere. And forcing a theatre company to employ women may not be in anyone's best interests.

> I think actually it causes more harm than good. On the one hand you want to say look, you really need to consider the numbers here and look at how imbalanced it is, but on the other hand none of us wants to be in a show because of the numbers, and some of us have been accused of only getting opportunities because of that sort of thing. So it's so complicated.... I'd rather have the conversation about being more open-minded to increasing diversity.

Ms. Toy Johnson is referring to the use of affirmative action to increase racial diversity among Broadway casts, but she could just as easily be referring to gender.

Negative connotations around positive discrimination exist when the assumption is made that that is the *only* reason the person has been given the job—when, for example, the director understands that political correctness demands he hire a certain number of non-white ensemble members. But who is to say that those ensemble members were not good enough to be there in the first place and that a traditional attitude towards the musical as a white industry was denying those performers a chance even to audition? It is undeniable that color-blind casting—another way of describing positive discrimination—increased the numbers of non-white performers in musicals. Would similar preferential treatment toward women do the same for the gender breakdown on creative teams? Beth Williams notes:

> Well, here's where I end up being almost obstructionist to the idea of what can be done. I take myself back to the conversation I had with the black American man about what can be done to change the under-representation of black performers. "If the actors don't come to the audition room, how can I hire them?" I asked. I know I wasn't the first person to ask that question, and his response was understandably frustrated. So I could say to myself, OK, I'm never going to produce a show without making sure that 50 percent of the people involved are women, or without having at least one or two women on the writing team. But is it that simple? Will my saying that make it achievable? Does it make sense to attempt to create new musicals by demanding equal participation by women? I'm afraid I don't think so. To be clear, I also don't think it makes sense to attempt to create new musicals by demanding equal participation by men. But we're right back where we started, without a clear solution.

It does seem to me that some form of positive discrimination is the only way that the gender imbalance in musical theatre can begin to change. Affirmative action is seen as a negative concept because it is regarded as a helping hand offered to recipients who are not good enough to get there on their own. Opponents argue that if women want to be considered as equals, they shouldn't expect special consideration.

But women in musical theatre are not regarded as equals and are therefore not given the same opportunities as their male colleagues. It's an ever-decreasing circle—without the opportunity to develop their skills, women will never be in a position where they are serious contenders for the top jobs. Nina Lannan notes:

> Can they go off Broadway and work? A potential woman director? Sure. Can they go to a regional theatre and work? Yes. But they are not working with all the tools of their craft, all the bells and whistles that Broadway can offer. And you've got to work with those tools to understand how to use them.

In the U.K. in the 1990s, Tony Blair's Labour party put a number of affirmative action strategies in place aimed at increasing the number of female MPs. One action in particular, the introduction of all-women shortlists (AWS), which ensured the selection of a female candidate to contest a safe constituency seat, caused controversy. AWS was condemned as undemocratic and discriminatory against men, and in 1995 two prospective candidates—Peter Jepson and Roger Dyas-Elliott—challenged the policy in court, claiming that all-women shortlists were illegal under the sex discrimination act of 1975. In 1996, an industrial tribunal found in favor of the two men, agreeing that the Labour Party had broken the law. However, the significant reduction in the number of female MPs after the 2001 general election caused the Labour Party to introduce the Sex Discrimination (Election Candidates) Act 2002, which allows political parties to positively discriminate in favor of female pre-selection candidates. All-women shortlists have been credited with increasing the number of female MPs—including the first female home secretary, Jacqui Smith—and challenging the prejudices that previously discouraged women from putting themselves forward as candidates. The result of a woman's voice being given a platform in parliament is that issues such as childcare, domestic violence, and women's health have now become priorities. For 50 percent of the population, this is a good thing.

The reason I cite this example of positive discrimination is to show what can be done when affirmative action is taken. Politics, like musical theatre, has traditionally been dominated by men, yet male politicians showed a willingness to change and to move with the times. Tony Blair was aware that a parliament in which women were so under-represented was not good government. And yes, there were women who opposed his affirmative action strategies, and some of those women were already MPs. Some women don't support other women—that is hardly groundbreaking news. Margaret Thatcher did little to encourage women into Parliament or to promote the women already there. But times have changed, and the evidence speaks for itself. More women in government resulted in women's issues gaining more prominence.

I believe the first step towards putting a woman's voice onstage is for producers to acknowledge that the audience is made up mainly of women. When producers get around to accepting that, it is a logical step to then question if what is onstage is really what that audience wants to see. If they have difficulty with that, then here's an easy way around it. Male producers need to ask themselves if they, as men, would go to a show that portrayed their sex as mindless and where the story bears no resemblance to the way they currently live their lives. Would a male producer commission a new musical with no roles for men and a woman in drag giving her impersonation of what it is to be a man? I think not.

And perhaps there is a new generation of producers and creators hovering in the wings, who will take over when the current fixtures retire, and who understand the importance of respecting women in an industry that depends upon them for survival. Beth Williams notes:

> I think that any one of us who is impactful at what we do will ultimately change the product—we just happen to be a group of women. I think it's women ourselves who have to want to change it individually, and who ultimately will wake up ten years from now and hopefully it will feel different. Or five years from now. Or thirty years from now.

Musical theatre is routinely accused of dumbing down in order to accommodate a less sophisticated audience, and I would include pandering to the kiddie dollar within that accusation. In the last 15 years or so we have been subjected to *Shrek the Musical, The Little Mermaid, Mary Poppins, Chitty Chitty Bang Bang, Beauty and the Beast, The Lion King, Wicked, Matilda, Newsies, Aladdin, Cinderella, Charlie and the Chocolate Factory, Annie* (again!), *Oliver* (again!), *High School Musical, Tarzan,* and *The Hunchback of Notre Dame.* Future Disney plans for Broadway include *Dumbo, The Jungle Book, Alice in Wonderland,* and *Pocahontas.* Musical theatre dumbing down? How could anyone who reads the above list even question that? Clearly there is money to be made out of children, especially when they are let loose on the merchandise stall. It saddens me that a genre that used to be regarded as an art form now appears to have morphed into an offshoot of Disneyland.

Let's look to the future for a moment, or at least the future audience. All these little girls sitting enraptured by *Chitty Chitty Bang Bang* or *Matilda* or the Disney juggernaut: what are they going to go and see when they become young women? What will their celebratory girls' night out be? A revival of *High School Musical*? God help them. If the kiddie dollar becomes the financial mainstay for producers, will there be a choice other than the "family show" left within the genre in ten years' time? Or will musical theatre be aimed primarily at the under-twelves? Statistics show that over 30 percent of women of child-bearing age in the first world are choosing not to have children, and those figures are rising. What will musical theatre have to offer in 2024 for the child-free, financially independent, thinking young woman? Very little, if it continues down the path it is moving toward, because those same young girls being taken to a musical as a birthday treat today are more aware of gender issues and their rights against discrimination than my generation ever was. When they grow out of the fantasy being sold to them by musicals, they may well grow tired of an industry that clearly has not kept pace with progress. They may not stay so quiet at the lack of women onstage or the stereotypical depiction of female characters. They may simply stay away because the genre does not speak to them. Part of me lives in hope. The other part is desperately sad at the prospect of the demise of a genre I love, and have spent my working life within, albeit under a very thick glass ceiling.

Thinking has shifted on the ways in which to tackle all forms of discrimination. It is now acknowledged that in order to combat racism or domestic violence, for example, there is little point in telling the victim it is unacceptable. They know that already. It is more important and effective to re-educate the perpetrator and to enlist the support of people who do not hold racist or abusive viewpoints. I do believe there are men in musical theatre who would support a call for a woman's voice to be heard within the industry. Perhaps they are simply unaware that it does not exist because it never occurs to them to question the status quo. If I give the male producers, directors, and artistic directors the benefit of the doubt and allow them the excuse that they have never really thought about the gender inequality within musical theatre, what could they do to effect change?

They could start by actively developing new female talent, particularly writers and composers and by actually going and seeing shows in regional theatres or fringe venues that have been created by the women who are now ready to move into the mainstream. Producers could invest in new shows by women, not necessarily with a view to bringing the show to Broadway or the West End, but as a way of widening the pool of potential talent for later productions. They could then prove themselves more open to the idea of a woman's voice by commissioning female writers, or shows about women, and by then hiring female directors and choreographers and musical directors to stage them. Or they could insist that a certain number of assistant roles on Broadway and the West End be filled by women to ensure a more balanced viewpoint and to lay foundations for a future industry in which both the male and female voices are present. None of these initiatives could be defined, or derided, as positive discrimination. They are not radical, like the all-women selection lists. They are merely ways of opening up opportunities for able, creative women to develop their talent. Susan H. Schulman notes:

> I didn't do it on my own, you know. I had to have someone like Stephen Sond-heim say OK. He could have said no. He could have said, "Really? A woman director for *Sweeney Todd*? Honestly?" But he didn't say that. He said, "This is swell." And that made other people say, "OK, we'll take a chance on this." It also happened to get very good reviews from male critics, and that was very helpful…. So you know, you can't ever do it by yourself. I also had a creative team that I worked with that were very much in my sensibility, so I was allowed to do it the way I wanted to do it. I didn't have a producer telling me, "Oh my God, you can't do *Sweeney Todd* that way." I had a producer who said, "Do *Sweeney Todd* the way you want to do *Sweeney Todd*." That's what's impor-tant. And when you have that kind of support then you can be courageous and you can go forward and not be timid about it. And I think that I was fortunate in those circumstances. Yes, I had training, yes I had the ability, and yes, I had experience because I had done a lot of regional theatre. But I still needed all those other people to come together at a certain point and go, "We know you can do this." You know, everybody needs to be brave in who they hire and look to the ability and forget about the gender.

If the men who currently hold the power within the musical theatre industry take issue with my claim that there is an inbuilt prejudice towards women, then prove to me that I am wrong. Please! Open doors to female cre-ative talent. Produce shows that resonate with a female audience. Discourage sexual stereotyping or a one-dimensional view of women onstage. Put the strong-willed, independent woman onstage. Stop putting drag queens into roles written for women. Allow women in the audience to feel empowered by the characters they see onstage—as they do with *Mamma Mia!* Make it possible for a woman's voice to share the stage with a male one, instead of being suffocated by it. Bring musical theatre in line with contemporary think-ing in society on gender equality and the perception of women. None of these are impossible or unreasonable requests. Susan Stroman adds:

> I think it goes back to what I said before, that if you really believe you have it, you've got to create it. You can't wait for someone to hire you. Because that phone won't ring…. And I think for women … they've got to figure that out. No matter what kind of artist you are, you've got to take control of it. It's tough out there, it's really tough. So you've got to take control of it. And be seen. And be heard.

Susan Stroman is absolutely right in exhorting women to take con-trol. And I believe that thinking should not solely apply to their career development. We, as women, need to take at least some control of musical theatre.

Women are too quiet within the profession because they fear for their jobs. But bitching among ourselves about the poor treatment in rehearsal rooms or the impossibility of being interviewed for a creative role will not change anything. We have to join forces and speak out. Perhaps the way in which women are represented onstage in musicals is a direct result of our passivity within the profession, where we smile dutifully and do what we are told, where we do not challenge inequality and co-operate with the sexism displayed both on and off the stage. Maybe we need to demonstrate to the men writing and producing musicals—who have obviously never encountered it—exactly how a strong, independent woman sounds and behaves, because change can never emerge out of silence. Was Ethel Merman quiet? Did Betty Comden, Dorothy Fields, Agnes de Mille, or Graciela Daniele never express an opinion? I doubt that very much. So why have we become mute? Why are we allowing a genre which once celebrated women to be taken away from us? If there is a malaise setting in, emanating from a feeling of helplessness, then we need to get over that, and get over it now, before musical theatre— a genre we have patronized and supported for decades—ceases speak to us or for us. We have to take some responsibility for the current male domination of the genre, because by not speaking out we have, in part, enabled it to occur. It is time to start fighting back. We have to stop being silent and passive and ask the question, how do we see *ourselves*. As Queen, the dismal victim from *The Life* wailing about how she's no good, because he's no good. Or as Mame? The feisty optimist flinging open metaphorical new windows and in complete control of her own life?

Throughout my interviews with women in the U.K., the same handful of male names cropped up over and over again in association with the behavior described at the beginning of this chapter—bullying, sexism, threats, and intimidation—"you'll never work again, dear"—sexual harassment, random firings, a dismissive attitude and general disrespect towards women. This is a handful of men who wielded enormous power in musical theatre in the late eighties and nineties and who, it could be argued, set the standards under which the industry subsequently operated. This, I believe—and I stress that this is my personal opinion—goes some way towards explaining why women in the U.K. feel less empowered than their American counterparts.

Society has changed enormously in the last 25 years, and the attitudes of the majority of men have changed with it. Many men now are as offended by sexism as women are. But there will always be the hardy few who see no reason to rethink their attitudes and who continue to operate as they always have. Unfortunately, those men remain incredibly powerful within musical theatre in London. The shows they create do not empower women onstage, and their production houses do not employ women in creative roles. But add to that their enormous wealth and almost complete domination of West End theatres, and it becomes more apparent why women struggle to find a voice within musicals in the U.K., because the attitudes from the top filter down. Bad behavior is replicated by a new generation because they have witnessed it as being perfectly acceptable among the men they seek to emulate. This is compounded by those same men in power consciously hiring people who will not challenge their directives and will do as they are told—the yes men. And, let's not forget, there is enough money to be made out of musical theatre these days to silence any hint of integrity or principles. Ironic that an industry that thrives on collaboration and support, that exists to entertain and lift spirits, exists under such tyranny, in the U.K., at least.

The good news is that those same men have all passed retirement age. At some point they will take the millions they have reaped from their male-centric musicals and sexist, bullying production houses and retire to the south of France, leaving the industry open to a more enlightened way of thinking, and, one hopes, more enlightened shows.

And let's celebrate the fact that in the U.S., at least, huge strides are being made towards a more gender-balanced and equal industry. Yes, women are still grossly under-represented at the creative level, but the signs are there that it is changing, that women are actively being supported and are no longer completely out in the cold. From little acorns, mighty oaks can grow!

I believe women are emotionally stronger than men. They have to be, in order to negotiate their way through a society that designates them second-rate. So let's unite forces and demonstrate exactly what women can do when they set their minds to it. Step by step, we can instigate reform in this industry and transform it into what we want, not what we are told we want. They are small steps, such as Nina Lannan raising the question of a woman's presence on the creative team of *Tootsie,* or Susan Stroman inviting a young woman to observe her work, or a group of women in the audience bombarding the producers of *Rock of Ages* with protests at how the women are portrayed. Small steps are only the beginning of a long journey. But unless we make them collectively, nothing will change.

There are new ways to dream. I believe that passionately. We, the women in the industry and the women in the audience, have the power to change musical theatre. So what's stopping us? Susan H. Schulman adds:

> Look, I've been very fortunate, you know, given when I started. I've been very fortunate to have had people recognize my ability at a certain stage. To be

given by, interestingly, a woman producer, Janet Walker at the York Theatre, the opportunity to do shows that were normally associated with a male director. And I think that ... that has become less difficult for women today. I think that is true. I think in my time ... when *Sweeney Todd* was received.. a major publication as a compliment said that ... I'm paraphrasing ... that the show is so good it's impossible to tell the gender of the director. That's a compliment? You know, I guess it's a compliment. People would be horrified if anybody wrote that now. But it was written in a major publication so, there you go. We have come a long way. I am very, very happy to say that we have. And I'm happy to have been a part of that. To have been someone who helped break through that prejudice.

NOTES

1. Tell you what I want, what I really, really want: genuine musicals," *The Independent*, June 30, 2012.

2. Rebeck was attached to the musical *Ever After* as book writer, but after being postponed in 2009, the show failed to make it to production.

3. girlrising.com.

4. http://www.missrepresentation.org/about-us.

5. http://www.mumsnet.com.

Bibliography

Askew, Emily. 2009. "Extreme Makeover and the Classic Logic of Transformation." In *You've Comea Long Way, Baby: Women, Politics and Popular Culture.* Edited by Lilly J. Goren. Lexington: University Press of Kentucky.

Bach, Steven. 2002. *Dazzler: The Life and Times of Moss Hart.* Cambridge, MA: Da Capo Press.

Bell, Marty. 1993. *Broadway Stories: A Backstage Journey Through Musical Theatre.* New York, NY: Limelight Editions.

Berger, John. 1972. *Ways of Seeing.* London: British Broadcasting

Block, Geoffrey Holden. 1997. *Enchanted Evenings: The Broadway Musical from Show Boat to Sondheim.* New York: Oxford University Press.

Bradley, Ian. 2004. *You've Got to Have a Dream: The Message of the Musical.* London: SCM Press.

Bryer, Jackson R., and Richard A Davison. 2005. *The Art of the American Musical: Conversations with the Creators.* New Brunwick, NJ: Rutgers University Press.

Clum, John M. 1999. *Something for the Boys: Musical Theatre and Gay Culture.* New York: St. Martin's Press.

Coleman, Bud and Judith Sebasta. 2008. *Women in American Musical Theatre.* Jefferson, NC: McFarland.

Faludi, Susan. 1991. *Backlash: The Undeclared War Against Women.* New York: Vintage.

Feuer, Cy, and Ken Gross. 2003. *I Got the Show Right Here: The Amazing, True Story of how an Obscure Horn Player Be-* came the Last Great Broadway Showman. New York: Applause Theatre and Cinema.

Fetterley, Judith. 1977. *The Resisting Reader: A Feminist Approach to American Fiction.* Bloomington: Indiana University Press

Gale, Maggie B., and Vivien Gardner. 2004. *Auto/biography and Identity: Women, Theatre and Performance.* Manchester: Manchester University Press.

Geraghty, Christine. 1991. *Women and Soap Opera: A Study of Prime Time Soaps.* Cambridge, UK: Polity Press.

Gottfried, Martin. 1990. *All His Jazz: The Life and Death of Bob Fosse.* New York: Bantam.

Harburg, Ernie, and Harold Meyerson. 1993. *Who Put the Rainbow in the Wizard of Oz? Yip Harburg, Lyricist.* Ann Arbor: University of Michigan Press.

Harris, Daniel. 1997. *The Rise and Fall of Gay Culture.* New York: Ballantine.

Ilson, Carol. 1989. *Harold Prince: From Pajama Game to Phantom of the Opera.* Ann Arbor: UMI Research Press.

Jeffreys, Sheila. 2005. *Beauty and Misogyny: Harmful Cultural Practices in the West.* London: Routledge.

Jones, John Bush. 2003. *Our Musicals, Ourselves: A Social History of the American Musical.* Hanover: Brandeis University Press, published by University Press of New England.

King, Catherine. 1992. "*The Politics of Representation: A Democracy of the Gaze.*" In *Imagining Women Cultural Represen-*

tations and Gender. Edited by Frances Bonner, Lizbeth Goodman, et al. Cambridge, UK: Polity Press.

Knapp, Raymond. 2006. *The American Musical and the Performance of Personal Identity*. Princeton, N.J.: Princeton University Press.

Lawrence, Greg. 2003. *Colored Lights: Forty Years of Music, Show Biz, Collaboration and All That Jazz*. New York: Faber and Faber.

Lerner, Alan Jay. 1994. *The Street Where I Live*. Cambridge, Mass: Da Capo Press.

Leve, James. 2009. *Kander and Ebb*. New Haven: Yale University Press.

Manfull, Helen. 1999. *Taking Stage: Women Directors on Directing*. London: Methuen Drama.

Mordden, Ethan. 2001. *Open a New Window: The Broadway Musical in the 1960s*. New York: Palgrave Macmillan.

Mulvey, Laura. 1999. "Visual Pleasure and Narrative Cinema. In *Feminist Film Theory: A Reader*. Edited by Sue Thornham. Edinburgh: Edinburgh University Press.

Naranch, Laurie. 2009. "Smart, Funny and Romantic? Femininity and Feminist Gestures in Chick Flicks." In *You've Come a Long Way, Baby: Women, Politics and Popular Culture*. Edited by Lilly J. Goren. Lexington: University Press of Kentucky.

Nolan, Frederick. 2002. *The Sound of Their Music: The Story of Rodgers and Hammerstein*. New York: Applause Theatre and Cinema.

Richmond, Keith. 1995. *The Musicals of Andrew Lloyd Webber*. London: Virgin.

Riddle, Peter, H. 2003. *The American Musical History and Development*. Oakville, Ont: Mosaic Press.

Robertson, Pamela. 1996. *Guilty Pleasures: Feminist Camp from Mae West to Madonna*. Durham: Duke University Press.

Rodgers, Richard. 1976. *Musical Stages: An Autobiography*. London: W.H. Allen.

Rutter, Carol. 1988. *Clamorous Voices: Shakespeare's Women Today*. London: Womens.

Secrest, Meryle. 1998. *Stephen Sondheim: A Life*. New York: Delta Trade Paperbacks.

Sinfield, Alan. 1999. *Out on Stage: Lesbian and Gay Theatre in the Twentieth Century*. New Haven: Yale University Press.

Smith, Susan. 2005. *The Musical: Race, Gender and Performance*. London: Wallflower.

Sontag, Susan. 1961. "Notes on Camp." In *Against Interpretation and Other Essays*. New York: Farrar, Straus and Giroux.

Stempel, Larry. 2010. *Showtime: A History of Broadway Musical Theatre*. New York: W.W. Norton.

Sternfeld, Jessica. 2006. *The Megamusical*. Bloomington: Indiana University Press.

Steyn, Mark. 2000. *Broadway Babies Say Goodnight: Musicals Then and Now*. New York: Routledge.

Thelan, Lawrence. 2000. *The Show Makers: Great Directors of the American Musical Theatre* New York: Routledge.

Vaill, Amanda. 2007. *Somewhere: The Life of Jerome Robbins*. London: Weidenfeld and Nicolson.

Vermette, Margaret. 2006. *The Musical World of Boublil and Schoenberg*. New York: Applause Theatre and Cinema.

Walter, Natasha. 2010. *Living Dolls: The Return of Sexism*. London: Virago.

Wolf, Naomi. 1990. *The Beauty Myth*. London: Chatto and Windus.

Wolf, Stacy Ellen. 2010. Changed for Good: A Feminist History of the Broadway Musical. New York: Oxford University Press.

_____. *A Problem Like Maria: Gender and Sexuality in the American Musical*. Ann Arbor: University of Michigan Press.

Zadan, Craig. 1990. *Sondheim & Co*. London: Nick Hern.

Index

Abbott, George 15, 45, 156, 159
The Addams Family 175, 177
Ahrens, Lynn 17, 147, 150
Aida 22
Aladdin 22
Albin *(La Cage aux Folles)* 122
Ali Hakim *(Oklahoma!)* 121
Andrews, Julie 8, 9, 35, 63
Angel *(The Rink)* 53, 81
Annie 51, 119
Annie Get Your Gun 13, 46, 50, 74, 137, 155, 164, 177
Annie Oakley *(Annie Get Your Gun)* 50, 72, 161
Antonenko, Aleksandrs 176
Anything Goes 13, 112, 151
Aspects of Love 22, 43, 44, 107, 121
Atkinson, Brooks 166
audience attendance statistics 15, 18, 19
Avenue Q 26, 123

Baby *(Dirty Dancing)* 101–102, 104
Bacharach, Burt 153
Baily, Pearl 141
Ball, Lucille 72
Barnes, Clive 72
Bat Boy 25
Beautiful 147
Beauty and the Beast 10, 22, 57, 91
Belle *(Beauty and the Beast)* 57, 105
Bennett, Michael 15, 128
Berger, John 85, 86
Berkeley, Busby 104
Berlin, Irving 15, 45, 50, 74, 151
Best Little Whorehouse in Texas 66–67
Betty Schaeffer *(Sunset Boulevard)* 42, 105
Billy Bigelow *(Carousel)* 52–53, 134, 135, 152, 166
Billy Elliot 10, 22, 38, 147
biological determinism 26, 27, 68, 131, 190

Black, Don 43, 44, 99, 107
Blair, Tony 143, 195
Blakemore, Michael 154
Block, Geoffrey 166
Blood Brothers 51, 52, 77
BMI workshop 58, 180
Bobby *(Company)* 121, 174
The Bodyguard 177
The Book of Mormon 19, 22, 24, 25, 26, 37, 38, 41, 46, 56, 80, 119, 123, 143, 186
Boublil, Alain 15, 18, 51, 63
Bourne, Matthew 119
Boy from Oz 36
Bradley, Ian 20, 45
Brantley, Ben 23, 24, 70, 113, 153, 154, 173
The Bridges of Madison County 147
Brigadoon 20
Broadway League 15
Brown, Jason Robert 150
Buckley, Betty 9
Bullets Over Broadway 14
Burch, Peter 157
Burns, Keith 142
Bye Bye Birdie 153

Cabaret 13, 42, 51, 80–81, 147
La Cage aux Folles 112, 115, 121
Caine, Rebecca 180; quotes 89, 96, 99, 113–114, 177–178
Calamity Jane 137
Call Me Madam 13, 72, 74, 112, 124
Camelot 14, 130, 131, 155
camp 13, 109, 112, 113
Camp, David 31
Carmen Jones 140
Caroline or Change 139
Carousel 14, 29, 38, 46, 51, 52, 53, 93, 134, 145, 152, 154, 164, 166, 167, 168, 189
Carvel, Bertie 117
Catch Me If You Can 10

Cats 34
Cavett, Wendy (quotes) 27, 37, 47, 56, 90, 133
Channing, Carol 9
Charlie and the Chocolate Factory 147
Chicago 10, 20, 22, 51, 81, 86, 87, 89, 98, 115, 119
childless women 51, 52
Chitty Chitty Bang Bang 10, 22, 196
A Chorus Line 20, 94, 100, 105
Church, Michael 118
Christine *(Phantom of the Opera)* 33, 43, 49, 72
Clara *(Light in the Piazza)* 72
Claudia *(Nine)* 65
Clinton, Hillary 18
Clum, John M. 44
Coleman, Cy 67
The Color Purple 20, 60, 61, 78, 80, 107, 131, 141
Comden, Betty 16, 17, 199
The Commitments 147, 177
communal experience 20
community 20, 46
Company 18, 110, 121, 174
Connick, Harry, Jr. 36
Cosette *(Les Misérables)* 72, 89
Countess Aurelia *(Dear World)* 106
Coward, Noël 45, 124, 128
Craymer, Judy 23, 29, 30, 182, 192
Crowley, Bob 168

Dame Edna Everege 115, 120
Damn Yankees 46, 98, 155
Danielle, Graciela 17, 199
De Mille, Agnes 16, 168, 174, 199
Desiree *(A Little Night Music)* 70, 135
Diana *(Next to Normal)* 43, 52, 57, 70–71
Dickstein, Mindy 80
Dirty Dancing 10, 89
Dirty Rotten Scoundrels 60, 147
Disney 45, 57, 188, 196
diva roles 13, 72, 112, 114
Dr. Zhivago 56, 87, 128
Donna *(Mamma Mia!)* 39, 43, 49, 78
drag queen 24, 77, 114–117, 119, 120
Dreamgirls 10, 77, 141
The Drowsy Chaperone 25, 26, 41
Dyson, James 16

Ebb, Fred 8, 15, 37, 57, 63, 73, 81
Ebersole, Christine 11, 59
Edna Turnblad *(Hairspray)* 120, 145
Effie *(Dreamgirls)* 77
Elder Price *(Book of Mormon)* 120
Elle Woods *(Legally Blonde)* 102, 106
Ellen *(Miss Saigon)* 52, 146

Eliza Doolittle *(My Fair Lady)* 169, 171
Elphaba *(Wicked)* 75, 101, 121
Em Cee *(Cabaret)* 121
Eponine *(Les Misérables)* 50, 51, 89
Eva Peron *(Evita)* 68, 70, 98, 99, 135–136
Evita 13, 37, 38, 39, 51, 68, 70, 79, 98
Eyre, Richard 147

Falsettoland 45
Falsettos 122
Faludi, Susan 10, 54, 127
Fanny Brice *(Funny Girl)* 94
female sexuality in musicals 13, 68, 81, 90, 98, 103
female victim 75
feminist musical 75, 79, 82
Fetterley, Judith 110
Feuer, Cy 15, 156, 159
Fiddler on the Roof 18, 139–140, 155, 176
Fields, Dorothy 16, 199
"Fifty Percent" *(Ballroom)* 77
Finian's Rainbow 163, 164
Finn, William 150
Flaherty, Steven 150
Flower Drum Song 114, 134, 141, 152, 168, 173
Follies 20, 105, 106, 112, 121
Fosca *(Passion)* 48, 50, 51, 76, 77, 91, 92, 107
Fosse, Bob 15
Foster, Sutton 11, 73
42nd Street 20
Freeman, Hadley 158
Frost, Vicky 87, 157
The Full Monty 52, 123
Funny Girl 13, 63, 94, 124
A Funny Thing Happened on the Way to the Forum 165

Ganakas, Greg 155
Gardner, Elysa 153
Gardner, Lyn 113
gay men and musicals 13, 73, 98, 109–111, 121, 124–125, 128–129
Gershwin, George 15, 18, 45
Gershwin, Ira 15, 18, 45
Ghost 175, 176
Gilbert and Sullivan 118, 119, 140, 176
girl power 29, 31, 74, 75, 81, 101, 182
Girl Rising 188
Glee 31, 183
Glinda *(Wicked)* 75, 101, 121
Global Creatures 157, 158
Godspell 45
Gooch *(Mame)* 96, 103
Gottfried, Martin 139
Grandage, Michael 155

Grease 19, 48, 189
Green, Adolph 16, 17
Grey Gardens 21, 29, 39, 59, 60, 113, 135, 137
Guettel, Adam 150
Guys and Dolls 137, 145, 155, 160, 165, 177
Gypsy 22, 37, 49, 60, 72, 112, 124

Hair 20, 45
Hairspray 10, 13, 48, 96, 109, 115, 116, 117, 145, 158
Hall, Carol 66
Hammerstein, Oscar 8, 15, 46, 140, 151, 161, 162, 168, 169, 176
Harris, Daniel 116
Harris, Neil Patrick 109
Harrison, Anneke (quotes) 12, 14, 17, 18, 44–45, 49, 61, 68, 82, 85, 95, 127–128, 132, 148, 187
Hart, Lorenz 45, 128
Hedwig and the Angry Inch 79, 115
Hello Dolly! 13, 112, 119, 124, 141, 155
Henry Higgins (*My Fair Lady*) 37, 130, 131, 149, 152, 164, 169, 170, 171, 172
Herbert, Kate 157
Herman, Jerry 8, 15, 37, 57, 63, 72, 73, 128
High Fidelity 177
High School Musical 10, 22, 196
Hilferty, Susan 17
Horrocks, Jane 155
How Do You Solve a Problem Like Maria (TV show) 10
How to Handle a Woman? 14
How to Succeed in Business … 21, 22, 36, 126, 154, 155, 156, 160, 164, 165
Hwang, David Henry 173
Hytner, Nick 168

If/Then 147
Into the Woods 22, 121, 145
Isherwood, Christopher 113

Jackman, Hugh 36
Jeffreys, Sheila 130
Jelly's Last Jam 119, 131, 141
Jersey Boys 10, 22, 35, 37, 46, 55, 58, 79, 175
Jesus Christ Superstar 72
Johnson, Catherine 39
Johnson, Christine Toy (quotes) 93, 94, 144, 145, 146, 148–149, 150, 152, 173, 177, 194
Jones, Chris 154
Jones, Deborah 87
Jordan, Julia 183
Joseph and the Amazing Technicolour Dreamcoat 113

juke box musical 10, 33, 58
Julie (*Carousel*) 53

Kander, John 8, 15, 37, 57, 63, 73, 81, 119, 150
Kaufman, George S. 45
Kellaway, Kate 169, 170
Kern, Jerome 15
Kim (*Bye Bye Birdie*) 134
Kim (*Miss Saigon*) 51, 52, 57, 65, 72, 146
King, Carol 147
The King and I 142, 152, 155, 161, 162, 164, 168, 176, 177
King Kong: The Musical 87, 157, 159, 192
Kinky Boots 22, 37, 38, 46, 55, 79, 115, 123, 147, 177
Kiss Me Kate 46, 155, 169, 170, 171
Kiss of the Spiderwoman 115, 122, 124
Krane, David 174

La Barrie, Melanie (quotes) 12, 46, 79, 93, 139, 144, 147, 173, 175, 179
Lacan, Jacques 85
La Chuisa, Michael John 150
Lady in the Dark 154
Landesman, Heidi 17, 79
Lannan, Nina (quotes) 32, 58, 59–60, 141–142, 156, 160, 185, 189, 190, 195
Lansbury, Angela 9, 112
Lapine, James 76, 104
Lara (*Dr. Zhivago*) 57, 88
La Rue, Danny 119
The Last Ship 147
Lauper, Cindi 147
Laurents, Arthur 155
Lawrence, Gertrude 72
Legally Blonde 10, 13, 21, 29, 39, 48, 68, 80, 90, 95, 100, 123, 144, 175, 176, 180
Leonowens, Anna 161
Lerner, Alan J. 15, 151, 169, 170, 176
Lewis, Norm 11
Liesl (*The Sound of Music*) 57
The Life 19, 22, 39, 50, 66, 67, 76, 81, 100, 143, 180, 199
Light in the Piazza 72
Lilly Award 181, 183
Lily Savage 119
Linda (*Flower Drum Song*) 134
The Lion King 22, 25, 34, 143, 175
Lister, David 35, 181–182
Litson, Jo 158
Little Edie (*Grey Gardens*) 59, 135, 137
The Little Mermaid 10, 22
A Little Night Music 22, 70, 112
Little Women 37, 47, 80
Lizzie (*110 in the Shade*) 43, 48, 49, 50, 103, 105, 106, 137

Lloyd Webber, Andrew 10, 11, 15, 36, 43, 44, 99, 107, 151, 154, 182, 187
Loesser, Frank 90, 151, 160
Loewe, Frederick 15, 151, 169, 170, 176
Longbottom, Robert 173
Longton, Carrie 188, 189
Love Never Dies 26, 42, 48, 51
Lucille *(Parade)* 54
Lucy the Slut *(Avenue Q)* 26
Luhrmann, Baz 158
Luker, Rebecca (quotes) 22, 58, 71, 82, 176
LuPone, Patti 9, 11, 24, 35, 72
Lysistrata Jones 19, 81–82, 127, 143

MacAnuff, Des 87, 155
Mack and Mabel 77, 105
Mackintosh, Cameron 11, 15, 18, 36, 63, 124, 151, 168, 174, 182
MacMillan, Kenneth 168
Mad Men 154, 165, 184
Made in Dagenham 147
makeovers in musicals 101–103
male gaze 13, 85–87, 89, 90, 103
Mame 22, 51, 52, 60, 96, 112, 124, 199
Mamma Mia! 10, 16, 20, 22, 34, 37, 39, 43, 49, 56, 77, 78, 80, 82, 89, 96, 145, 187, 198
Mamma Rose *(Gypsy)* 49, 71–72, 110, 135
Maria Von Trapp *(The Sound of Music)* 82, 136
Marian *(The Music Man)* 48, 105, 137
Marshall, Kathleen 17
Martin, Mary 8, 35, 72, 73
Martin Guerre 76
Mary Poppins 10, 22, 59
Matilda 21, 79, 115, 116, 117, 120, 147, 182, 196
Max *(The Sound of Music)* 121
Mayer, Michael 87
Maysles, Albert and David 59
McDonald, Audra 93, 144, 145, 146
McGregor, Ewan 155
mega musical 33
Memphis 20, 38, 131, 141
Menzel, Idina 9, 35, 73, 147
merchandise 34
Merman, Ethel 8, 9, 72, 73, 74, 112, 199
Merrick, David 141, 156, 159
Merrily We Roll Along 121
Messing, Debra 183
The Mikado 140
Minnelli, Liza 9, 72, 73
Les Misérables 7, 10, 19, 33, 34, 45, 50, 51, 53, 74, 89, 93, 145, 146, 182
Miss Celie *(The Color Purple)* 61, 78, 107
Miss Mona *(Best Little Whorehouse in Texas)* 66–67

Miss Representation 188, 189
Miss Saigon 19, 33, 39, 50, 51, 52, 53, 56, 57, 65, 79, 142, 143, 146, 147, 148, 180
Miss Trunchbull *(Matilda)* 116, 117, 119
Mme. Thernardier *(Les Misérables)* 96, 119
Monroe, Marilyn 183
Most Happy Fella 90, 160, 176
Mrs. Johnstone *(Blood Brothers)* 77–78
Mrs. Lovett *(Sweeney Todd)* 37, 114
Mrs. Lyons *(Blood Brothers)* 52
Mulvey, Laura 85
Mumsnet 188, 189
The Music Man 20, 46, 48, 137–138, 155, 169, 174, 175
music theatre critics 82
My Fair Lady 14, 37, 46, 80, 110, 126, 130, 152, 154, 164, 169–171, 172, 176, 177

Nancy *(Oliver!)* 75, 76, 77
Needham, Alex 158
Newsies 22, 37, 55, 147
Newsom, Jennifer Siebel 188
Next to Normal 19, 21, 22, 23, 29, 39, 43, 52, 57, 61, 70–71, 81, 130, 131, 134, 180, 186
Nine 10, 65–66, 67, 81, 98, 143
9 to 5 177
Norma Desmond *(Sunset Boulevard)* 65, 98, 99, 100, 103, 119, 137, 179
Norman, Marsha 147, 182
#NotBuyingIt 188
Nunn, Trevor 162, 169, 174

O'Hara, Kelli 73
Oklahoma! 16, 20, 30, 46, 121, 151, 154, 160, 164, 166, 168, 174, 177
older women in musicals 99, 100, 107
Oliver! 75
On a Clear Day 23, 24, 36, 61, 126, 163
Once 38
Once on This Island 50
110 in the Shade 43, 48, 49, 50, 93, 94, 137, 145, 172
Opera Australia 142
Orange Prize for Fiction 80
Othello 176
overweight women in musicals 95–97, 98, 107

Pacific Overtures 176
Paget, Clive 158
The Pajama Game 46, 147, 155
Parade 54, 139
Parks, Suzan-Lori 162
Passion 48, 49, 51, 76, 91, 121, 180
Paul *(A Chorus Line)* 122
Paulette *(Legally Blonde)* 101
Paulus, Diana 162, 163, 168

Pavlovic, Carmen 88, 192
Penny *(Dirty Dancing)* 89
Peters, Bernadette 9, 43, 72, 126, 155
Peters, Clarke 145
Phantom of the Opera 33, 34, 35, 45, 47, 48, 49, 50, 53, 74, 187
Phillips, Lou Diamond 155
Pippin 45
The Pirates of Penzance 117, 193
Platt, Mark 182
Porgy and Bess 13, 119, 131, 155, 162, 164, 168, 172
Porter, Cole 15, 45, 124, 128, 151
Prince, Hal 15, 155, 156, 159
Priscilla Queen of the Desert 52, 113, 115, 127
The Producers 17, 36, 98, 105, 117, 123
Promises, Promises 153, 154, 165
Pryce, Jonathan 35, 142, 148, 172
Purlie 45, 141

Queen *(The Life)* 67, 76, 144, 199
Queenie *(The Wild Party)* 76, 77

race in musicals 13, 86, 93, 94, 96–97, 140–149, 162, 164
Radcliffe, Daniel 22, 36, 155, 156
Rags 140
Ragtime 51, 52, 140
Raisin 141
Rebeck, Theresa 183
Rees, Jasper 172
Regan, Sasha 117
Rent 20, 122
revivals 14
Rice, Condoleeza 18
Rice, Tim 8, 70, 143
Rich, Frank 29, 37, 44, 72
The Rink 22, 51, 53, 80–81
Ripley, Alice 70
Rivera, Chita 8, 9, 35, 72, 73
Rivers, Joan 106
Robbins, Jerome 15, 18, 128
Roberts, Justine 188, 189
Robinson, Bill "Bojangles" 140
Rock of Ages 10, 19, 25, 60, 61, 81, 87, 89, 104, 177, 186, 200
Rocky 22, 79, 147, 177
Rocky Horror 115
Rodgers, Richard 8, 15, 45, 46, 151, 161, 162, 168, 169, 176
romance in musicals 19, 46, 47, 65
Rooney, David 24, 158
Rose *(Aspects of Love)* 43
Roundabout Theatre 93, 172
Russell, Rosalind 72
Russell, Willy 51, 78

sacrificial women 50, 51, 52
Sally *(Follies)* 106
Sally Adams *(Call Me Madam)* 71, 72
Sally Bowles *(Cabaret)* 42, 81, 98, 99, 110, 137
Salonga, Lea 93
Sandy *(Grease)* 48, 72, 103, 104, 144
Sarah *(Ragtime)* 52
Sawyer, Miranda 30
Scatliffe, Kyle 146
Scheck, Frank 154
Schönberg, Claude-Michel 7, 15, 18, 51, 63
Schulman, Susan H. 17, 29, 37, 73, 79, 80, 133, 155, 175, 177; quotes 11, 15, 20, 28, 33, 129, 148, 167, 169, 198, 200–201
The Scottsboro Boys 59, 60, 140
The Secret Garden 37, 47, 79
Seven Brides for Seven Brothers 155, 164
Showboat 13, 155, 163, 164, 174
Shrek the Musical 10, 22, 36, 175, 176, 177
Shuttleworth, Ian 118
Silverman, Leigh 147
Simon, Lucy 17; quotes 39, 56, 57
single women in musicals 49
Sister Act 29, 144
Smash (TV series) 111, 159, 183, 184
soap operas 20, 21
Sommer, Elyse 59
Sondheim, Stephen 15, 18, 25, 30, 31, 57, 72–73, 76, 104, 121, 127, 128, 162, 163, 176, 198
Sonja *(The Life)* 66
sons in musicals 52–53
Sontag, Susan 112
The Sound of Music 10, 20, 25, 51, 57, 63, 82, 138–139, 150, 154, 168, 175, 176, 177
South Pacific 13, 29, 51, 105, 115, 116, 150, 151, 154, 156, 160, 164, 168, 176
Spamalot 25, 26, 29, 36
Spencer, Charles 30
The Spice Girls 22, 29, 30, 74, 75, 101, 175, 181
Spiderman: Turn Off the Dark 22, 32, 35, 157, 158, 159, 175, 177
Spring Awakening 20, 22, 88, 127
Stone, David 182
Streisand, Barbra 8, 9, 63, 72
Strictly Ballroom 20, 158, 159, 192
Stroman, Susan 17, 59, 147, 174, 200; quotes 23, 25, 28, 29, 41, 58, 72–73, 140, 163–164, 174–175, 181, 182, 192, 198
Sunday in the Park with George 18, 126
Sunset Boulevard 13, 21, 42, 44, 51, 65, 99, 100, 124, 179, 180
Sweeney Todd 22, 29, 37, 121, 167, 176, 198
Sweet Charity 13, 46, 67, 81, 87, 174
Sydney Theatre Company 118, 193

Taboo 115
Taylor, Paul 30
Taymor, Julie 17, 32
Technology in musicals 32, 34
Tell Me on a Sunday 43, 44
Tesori, Jeanine 17, 37, 80, 150
Thatcher, Margaret 18, 132, 195
Thirteen 22
Thriller Live 177
Ti Moune *(Once on This Island)* 50, 72, 134–135
"Time Heals Everything" *(Mack and Mabel)* 77
Tracy Turnblad *(Hairspray)* 96–97, 102
Turner, Geraldine (quotes) 34, 54, 63, 74, 77, 115–116, 123

Verdon, Gwen 9
victim song 76
Vincentelli Elisabeth 59, 153
Violet 37, 80, 92, 107, 147
Violet *(Violet)* 80, 92
Viva Forever! 22, 29–31, 35, 128, 175, 181, 192

We Will Rock You 10, 25, 36, 58, 175
Wendla *(Spring Awakening)* 88
West Side Story 18, 30, 87, 139–140, 155, 172, 175
Wicked 22, 25, 29, 34, 37, 39, 48, 74, 75, 82, 110, 175, 182, 183
The Wild Party 76
Williams, Beth (quotes) 7, 32, 152–153, 165, 172, 181, 191, 194, 196
The Witches of Eastwick 20, 22, 56, 65, 98, 99, 145
The Wiz 45, 131, 141
Wolf, Naomi 97, 99, 107
Wolf, Stacy 48, 74, 75, 110
woman's voice 37, 39, 56, 63, 80, 81, 179, 182, 197
women as mothers 51–52
Wong, B.D. 142
Woodhead, Cameron 87, 157

Xanadu 25, 26, 36

Zambello, Francesca 155